Old Testament In

HISTORY OF ISRAEL

TEF Study Guides

This series is sponsored and subsidized by the
Theological Education Fund in response to requests
from Africa, Asia, the Caribbean, and the Pacific.
The books are prepared by and in consultation with
theological teachers in those areas. Special attention
is given to problems of interpretation and applica-
tion arising there as well as in the West, and to the
particular needs of students using English as a
second language.

General Editor: Daphne Terry

TEF Study Guide 7

Old Testament Introduction 1
HISTORY OF ISRAEL

DAVID F. HINSON

PUBLISHED IN
ASSOCIATION WITH THE
UNITED SOCIETY FOR
CHRISTIAN LITERATURE
FOR THE
THEOLOGICAL EDUCATION FUND

LONDON
S·P·C·K

First published in 1973
by the S.P.C.K.
Holy Trinity Church
Marylebone Road, London, NW1 4DU

Reprinted 1975

Made and printed in Great Britain by
Hollen Street Press Ltd, Slough, Berks.

SBN 281 02762 5 (net edition)
SBN 281 02763 3 (non-net edition for Africa, Asia, S. Pacific and Caribbean)

Contents

Illustrations, Maps, and Charts

ACKNOWLEDGEMENTS

MAPS
The Lutterworth press have generously allowed some of the maps in their Students' Bible Atlas by H. H. Rowley to be used as the basis for the maps in this book.

PHOTOGRAPHS
The photographic material is reproduced by courtesy of Camera Press Ltd (8.4 and 9.3) and the Mansell Collection, London.

Preface

It is with great pleasure that I acknowledge the advice and help I have received from so many who are interested in this project. First and foremost from Miss D. Terry, Publications Secretary of the Theological Education Fund, because without her interest and enthusiasm the work on this book would never have begun. Closely related with her has been her secretary. Mrs J. Chapman, who has kept the correspondence flowing, and has retyped the whole manuscript in its final draft.

Several men with experience of teaching in theological colleges in various parts of the world, have sent in their comments and suggestions which have been given careful consideration. These include John H. Dobson of Bishop Tucker College, Uganda, and Norman Kingston of Kenyatta College, Kenya. I was especially glad to have the interest and support of W Vernon Stone with whom I shared the work of the United Church of Zambia Ministerial Training College at Mindolo, in Kitwe, in former days. It was a special honour to receive comments on my manuscript from Professor P. R. Ackroyd of King's College, London, an acknowledged scholar in Old Testament studies.

I am only too conscious that what I have written will not fully satisfy those who have advised me: for they have written from somewhat different standpoints, not only from my own, but from each other as well. It is my hope that what I have written will be seen as a coherent and helpful presentation of the history of Israel which will be acceptable to most teachers, and intelligible to most students. If I have failed in this then the fault is wholly mine.

Hemel Hempstead 1972   DAVID F. HINSON

Author's Note: Using This Book

This is the first book in a three-volume course on the Old Testament. In this volume we study the history of Israel. In the second book we shall study the way in which the books of the Old Testament came to be written. In the third book we shall study the ideas about God, man, and the world which are contained in the Old Testament.

Why do we study the Old Testament in this way? Some students may think that we ought to read each of the books of the Old Testament in turn, and so come to know all that is in it. But that would be impossible in a college course. You will need to go on studying the Bible long after you have left college, in order to reach a deep understanding of it. Even people who have studied the Old Testament for many years know that they still have many things to learn. There is always some new insight, and some new understanding for those who go on with their studies.

An experiment will show that this is true. Look in the Bible for the book of Isaiah. You will see that it has sixty-six chapters. Read through the first chapter. Then read it again, noting the things in it which seem to you to need an explanation. Perhaps somebody whom you know could explain these things to you. If he did so, it would take the whole of a lesson period, or even longer. But this is only one chapter out of sixty-six, in one book out of a total of thirty-nine books in the Old Testament. For one period on each chapter of the Old Testament, you would need nearly a thousand lessons to complete your study. And this is only one of the many important subjects you need to study in college. Most students have less than half this number of lessons on the Old Testament in a three-year course. So we have to find other ways of study which will help students to understand the whole of the Old Testament, and to go on reading after leaving college, without being faced by too many things which they do not understand.

If you go back now to the list of questions or difficulties which you found in Isaiah 1, you will probably find that they can be grouped into three sorts, as follows:

1. *Historical questions*, e.g. who were the people mentioned in v. 1: Uzziah, Jotham, Ahaz, and Hezekiah? Who were the 'aliens' who had overthrown Judah (see v. 7)? What happened at Sodom and Gomorrah, that was worse than events in Judah (see v. 9)? These questions are matters of history. If we know the history of Israel we shall understand these references in Isaiah. This first volume in the course deals chiefly with this sort of question.

2. *Literary questions*, e.g. who was Isaiah? Do we know anything more about him than that he was 'the son of Amos' (see v. 1)? Did he himself write these words, or did he preach them? If he was a preacher, how did his words come to be written in the book of Isaiah? Why did he feel that he must say these things? What else did he say on similar subjects? This sort of question will be discussed in the second volume of this course. This sort of Bible study is often called 'Introduction', because it tells us what we need to know when we begin reading a book of the Old Testament for the first time, just as an introduction to a person tells us what we need to know about him when we meet him for the first time.

3. *Theological questions*, or questions of interpretation, e.g. why does Isaiah call God 'the Lord of Hosts' (see v. 9, etc.)? What does he mean when he uses the words 'sin', and 'iniquity' (v. 4), and 'justice' (v. 17), and 'righteousness' (v. 26)? Why does he condemn sacrifices, and other kinds of religious ceremony (see vv. 12 to 15)? This sort of question can only be answered by a careful study of the ideas held by the Old Testament writers. We call this sort of study 'Old Testament theology', and it is the subject of the third book in this course.

HELPS TO BIBLE STUDY

We shall read many different parts of the Old Testament as we work through this course, but we shall not read everything that it contains. You will need to study the various books of the Bible during the years ahead until you have read it all once with careful thought; and later you will want to read many parts of it again and again. For serious study you will need at all stages to consult certain 'reference tools', i.e. books which provide basic information about the Bible and its contents. These are of four main sorts: commentaries, Bible dictionaries, concordances, and Bible atlases.

(a) *Commentaries* are written by scholars who have themselves studied the historical and literary background to the Bible, and the theological teaching which it contains. Usually they deal with each book chapter by chapter, explaining each verse, and interpreting the writer's message. If you have access to a library, look for a commentary on the book of Isaiah, and see how the author uses his knowledge to explain the problems of Isaiah 1. There may be several different commentaries on the same subject, and you may need to consult a number of them in order to find all the answers that you need.

When you prepare sermons, it is useful to make a habit of looking into at least one commentary to make sure you have fully understood your text, or the passage that you wish to expound. Students working alone will find it helpful to supplement this course, if they can, by studying at least one complete book of the Old Testament alongside each volume, using suitable commentaries.

(b) *Bible dictionaries* generally contain explanations and short articles on the meaning, background, and setting of the more important words and names of people and places used in the Bible. Most theological libraries contain at least one large standard Bible dictionary, but students should if possible have their own copy of one of the shorter ones, such as the *Concise Dictionary of the Bible* in the World Christian Book series (see p. xv).

(c) *Concordances* are alphabetical lists of words and names used in the Bible, with chapter and verse references to show where each occurs. Like dictionaries, they vary in size, and are usually related to a particular Bible version. Most theological libraries hold a complete concordance of the Revised Standard Version, and for use with this Guide, the Oxford *Concise Concordance to the RSV* is probably the most useful shorter one for readers to possess for themselves (see p. xv).

(d) *Bible atlases*. Most of the place-names mentioned in this Guide can be found on one or other of the maps provided as a background to each chapter. Some Bibles contain maps of Palestine and the Near East as it was in ancient times, and most libraries have standard atlases showing how place-names and national and tribal boundaries have changed at different times in the history of Israel. H. H. Rowley's *Students' Bible Atlas* is a simple and inexpensive introductory atlas, with explanatory notes as well as an index.

STUDY SUGGESTIONS

Suggestions for further study appear at the end of each section. They are intended to help readers to study more thoroughly, and to understand clearly what they have read, and also to check the progress made. Topics for research and discussion are included.

The best way to use these study suggestions is: *first* read the appropriate section of the Guide carefully once or twice, looking up all the Bible references as you go along; *then* do the work suggested, in writing or group discussion, without looking back at the Guide except where there is an instruction to do so.

Please note that the study suggestions are only *suggestions*. Some readers may not want to use them at all. Some teachers may want to use them selectively, or to substitute questions of their own.

The *Key* (p. 201) will enable readers to check their own work on questions which can be checked in this way. In most cases the Key does not provide the answer to a question; it shows where to find an answer.

SUBJECT INDEX

The Subject Index (p. 214) includes most names of people and places mentioned in the Guide, but only the more important references to each subject.

BIBLE REFERENCE INDEX

The Bible Reference Index (p. 220) gives (a) the chapter of this Guide that contains the majority of references to any book of the Bible, and (b) page numbers for references to it in other parts of the Guide.

BIBLE VERSION

The English translation of the Bible used and quoted in the Guide is the Revised Standard Version.

TIME CHARTS

The six Time charts show in outline only the comparative dates of kings and other leaders, and of important events, in the history of Israel and of neighbouring nations.

Bibliography

The books listed below for further reading provide additional information, at a rather more advanced level, on the various subjects covered by this volume, i.e. archaeology, geography, Israelite religion, peoples of the ancient world, and peoples and places of Israel. The reference books are such as most serious students of the Bible will want to possess for themselves, and will serve for New Testament as well as Old Testament Study.

FURTHER READING

Archaeology and the Living World, J. Vardaman, Broadman Press

Archaeology of the Old Testament, R. K. Harriscn, English Universities Press

Archaeology and the Old Testament World, J. Gray, Nelson

The Ancient World, R. K. Harrison, Edinburgh University Press

God's People among the Nations, L. E. Toombs. Lutterworth

The People of the Old Testament, P. R. Ackroyd, Christopher

Everyday Life in Bible Times, National Geographic Society

Worship in Ancient Israel, H. H. Rowley, SPCK

Sacrifice in the Bible, H. Ringgren, Lutterworth

REFERENCE BOOKS

Student's Bible Atlas, Edited by H. H. Rowley, Lutterworth

Nelson's Complete Bible Concordance of the Revised Standard Version, Nelson

Oxford Concise Concordance to the RSV, Oxford University Press

Concise Bible Dictionary, Edited by S. C. Neill, J. Goodwin, and A. Dowle, Lutterworth

The Bible Dictionary, M. S. and J. L. Miller, Black

Dictionary of Bible Personal Names, H. H. Rowley, Nelson

Dictionary of Bible Place Names, H. H. Rowley, Oliphants

Geographical Companion to the Bible, D. Baly, Lutterworth

Introduction

1. THE IMPORTANCE OF HISTORY

We have seen (p. xi) that by studying Old Testament history we shall be able to answer some of the questions which arise as we read the Bible. Taking Isaiah 1 as our example, we saw that a study of history would help us to understand about the kings Uzziah, Jotham, Ahaz, and Hezekiah who reigned at the time of Isaiah. We saw that a knowledge of history would help us to understand who had attacked Judah, and would show us the reason why Isaiah compared Judah with Sodom and Gomorrah.

But some readers may want to know *why* these things matter. They happened so long ago, that it doesn't seem possible that they can affect people today who live in countries so far away from Palestine. We are willing to read the Bible because it is God's book, and has always been used in the Church. But some of us expect its meaning to be quite plain when the writers are dealing with subjects and ideas which are important to us. We feel that it does not really concern us how the writers related these ideas to the needs of the people of their own time. Our interest is in the message of God for our own day.

It is easy for us to take a verse and to use its message of rebuke for people of our own time who behave in a similar way, e.g.:

> Your princes are rebels
> and companions of thieves.
> Every one loves a bribe
> and runs after gifts.
> They do not defend the fatherless,
> and the widow's cause does not come to them.
>
> (Isa. 1.23)

It is easy to use the words of Isaiah to describe the ideal society, and to tell people that God is working for the day when all men will live at peace, e.g.:

> I will restore your judges as at the first,
> and your counsellors as at the beginning.
> Afterwards you shall be called
> the city of righteousness, the faithful city.
>
> (Isa. 1.26)

These are fine ideals, and it is a glad act of faith for us to declare such a hope to our own people today. We can understand how Isaiah felt when he stood before his people and preached this message. We can appreciate the fact that he applied these ideas to his own time, referring to his own people 'Israel' (v. 4), and to their capital city 'Zion' (v. 8), and to a great disaster known to them all which had happened at Sodom and Gomorrah (v. 9).

But some people will say that Isaiah was referring to local people, places, and events only in order to make his message vivid to his own people and that we should replace them by our own local references which will help our people to understand God's purposes for them today. They will ask, 'Why should we spend a long time, the time taken to study a whole book, trying to understand what happened in Israel so many centuries ago? The things which made Isaiah's message clear to Israel won't help our people.'

GOD'S REVELATION TO ISRAEL

The answer is that God made himself known through history, in the life of a particular nation. Isaiah did not mention local people, places, and events only as illustrations which would be helpful to the Israelites. They are part of the story of how God first made Himself known to men. Isaiah spoke as he did because he shared in the experience of God's revelation. Through this experience he came to understand more about God's ways with men, and he was able to interpret them to the people of his own time.

If we try to replace the names Israel, Zion, Sodom, and Gomorrah by our own local illustrations we shall change the whole meaning of this chapter of Isaiah. God was 'the Holy One of Israel' (v. 4) in a different sense from the way in which He is the Holy One of any other country. Israel was the nation whom God chose with the purpose of making himself known to them, so that through them He would make Himself known to all other nations. No other country can claim the same position as Israel in God's plans.

Isaiah's rebuke had a special meaning because he was speaking to the Israelites. They had been chosen for this very special responsibility, and yet they had 'forsaken the Lord'. God's whole plan of salvation was endangered by their disobedience. Other peoples may forsake the Lord, and may hinder the spread of the Gospel, but they cannot do as much damage by their disobedience as the Israelites could. 'Zion' and 'Sodom and Gomorrah' have a place in the history of how God revealed Himself to the Israelites. We need to know about them if we are to share in that revelation.

PREPARATION FOR CHRIST'S COMING

Some people may ask, 'Why did God delay so long before sending

Jesus Christ into the world? Was it really necessary for the Israelites to experience two thousand years of history before they could welcome Jesus among them?'

The answer is that it was necessary for men to know many things about God before Jesus came. Without this preparation nobody could have understood the things which He said, and the things which He came to do. Jesus was able to use the knowledge of God which the Jews already possessed in order to teach them further. He did not have to explain that there is only one God; or that the world belongs to God, and men were created by Him; or that God is righteous, and intends men to love one another. The Jews knew these things already. They had learnt them through their experiences of God in history.

Even Isaiah was not in a position to understand all that God wanted to reveal to mankind. He believed that Jerusalem was to be re-established as the centre of an earthly kingdom 'as at the first' (v. 26). This never did happen. A hundred years later Jeremiah had to teach the Israelites that they must submit to foreign rule, because of their continuing disobedience to God (Jer. 16.10–13). Even after the Exile, Isaiah's understanding of God's plans was not fulfilled. In the end the 'judges' and 'counsellors' of Jerusalem arranged the death of Jesus.

Isaiah was correct in believing that God intended to establish a righteous kingdom. But his understanding of that kingdom was limited by his knowledge of earthly kingdoms. It was not until the Exile that the Israelites began to see that God could rule in men's hearts, even when Israel had no human king, and there was no Israelite capital city where the worship of God could be conducted. (The Kingdom of Heaven proclaimed by Jesus was very different from the kingdom of Israel preached by Isaiah. But the teaching of Isaiah was one step on the way to understanding the message of Jesus.)

So we see that God revealed the truth stage by stage as people were ready to receive it. The experiences of the Israelites in the course of their history were God's way of educating His people and leading them to the truth. God led Israel through a long series of new experiences, and spoke in the hearts and minds of the leaders of Israel, in order to make His purpose and plans more fully known to them. They in turn shared these fresh insights into the truth with their fellow Israelites. In this way, step by step, men's hearts were slowly prepared for the coming of Christ and for God's fuller revelation through all that He was, and said, and did.

ISRAEL AND OURSELVES

We ourselves are very much like the Israelites. We have grasped some part of the truth about God, and about man, and about the world. We too need to be led forward by the Spirit of God toward fuller understanding of His ways. Often we shall find that the new experiences of life

3

teach us deeper truth, but we are also able to benefit from the experiences of others. If we try to place ourselves where the Israelites stood, and to enter into their experiences of God, we can begin to share their deepened insight into reality. As a result, we ourselves come closer to God.

This means that it is not sufficient for us to pick out from the Old Testament those ideas which are already 'in tune' with our own knowledge of God. We need to discover why and in what ways the Israelites' ideas changed, as God led them forward into fresh understanding. We have to recognize that at times they reached a far deeper understanding of the mind of God than we as individuals have yet done. We must work to understand *why* they thought, acted, and believed in the way they did. Our own understanding will be deepened and enriched by the effort we make to share with them their experiences of God at work in history.

STUDY SUGGESTIONS

WORDS

1. How would you yourself define the word 'history', if asked to do so by a student who had never studied the subject?

REVIEW OF CONTENT

2. Give two reasons why Christians today should study the history of Israel.
3. Which of the following statements are true and which are untrue?
(a) Events which happened long ago cannot affect us today.
(b) Other peoples who forsake God cannot do as much damage by their disobedience as the Israelites could.
(c) Isaiah referred to local people and places only in order to make his message vivid for his own people.
(d) If we replace the place-names mentioned by the prophets by our own local illustrations, we shall help our people to understand God's purposes for them today.
(e) The details of Israel's history are important because they are part of the history of how God made Himself known to men.
4. Why was it necessary for the Israelites to experience 2,000 years of history before they could welcome Jesus among them?
5. 'Even Isaiah was not in a position to understand all that God wanted to reveal' (p. 3).
Give examples of:
(a) One way in which Isaiah's understanding of God's plan for mankind was correct, and
(b) One way in which his understanding of God's plan was limited.

4

6. In what way or ways does the Kingdom of Heaven proclaimed by Jesus differ from the kingdom of Israel described by Isaiah?

FURTHER STUDY AND DISCUSSION

7. (a) In what ways are we today like the Israelites in our approach to God?
   (b) In what ways are we *unlike* them?
8. People can approach the study of history in many different ways. Which *five* of the following words best describe the spirit in which we should study the history of Israel:
   receptive obedient prejudiced perceptive humble controversial open-minded conceited impatient?
9. Read again Isaiah 1.1. Look up in a Bible dictionary the names of the kings mentioned in the passage: Uzziah, Jotham, Ahaz, and Hezekiah. Then answer the following questions:
   (a) What was the great foreign power which Judah had to contend with during the time of Isaiah?
   (b) Which of the two Jothams mentioned in the dictionary belonged to the time of Isaiah?
   (c) Which two of the four kings led revolts against the Assyrians, and which one welcomed the help of the Assyrians?
   (d) How did Hezekiah react to the siege of Jerusalem by the Assyrians, and what new insight into the ways of God did he gain through the experience?
   (e) What difference, if any, was there between the relationships of Israel with Syria in the reign of Uzziah, and those in the reign of Jotham? How did this affect Judah?
   (f) Which one of the four kings made the greatest improvements in the everyday life of Judah?
   (g) What difference was there between Ahaz and Hezekiah in their attitude to idols? Do you think that fear of the power of Assyria affected the attitude of each to worship of idols?
10. List the most important events in the history of your own country.
   (a) What, if anything, do you think can be learned from them about the ways of God?
   (b) What single event or series of events do you think has most affected the religious life of your people, and in what way?

2. HOW DO WE KNOW WHAT HAPPENED?

In this book we are concerned with the history of Israel, which is important for Christians because God revealed Himself and His purposes to the Israelites through the things which happened to them as a nation. It is important for us to know about these events so that we

5

can understand the Israelites' experiences, and share their deepening knowledge of God. But how do we *know* what happened three thousand years or more ago? The history of very few countries goes so far back into time. How can we say anything definite about what happened in Israel so long ago?

I. THE BIBLICAL RECORDS

The Bible itself contains records of some of the events, especially the two most significant events, of Old Testament times, i.e.:

1. the *Exodus*, when the Israelites escaped from slavery in Egypt, and

2. the *Exile*, when they were defeated and their leaders taken away to Babylon.

We must make use of the historical evidence which the various writers of the books of the Old Testament give us. And we must understand how to use this evidence. We must recognize the different sorts of writing by which the story of Israel is told. And we must remember that the Bible does not give us a full account of everything that happened throughout the life of ancient Israel.

Most scholars recognize three different kinds of story-telling in the Biblical records. They speak of 'myths', 'legends', and 'history'. What is the difference between them?

(a) *Myths* are the stories which people in ancient Israel composed to try to explain life as they knew it. These stories *were not based on people's memories* of actual events. The story of Creation in Genesis 1, for example, cannot be a record of what men actually remembered, because according to the story itself man was not created until *after* all the other things had happened. Whatever explanation we like to give about the origin of the story, we cannot call it history: for history depends upon the memories and records of men. There are a number of stories in Genesis which most people today, including most Christians, regard as myths. Some examples are the stories of: Adam and Eve and the serpent; Noah and the world-wide flood, the tower of Babel. These stories are valuable because they express important truths about the nature of man, and about the ways of God. But they are not historical records, and we must not treat them as though they were.

(b) *Legends* are stories which are based upon the memories of men, and which were preserved for a long time by memory and the spoken word alone, before they were ever written down. A father told his children what his father had told him, and so the story was passed on from generation to generation. Often the story was only written down *several hundred years after the event which it recorded had actually happened.*

As a result the written account was often different in some way from the actual event. Perhaps somebody forgot the details, or misunderstood what they had been told, and passed the story on to their children in a slightly different form. We know that this happened because in parts of the Bible we find two differing accounts of the same event. Each account had been handed down by a different family or tribe in Israel. The event had been remembered differently in each, and when the books of the Bible were finally written nobody knew which was the most accurate account, so both were included.

Such stories, when they are found in the Bible, are known as 'legends'. Even today we cannot be certain what actually happened to create the memories which are contained in these legends.

(c) *History* is an account of actual events which occurred in the past, and which were *recorded in writing at the time or fairly soon afterwards*, while people still living remembered them. The importance of writing is that information can be preserved from generation to generation in the exact form in which it was first recorded. Later writers may add to it, but the story is not so likely to change with the passage of time as the memories which people carry in their heads. Many parts of the Old Testament are 'history' in this sense. They are records which were prepared soon after the event took place, and were preserved for later ages in this way.

We can be much more sure of what happened in Israel when we are reading records of this kind. But even here we must remember that each writer recorded what he thought was important; not every single thing that happened. This is true of all historians and all history. In many of the books in the Bible the writer included those events which had most helped him to understand God's ways, and His purposes for man. So we can benefit by sharing his experiences. But sometimes a writer failed to understand things which happened and so did not include them, even though they were really of great importance. We need to know about these things also if we are to gain a full grasp of God's work in Israel.

2. OTHER SOURCES

Can we in fact add to our knowledge of the history of Israel from sources other than the Bible itself? One way to do so is through the study of archaeology. Archaeology is the discovery and study of things which remain from earlier times. It has been developed during this century as an important way to verify and supplement written history.

Biblical archaeology is the search and study in the Near East of remains of buildings and objects from ancient times. Biblical archaeologists have found a wide variety of things which were actually made and used in Biblical times. Their work has been greatly helped by the fact that in Palestine there are many 'tells'. These are small hills, which have

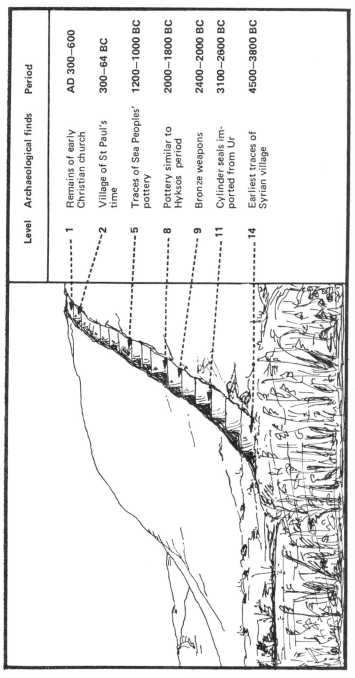

Level	Archaeological finds	Period
1	Remains of early Christian church	AD 300–600
2	Village of St Paul's time	300–64 BC
5	Traces of Sea Peoples' pottery	1200–1000 BC
8	Pottery similar to Hyksos period	2000–1800 BC
9	Bronze weapons	2400–2000 BC
11	Cylinder seals imported from Ur	3100–2600 BC
14	Earliest traces of Syrian village	4500–3800 BC

Introd. 1 'By digging into mounds or "tells," where ancient towns or villages were built, archaeologists discover remains dating from different times. (See p. 9.) This drawing of an experimental trench dug into a tell in northern Syria shows examples of the different sorts of pottery and other objects found at different levels. In this way it is possible to check the dates of the different villages built there.

come into being because for thousands of years there have been villages or towns built on the same piece of land. Each new village was built on the ruins of the previous one, and so the 'tells' have been formed.

A skilled archaeologist can dig into a 'tell' and discover the remains of each ancient village. The deeper he goes into the hill, the more ancient are the remains which he discovers. He is helped in his work by the fact that there are always plenty of pieces of broken pottery. Pots can be made in many different shapes, and decorated in many different ways, and each different age had its own distinctive styles. Thus archaeologists can discover the date of each level of the 'tell' by studying the pieces of pottery there. They can check the accuracy of these dates by other methods also. The things that they find at each level help them to discover and describe the kind of life that was lived in the village at each age.

These discoveries are of widely different kinds. The archaeologists uncover city walls and gates; they reveal the foundations of houses, stables, and palaces; and examine water supplies, food stores, and graveyards. They find many smaller objects such as coins, weights, tools, and toys. Sometimes they see direct evidence of warfare and destruction, especially where the walls and houses have been burnt by fire.

By studying such discoveries we can learn a great deal about the various tribes and nations who lived in the ancient Near East. We can fill in the background details about the peoples amongst whom the Israelites lived, and with whom they fought or intermarried.

Perhaps the most exciting discoveries are written records. These may be letters written on papyrus, or on wood or silk or animal skins, which were stored in some dry place and were then forgotten, and were only rediscovered in modern times. They may be clay tablets, or engravings in stone. Sometimes they record the religious ideas of their writers. Sometimes they report great victories in battle, or treaties between nations; sometimes they tell of personal and domestic matters. Some of them may simply help us to understand the ancient languages and ancient forms of writing. Sometimes they fill out our knowledge of the life and customs of an ancient people. Very occasionally they refer directly to events in Israel, which are also recorded in the Bible. For example, the Assyrians' accounts of their battles against Israel and Judah have been found, and help us to understand more clearly some of the events described in 2 Kings.

In this book we shall not make a systematic study of archaeology itself, but we shall use its results wherever possible to deepen our understanding of the experiences of Israel, which is our chief concern. We need to remember that fresh discoveries are being made by archaeologists every year. New evidence sometimes makes it necessary for archaeologists to alter or adapt their explanation of the significance of

'Perhaps the most exciting discoveries are written records' (p. 9). Two examples of records engraved in stone are:

Introd. 2   The *stele* or monument inscribed with a code of laws in the time of King Hammurabi of Babylon, about 1700 BC, with a relief at the top depicting the king standing to worship the sun god.

Introd. 3   The black basalt obelisk recording the military successes of the Assyrian king Shalmaneser III, with reliefs of the kings whom he defeated bringing him their tribute.

their discoveries. So sometimes one book will tell us one thing, and another book published later will tell us something different. It is the responsibility of authors to keep up to date with discoveries. The information on archaeology which we find in the most recently published book is likely to be the most accurate, and later books may lead us to fresh information and knowledge.

STUDY SUGGESTIONS

WORDS

1. Give a brief description of each of the following, in such a way as to show the difference between them:
   Legends   History   Myths
2. What is a 'tell'?

REVIEW OF CONTENT

3. What were the two most significant events in the history of Israel, as recorded in the Old Testament?
4. 'The story of creation in Genesis 1 cannot be a record of what people actually remembered' (p. 6).
   (a) Is this statement true or untrue?
   (b) On what evidence do you base your answer to (a)?
5. 'In parts of the Bible we find two differing accounts of the same event' (p. 7).
   What explanation can you give for this fact?
6. Which of the following statements are true and which are untrue?
   (a) Many parts of the Old Testament are 'history'; they are records which were written down soon after the events took place.
   (b) Each writer in the Old Testament wrote down every single thing that happened.
   (c) We do not need to know about things which writers in the Old Testament did not include.
   (d) Our knowledge of the history of Israel comes only from the Bible itself.
7. Describe some of the ways in which archaeology helps us to understand how people lived in ancient times.
8. Name three different sorts of written record found by archaeologists.

BIBLE

9. Look up the name Jericho in a concordance. Read all the verses from the Old Testament listed under this name, and make a summary of the information which these verses give.

10. Read the article on Jericho in a Bible dictionary (ignoring the New Testament references).
    (a) What extra information is given in the dictionary which, so far as you can tell, is not taken directly from the Bible?
    (b) What do you think was the source of this extra information?
11. Look up Ur and Samaria in a concordance and Bible dictionary. Summarize the information given in the dictionary and compare it, in the same way, with that given in the Bible.

FURTHER STUDY AND DISCUSSION

12. (a) What 'myths' about the creation of the world are told by people of other religions in your country?
    (b) In what ways, if any, are these myths like the stories about the creation in Genesis 1, and in what ways are they different?
13. (a) In what ways, if any, are 'mythical' stories of creation like the explanations of the beginning of the world given by scientists today?
    (b) What is the chief *difference* between all these stories of creation and the accounts of the beginnings of the world given by scientists today?
14. Give two examples of 'legends', either from other religions of which you know, or from the folklore of your own country.
15. Find out what you can about the work of archaeologists in your own country.

3. A BIRD'S EYE VIEW OF ISRAELITE HISTORY

A bird of prey, e.g. a hawk, often flies high in the sky where it can see the whole countryside set out beneath it like a map. The bird can see the movement of its prey, and can come quickly down to earth just where it will find food. The history of Israel as recorded in the Bible is long, and sometimes quite complicated. In this book we shall study the whole period of God's revelation to Israel, in order to understand the Old Testament. But first we need a bird's eye view of the history as a whole, so that we know where to come to earth in the book for the particular information we need concerning some major period in Israelite history. Time chart 1 (pp. 14 and 15) gives this sort of view.

If, for example, we want to know something about the Exile, we need to know that it happened in the time of the Babylonian Empire. Then we shall know that chapter 7 contains the information we need, because that chapter covers the period of the Babylonian Empire. In this way we shall avoid wandering backwards and forwards through the pages of the book, searching desperately for some mention of the Exile.

Time chart 2 (p. 21) sets the history of Israel in its place within the history of mankind. That chart begins with the cave-dwellers of 10,000 BC and ends with our own time close to AD 2000. In all, it covers 12,000 years of history. But the history of Israel only took up about one-sixth of that time: from about 2000 BC until shortly after the birth of Jesus Christ. Time chart 1 divides up the period of Old Testament history into its most important parts, and shows how these relate to the periods covered by the chapters of this book.

Notice that for almost the whole of the period of Israelite history we count the years backward. We begin from the time of Jesus Christ, and then say how many years *before* that time something happened. As a result of this system of counting, an event in the year 920 BC (Before Christ) happened *before* an event in 870 BC, i.e. further back into history from the time of Jesus Christ. It is important to remember this, because we who live in the period after Jesus Christ are used to the fact that, for example, AD 1920 *followed* AD 1870. So it is easy for us to get muddled. The years AD (from Anno Domini, Latin for 'in the year of the Lord') are counted in the time of Christ and *after*, so that the larger the number the more recent the event. But the years BC are counted from *before* the time of Christ and backward. Thus in both 'BC' and 'AD' the smaller the number the closer the event to the time of Christ.

Notice also that the years 99–0 are counted as the 'first century BC', 199–100 are the 'second century BC', and so on. As a result, the 'thirteenth century BC' included the years 1299–1200. Care is needed to avoid the mistake of supposing that the thirteenth century BC included the years that begin with 'thirteen', e.g. 1350 EC. This date in fact belongs to the fourteenth century. The same kind of reasoning leads to the fact that we are now living in the twentieth century, even though the years begin with 'nineteen', e.g. 1972.

The following summary of the ten chapters of this book will provide us with our bird's eye view of the history of Israel (study this summary alongside Time chart 1):

CHAPTER ONE (about 2000–1550 BC)

In this period nomadic peoples were seeking to settle in the fertile lands of Mesopotamia and Egypt, and to share the advantages of agriculture. Among them were Abraham, and his descendants Isaac, Esau, and Jacob, and the twelve sons of Jacob, including Joseph. They moved from Mesopotamia to Palestine, and then into Egypt. After 1550 BC the Egyptians regained their independence from nomadic settlers, and the Israelites became slaves in Egypt.

CHAPTER TWO (about 1550–1250 BC)

In this period the Egyptians were the most powerful nation, and they had control of Palestine for most of the time. The descendants of

TIME CHART 1: A bird's eye view of Israelite history

Year BC	WORLD HISTORY	ISRAELITE HISTORY	ISRAELITE LEADERS	CHAPTER
2000				
1900				
1800	Nomadic peoples settle in Mesopotamia and Egypt.	The Patriarchs travel from Mesopotamia to Egypt.	Abraham Isaac Jacob Joseph	1
1700				
1600				
1500				
1400	Egypt strong, ruling over Palestine.	The Israelites leave Egypt and travel to Sinai to make Covenant.	Moses	2
1300				
1200	Egypt weak, many conflicting tribes in Palestine.	The Israelites settle in Palestine and battle with many enemies.	Joshua The Judges	3
1100				
1000				

14

Year BC	WORLD HISTORY	ISRAELITE HISTORY	ISRAELITE LEADERS	CHAPTER
1000	Israel controls Palestine and lands beyond Jordan.	Philistines defeated. United Kingdom of Israel with Jerusalem as capital.	Saul David Solomon	4
900	A time of small nations. Brief invasions of Palestine by Egypt and Assyria.	Israel and Judah as rival kingdoms.	See Chart 3	5
800				
700	The Assyrian Empire	Israel attacked, Samaria destroyed, her people exiled. Judah defeated but later rebels.	Amos Hosea Isaiah	6
600	A time of great nations	Judah attacked, Jerusalem destroyed, her people exiled in Babylon.	Jeremiah Ezekiel	7
500	The Persian Empire	People of Judah freed. Some return to Jerusalem and rebuild city and Temple.	Haggai Zechariah Nehemiah Ezra	8
400				
300				
200	The Greek Empire	Judah ruled by Greeks. Maccabees lead revolt against enforcement of Greek culture.	Judas Maccabeus	9
100 BC				
0	The Roman Empire	Family of Herod share rule of Palestine with Procurators. The Jews rebel, Jerusalem destroyed.	JESUS CHRIST	10
AD 100				

15

Abraham were slaves in Egypt. Then God called Moses to bring them out of Egypt to Mount Sinai, where they entered into a Covenant, or agreement, with God. They received the Ten Commandments as a guide for their service to God and their behaviour toward each other. This whole experience is known as the Exodus.

CHAPTER THREE (about 1250–1000 BC)

In this period the Egyptians were weak, and had little control over events in Palestine. Many nomadic tribes, including the Israelites, were fighting for control of land there. Joshua led the Israelites into Palestine, and a number of the Judges, as their leaders were called, helped them in their conflicts with foreign tribes. The Philistines were their most dangerous rivals.

CHAPTER FOUR (about 1000–922 BC)

By this time the Philistines had become such a serious threat that the Israelites needed new and more powerful leaders. None of the Judges had been able to restrict the Philistines' increasing control of territory in Palestine. Samuel appointed Saul, and later David, to be kings over Israel, so that they could form permanent armies, and conquer the Philistines. Saul was unsuccessful, but David had great success not only over the Philistines, but also over many of the neighbouring kingdoms. Israel was at its most powerful in this period. Solomon, David's son, built the Temple in Jerusalem, and many other fine buildings; but he taxed his people too severely.

CHAPTER FIVE (922–802 BC)

After the death of Solomon there was civil war among the Israelites, and their kingdom was split into two parts: *Judah* in the south ruled by kings of the family of David, and *Israel* in the north ruled by kings chosen by the prophets, or who came to power by revolution. As a result, the Israelites lost their power over other nations in Palestine and across the Jordan. There was a period of conflict. Syria became one of the stronger of the small nations at this time. Both the Egyptians and the Assyrians raided Palestine, but neither stayed on to rule the countries they had attacked.

CHAPTER SIX (802–610 BC)

In the early part of this period there was no nation strong enough to conquer and control the Israelites. It was a time of peace and prosperity for Judah and Israel. But the prophets Amos and Hosea condemned the injustice and false worship which marked the life of Israel at this time. They warned of trouble to come. New and powerful kings came to rule in Assyria, who conquered Israel in 721 BC, and took its people into exile. This was the end of the Northern Kingdom. Judah submitted to the Assyrians, but several times rebelled against their control, relying on Egypt for help. Each time, the Assyrians regained control, and punished the people of Judah. Egypt could give no help. Isaiah the prophet urged the kings and people to put their trust in God, not in foreign alliances.

CHAPTER SEVEN (610–539 BC)

After a time the Assyrians found that they were unable to control the vast empire which they had created for themselves. Three nations fought against Assyria: Egypt, Media, and Babylonia. Assyria was defeated, and its empire was divided between the victorious nations. The Egyptians tried to regain control of Palestine, but were defeated by the Babylonians at Carchemish in 605 BC. The people of Judah tried to claim their independence, but were defeated by the Babylonians in 597 BC. After a period of rebellion, the Babylonians attacked Judah again in 586 BC and destroyed Jerusalem and the Temple. After each victory the Babylonians took some of the leading people of Judah into Exile in Babylon.

CHAPTER EIGHT (539–331 BC)

Cyrus, king of Persia, conquered Babylon in 539 BC, and gave permission for the Jews to return to Judah, and to rebuild the Temple in Jerusalem. They met with such difficulties that the work was not completed until 516 BC. In 445 BC Nehemiah was permitted to return to Judah to repair the walls of Jerusalem, and to establish a Jewish sub-province there. Probably in 397 BC Ezra came from Babylon, bringing a written record of the Law of God, which was perhaps the first five books of our Bible. These were to be used as the rules for the life of the Jewish community in Jerusalem.

CHAPTER NINE (331–65 BC)

Alexander the Great of Greece conquered a large area of the Mediterranean and the Near East, including the Persian Empire. After his death the Greeks continued to rule, though the area was divided into several separate kingdoms. From 323 to 198 the Jews were ruled from Egypt by a Greek family, the Ptolemies. In 198 the family of Seleucus took control of Judah, and ruled the Jews from Antioch. King Antiochus IV attempted to destroy the Jewish religion, and to enforce Greek customs upon the Jews. A group of Jews known as the Maccabees led the resistance to Antiochus IV, and they were eventually able to appoint their own kings over Judah, even though their country was still part of the Greek Empire.

CHAPTER TEN (65 BC–AD 70)

Conflict among the Maccabees about the appointment of a new king led them to invite the Romans to settle the matter for them. After a time the Romans appointed Antipater, an Idumean prince, as ruler over Judah. His son, Herod the Great, was the first of several men called Herod whom the Romans appointed to rule Palestine. In his reign Jesus Christ was born, and the new religious movement called Christianity sprang from the life and work of Jesus Christ. The Jews officially opposed this new movement, and asked for Roman help to destroy it. Later the Jews rebelled against the rule of harsh Roman procurators. The Romans punished this rebellion by destroying Jerusalem, and the Jewish state came to an end.

The history of Israel is very largely a story of conflict with other nations great and small. But through it all there runs a story of God's revelation of Himself, and of His purposes, to those who sought to know Him. Out of the bitterness of conflict and defeat new understanding was reaching those who were humble enough to receive it.

In this book we shall try to see something of God's revelation as it was experienced by the people who lived through each stage of this history. In volume 3 of this course we shall try to gather together all that they learned of God and His purposes, in order to see the way in which God prepared the hearts of men to receive Jesus Christ.

STUDY SUGGESTIONS

REVIEW OF CONTENT

1. (a) In what century is the year 721 BC counted?
   (b) What years are covered by the fourth century AD?
   (c) What years are covered by the second half of the sixteenth century BC?
   (d) In what century is the year 470 AD counted?
2. At what periods in the history of Israel were the following nations most powerful?
   Assyria   Palestine itself   Greece   Egypt   Babylon
3. In what nations were the following men or groups of men leaders?
   Alexander   The Maccabees   Cyrus
4. List the following ten events in the order in which they happened in the life of Israel:
   (a) Joseph and his brothers brought their father and their families to live in Egypt.
   (b) Cyrus, King of the Persians, set God's people free.
   (c) Moses led the Hebrews to Mount Sinai to make a Covenant with God.

(d) The Assyrians destroyed Samaria, and took Israel into Exile.

(e) Joshua and the later Judges helped the people settle in the Promised Land.

(f) The ten northern tribes broke away from the king and formed their own nation.

(g) The Babylonians destroyed Jerusalem and took the people of Judah into Exile.

(h) Abraham was called to find a new home, and create a new nation.

(i) Samuel anointed the first king for God's people.

(j) A new community was formed in Jerusalem, led by Nehemiah and Ezra.

CHAPTER 1

The Patriarchs

1. THE BEGINNINGS OF HISTORY

The biblical account of the history of Israel begins with God's call to Abraham to be the father of a new nation (Gen. 12.1f). The earlier chapters of Genesis contain the kind of stories which some scholars called myths (see p. 6), together with several ancient accounts of the beginnings and relationships of various other tribes and peoples. But in Genesis 12 we find the first of a connected series of stories, leading on from God's call of Abraham, through the birth of Isaac (Gen. 21.1–7) and of Jacob (Gen. 25.19–26), to the ancestors of the twelve tribes of Israel (Gen. 29.31—30.24). These people are known as the Patriarchs (from the Latin word for 'great fathers'), and we shall study their stories in this chapter. But first we must try to fill in the background against which these stories can be understood. Time chart 2 (p. 21) will help us to do this.

The earlier chapters of Genesis remind us that the people of Israel were not the first people on earth. And archaeological studies show that there had been several great civilizations before the time of Abraham, who lived at about 1900 BC. There is evidence of cave-dwellers living in the ancient Near East as far back as 10,000 BC. The oldest city whose remains have been uncovered in recent times is Jericho. People first built there about 8000 BC. The earliest signs that people were living a civilized life in Mesopotamia come from around 5000 BC, and in Egypt from around 4000 BC. The earliest known writings come from southern Mesopotamia, and are thought to belong to about 3300 BC. They were written by a people known as the Sumerians.

For a long time the normal centres of tribal life were single cities, each with its own king who had authority over the neighbouring farm land. The first larger political grouping existed in Egypt about 2900 BC, and is known as the Old Kingdom. There, three hundred years later, the first Pyramids were built. These are enormous tombs, and it is difficult to realize that they were built at a time when men had to depend almost entirely upon human strength, since the use of wheels and pulleys had not yet been discovered. The largest of them, known as the Great Pyramid, for example, is 481 feet high, and stands on a square base, with sides 755 feet long. There are 2,300,000 blocks of carved stone in it, each weighing about two and a half tons. The Egyptian kings for whom the Pyramids were built were known as Pharaohs, and were worshipped

```
Years
BC
10,000   Cave dwellers
 |
 |
9,000
 |
 |
8,000    Earliest known city dwellers
 |
 |
7,000
 |
 |
6,000
 |
 |
5,000    Civilization in Mesopotamia
 |
 |
4,000    Civilization in Egypt
 |
 |       Earliest known writings
3,000
 |       Old Kingdom in Egypt
 |
2,000    Abraham
 |
 |
1,000    David
BC
 |
0        Jesus Christ
 |
AD
1,000
 |
 |
2,000    Today
```

TIME CHART 2:
The place of Israel's history
in the history of mankind

as 'God-on-earth'. Their bodies were embalmed and placed in Pyramids to preserve them for their life beyond death. The Egyptians believed that ordinary men and women had no hope of sharing this renewed life beyond the grave.

The first large state in Mesopotamia was established by the Akkadians, who conquered the less well organized Sumerians in about 2600 BC. The Akkadian leader, Sargon, conquered the whole of Mesopotamia, and carried out raids far beyond its borders. In this area religion remained centred upon the various cities, each of which had its own god. The authority and power of each god was measured by the political power of the city which was supposed to be under his care. People believed that victory over an enemy showed that the god of the

21

victorious city or tribe was extending his power over the defeated nation or tribe and its territory. They also believed that it showed the failing power of the god of the defeated people.

Thus we see clearly that Abraham was not the first civilized man, and that his adventures were not the beginning of human history. In fact there had been as much time, and as many changes in human life and experience, *before* the time of Abraham, as there have been between his day and our own. We think of Abraham as belonging to a time long ago. But we should remember that the history of the human race began at least twice as long ago, and also that there had been human life on earth long before any records were written which could be formed into history.

The Bible writers make it clear that God had been at work among men long before the time of Abraham. But He began a new work in Abraham's time. He made Himself known to Abraham and his descendants in a deeper and fuller way, so that they in turn could share their knowledge of God with other peoples. 'By you all the families of the earth shall bless themselves' (Gen. 12.3). Or in other words, 'They will find help from their knowledge of your experience of God.'

STUDY SUGGESTIONS

WORDS

1. What is the meaning of the word 'Patriarch'?

REVIEW OF CONTENT

2. Who or what were the following?
   (a) the Patriarchs   (b) the Pyramids   (c) the Akkadians   (d) the Sumerians
3. Give approximate dates for the following:
   (a) The life of Abraham.
   (b) The first buildings on the site of the city of Jericho.
   (c) The Old Kingdom in Egypt.
4. (a) What did the Egyptians believe about life after death?
   (b) What did the people of Mesopotamia believe about the power of their gods?
5. 'The biblical account of the history of Israel begins with God's call to Abraham' (p. 20).
   (a) How do we know that Abraham's adventures were not the beginning of human history?
   (b) What 'new work' did God begin in Abraham's time?

FURTHER STUDY AND DISCUSSION

6. Draw a large sketch map of the Near East. Mark on it in the appropriate places:

(a) the following dates and the place-names associated with them (which are mentioned on pp. 20 and 21).

8000 BC   5000 BC   4000 BC   3300 BC   2900 BC   2600 BC

(b) the following (which are also mentioned on pp. 20 and 21).

(i) oldest city   (ii) first known writings   (iii) first kingdom   (iv) Pyramids.

2. WHO WERE THE PATRIARCHS?

An ancient creed of the Hebrew people begins, 'A wandering Aramaean was my father' (Deut. 26.5). The Hebrews evidently believed that their nation had come into being as an offshoot of a much more ancient people: the Aramaeans.

THE PATRIARCHS AND HISTORY

So far, in looking at the historical background to the Old Testament, we have only dealt with the development of civilization in Egypt and Mesopotamia before the time of Abraham. The Aramaeans were among the peoples who had not yet built cities, or developed powerful states. They were still nomads, keeping herds and living on the edges of the wilderness, but finding opportunity to trade with the more developed peoples of the cities.

Abraham's father, Terah, and his family seem to have been friendly with the people of the city of Ur in the southern part of Mesopotamia (Gen. 11:31). Ur had been a powerful and important city from about 3000 BC. At times its people had been able to gain control over large parts of southern Mesopotamia. But its power was finally broken, and the city destroyed, in about 1950 BC. Perhaps Abraham's people moved from Ur at that time because they could no longer trade there, or because they were no longer protected by a powerful ally.

Later Abraham left his 'kindred' and his 'father's house' in Haran to search out new pastures for his animals, and a new home for his own immediate family (Gen. 12.1). Later in the book of Genesis we find mention of Bethuel, the son of Nahor and Milcah (Gen. 24.24), and of Bethuel's children, Rebekah and Laban. These were all relatives of Abraham, and were living in the city of Nahor, which was near to Haran.

This supports the idea that the tribe had had a fairly permanent home there in northern Mesopotamia, and that the tribe had split into two sections when Abraham left for Palestine. It also suggests that respect and goodwill continued between the two parts of the tribe. The movements of the Patriarchs into Palestine, and later into Egypt, fit in well with what is known of the activities of nomadic peoples of those times. Everywhere they wanted to share the advantages of settled peoples.

They wanted land that they could use as their own, and the opportunity to trade with other people.

So far we have tried to find a connection between the Biblical stories of the Patriarchs, and the history of the world in which they lived. But we cannot do more than guess how they fit into the history of ancient times, because there is no mention of the Patriarchs in the ancient records preserved from Egypt or from Mesopotamia which might show us a direct link between them. In fact there are no written records or material possessions still remaining from the Patriarchs themselves. This should not surprise us, because nomads do not normally use writing, nor do they leave any permanent evidence of the places where they lived.

All that we know about the Patriarchs are the stories preserved for us in the book of Genesis, and these are legends (see p. 6) which were probably written down in their present form a thousand years after the death of Abraham. The Hebrews preserved these stories because, like men of other tribes, later generations regarded their ancestors with great respect and wished to know as much about them as they could.

But also the story-tellers in Israel felt that the stories contained important teaching about God, and about God's ways with men. The Israelites never doubted that God had chosen Abraham and his descendants, and had revealed Himself to them, and had established His Covenant with them. The stories were no doubt used in later times to teach these things to the new generations, and we too can value them because of the important truths which they contain about God and His plan for mankind.

Nevertheless, we can never be absolutely sure of the historical events which underlie these stories. The archaeologists cannot do more than tell us that there was a definite time in the history of the world when these things could have happened among the Israelites. They have discovered that the customs followed by the Patriarchs are very much like customs known to have existed among similar people who lived at about that time.

As we study the lives of the Patriarchs, we must always remember that we are dealing with legends, and not with history. The stories were not recorded in writing soon after the events. They existed for many centuries as memories which were passed on from father to son through many generations. We do not now possess the first written record of these memories. We shall see in volume 2 of this course that these stories were written and rewritten many times in the course of history. Thus the editions we now possess have been revised and adapted many times. We cannot discover now the original form of each of the stories, although scholars find it necessary to suggest what might really have happened. We shall restrict our study to the form in which we possess the stories today.

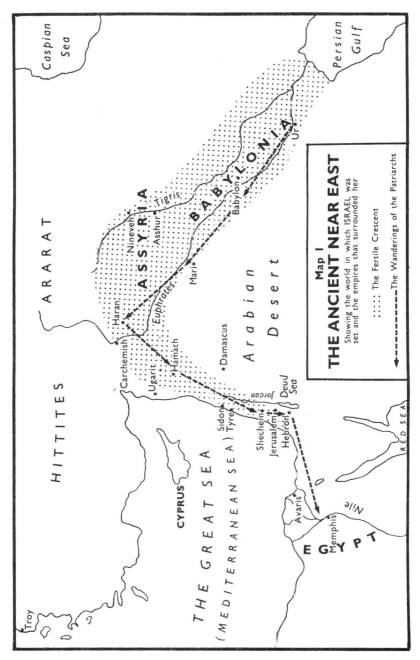

Map I
THE ANCIENT NEAR EAST

Showing the world in which ISRAEL was
set and the empires that surrounded her

:::::: The Fertile Crescent

- - - - - The Wanderings of the Patriarchs

ABRAHAM

The story of Abraham is recorded in Genesis 12—25. It begins with a command and promise of God, and goes on to show their fulfilment. God commanded Abraham, 'Go . . . to the land that I will show you' (Gen. 12.1). God promised Abraham, 'I will make of you a great nation' (Gen. 12.2).

As we read the chapters of Genesis which follow, we find that Abraham made his way to the land of Palestine, and that God assured him that this territory would belong to his descendants (Gen. 12.7; 15.18-21). But Abraham himself did not change his way of life in the new land. He remained a nomad travelling from place to place in search of pasture and water for his herds. Map 1 (p. 25) gives some idea of the area he covered in his travels. Shechem (Gen. 12.6), Bethel (Gen. 12.8), Hebron (Gen. 23.2), and the nearby Mamre (Gen. 18.1; 23.17f) were all on the central highlands, which in those days were not controlled by any city-dwellers, so that nomads could wander freely there.

Abraham also travelled in the Negeb (Gen. 12.9; 24.62), the territory to the south of Palestine, which includes Gerar (Gen. 20.1f), and Beersheba (Gen. 21.31-33; 22.19). He seems to have made a treaty with Abimelech, king of Gerar, which gave him freedom to travel where he liked (Gen. 20.15) and the right to use the water-holes of the area (Gen. 21.25-34).

Abraham also made one journey into Egypt in a time of famine, but he got into trouble there for behaving dishonestly to Pharaoh and to his own wife, and was expelled (Gen. 12.10-20). In any case Egypt was beyond the limits of the land God had given to him (Gen. 15.18).

Many of the stories preserved about Abraham are concerned with the problem: how could God's purposes be fulfilled unless he had descendants? It might have seemed sufficient for a close relative to inherit the promises of God, perhaps Abraham's nephew Lot. But Abraham parted company with his nephew (Gen. 13.8-13). They remained on good terms, and Abraham came to the rescue of Lot more than once, both by fighting for him (Gen. 14.14) and through prayer (Gen. 18.22-33). But Lot was to be ancestor of the Moabites and the Ammonites, not of the Israelites (Gen. 19.36-38).

According to the custom of those times a man who had no children would pass on his inheritance to a favourite slave. But Abraham was told that this would not be the case in his family (Gen. 15.3-6). Also according to custom, Sarah offered Abraham a slave woman to bear a son in her place (Gen. 16.1f), but this was not God's plan either (Gen. 17.15-19). At last in extreme old age Sarah did bear a son to Abraham, and they called him Isaac (Gen. 21.1-3).

Yet even this answer to God's promises could have failed. It seems that Abraham knew that some of the people of his time honoured their gods by sacrificing children to them. Probably he did not want to fall short in his own devotion to God, and so he was prepared to sacrifice Isaac. God prevented him from doing so, and provided a substitute (Gen. 22.9–14).

One final problem remained: Abraham married again after the death of Sarah, and more children were born to him by Keturah. These children might have contested Isaac's right to be sole inheritor of God's promises. Abraham therefore provided for their needs and sent them away (Gen. 25.5f). Thus when Abraham died he had seen the land which God had promised him, and also the child through whom a nation of his descendants would come into being.

ISAAC

We have already seen that Isaac's birth was important because he was to be the inheritor of God's promises. He was the one through whom they would be fulfilled. We have also noticed that Abraham came close to sacrificing Isaac while he was a child. Before Abraham died he made arrangements for Isaac's marriage. He sent a trusted servant back to northern Mesopotamia to his own people to find a suitable wife (Gen. 24). The servant found a way to select a generous, hospitable, and hard-working girl (Gen. 24.18f: few girls would want to water thirsty camels). He felt sure that God had chosen Rebekah for Isaac. They married, and after some delay Rebekah bore twins to Isaac, and they were called Esau and Jacob (Gen. 25.21–26). In time of famine the family moved down to Gerar in the Negeb, where Isaac successfully grew crops as well as continuing to care for his flocks and herds (Gen. 26.12–14). This seems to have led to conflict with the local inhabitants, so Isaac returned to the nomadic way of life after moving to Beersheba. As a result he was able to renew his treaty with the king of Gerar (Gen. 26.26–31). The happiness of Isaac's later years was spoilt by the quarrels between Esau and Jacob, in which Rebekah sided with Jacob, while Isaac preferred Esau (Gen. 25.28).

ESAU AND JACOB

The story of these two brothers is recorded in Genesis 25—36. It seems that they quarrelled even before they were born (Gen. 25.22f). The men who preserved the memories of Esau and Jacob did not attempt to hide their faults We can read in the book of Genesis how Esau held his responsibilities as the elder son too lightly, and could be provoked into actions which he later bitterly regretted. We can also read how Jacob was very ambitious, and how he used cunning in order to gain power for himself. God chose Jacob to be the inheritor of the promises which He had made to Abraham. Yet Jacob was a violent and deceitful person,

27

and did not respond willingly to God's call. Some scholars think that the new name 'Israel' which was given to him at the stream Jabbok (Gen. 32.28) may mean 'God strives' (see footnote to this verse in the RSV), i.e. one who caused God to work hard to bring him to repentance and obedience.

If we study the details of the story we find Jacob constantly in the middle of conflict. He successfully cheated his brother Esau of his rights as the eldest son (Gen. 27.33), but then found that his own life was endangered by Esau's anger (Gen. 27.41). Jacob escaped to his mother's home and in a time of conflict with his uncle Laban gained for himself two wives, Leah (Gen. 29.21–23) and Rachel (Gen. 29.28), and considerable wealth (Gen. 30.43).

Even though he was still in great dread of his brother's anger (Gen. 32.11), he returned to his homeland, because he knew that he would never find peace and independence while he stayed with Laban (Gen. 31.1f). On the way, Jacob had the strange experience of the fight at the stream Jabbok. Perhaps for the first time he recognized that God had been leading him through all the conflicts that had surrounded his life. He saw that God had been working to make him a worthy inheritor of His promises. His brother Esau welcomed him gladly, though Jacob remained uneasy about their relationship (Gen. 33.4; 33.15–17). Eventually Esau's descendants made their home in Edom, leaving Palestine to the Israelites, i.e. the descendants of Jacob whose new name was Israel.

JOSEPH

Part of the trouble in which Jacob was involved was the conflict between his two wives, Leah and Rachel (Gen. 29.31—30.24). The remainder of the book of Genesis contains the story of Rachel's son, Joseph. He aggravated the family disputes by telling his father and brothers of his dreams of greatness (Gen. 37). The brothers did not understand that God was revealing His purposes to Joseph in these dreams. In revenge they decided to get rid of him.

The story is a little confused at this point; probably because more than one source of information has been used in writing this chapter of Genesis. But the outcome is clear: Joseph found himself a slave in Egypt. By honesty and hard work he reached a position of responsibility, but was falsely accused of adultery and sent to prison. While there he showed himself able to interpret dreams, and was eventually released in order to use this gift for Pharaoh.

As a result, Pharaoh appointed Joseph to a position of power and authority. He was able to save Egypt from the worst effect of seven years of famine, and increased the power of Pharaoh over his people. Joseph was also able to relieve the starvation of his own family, and persuaded

1.1 'Ur had been an important city from about 3000 BC' (p. 23). A mosaic panel of about 2500 BC found there shows a king and his guests at a victory banquet, with men bringing food, animals, and other spoils captured from the enemy.

1.2 'Movement of the Patriarchs into Palestine and Egypt fits with what is known of nomadic peoples at that time. They wanted land, and a chance to trade with more settled peoples' (p. 23). Semitic traders in a wall-painting of 1890 BC (here shown in two sections) were bringing eye-paint to the king of Egypt.

them to settle in Egypt where he could take care of them all. He seems to have seen the whole course of his life as fulfilling God's purposes (Gen. 45.5).

STUDY SUGGESTIONS

REVIEW OF CONTENT

1. Who or what were the following?
   The Aramaeans   The Negeb
2. (a) At about what date did the city of Ur become powerful?
   (b) At about what date was it destroyed?
3. Name two general advantages enjoyed by settled peoples, which nomadic tribes of ancient times wished to share.
4. Name two special reasons why Abraham moved with his family from Haran into Palestine.
5. (a) Which of the three names for different kinds of writing: myth, legend, or history, should be used to describe the biblical account of the lives of the Patriarchs?
   (b) For what two chief reasons did the Israelites preserve the stories about Abraham and his descendants?
6. Read Genesis 13 and 20. Name *four* of the places visited by Abraham during his travels in Palestine.
7. 'The story of Abraham begins with a command and promise of God' (p. 26).
   What were this command and promise?
8. (a) Name two problems which might have prevented God's promise to Abraham being fulfilled.
   (b) Explain how the two problems which you have chosen in answer to (a) were overcome.
9. (a) For what reason was the birth of Isaac important?
   (b) What arrangements did Abraham make for Isaac's marriage?
10. 'It seems that Jacob and Esau quarrelled even before they were born (Gen. 25.22f)' (p. 27).
    Give two examples of conflict between the two brothers, with chapter and verse reference from the book of Genesis in each case.
11. What did Jacob learn from his experience at the stream Jabbok?
12. (a) In what way did Joseph add to the conflict in Jacob's family?
    (b) What reason can we give for the fact that two different accounts of how Joseph's brothers planned to get rid of him are included in Genesis 37?
13. (a) What did each of the following pairs of people described in the book of Genesis have in common?
    (b) Which one of the pair came first in time?

(Example: Rachel and Leah: (a) Both were wives of Jacob.
(b) He married Leah first.)

(i) Isaac and Jacob	(vi) Sarah and Keturah
(ii) Esau and Jacob	(vii) Abraham and Terah
(iii) Rachel and Rebekah	(viii) Joseph and Benjamin
(iv) Bethuel and Lot	(ix) Reuben and Simeon
(v) Potiphar and the Keeper of the prison	(x) The Baker and the Butler

FURTHER STUDY AND DISCUSSION

14. Abraham, Isaac, and Jacob each had another man of his tribe who shared some of his experiences with him (Abraham had Lot, Isaac had Ishmael, and Jacob had Esau). Do the writers of Genesis suggest that God had no interest in these other men, or was there an important role for each of them to play in the later history of mankind? What use did the writers of the New Testament make of the stories of these three men? (Use a Bible dictionary and concordance in preparing your answer.)

15. Many scholars believe that some of the stories of Genesis were preserved chiefly in order to provide an explanation of the relationship between Israel and some of the other tribes of similar origin. For example the Ishmaelites were said to be descended from Abraham through his slave-wife Hagar.
How did the story-tellers of Israel explain the connection between Israel and each of the following tribes?
Ammon   Aram   Edom   Moab
(Use a Bible dictionary and concordance in preparing your answer.)

3. THE GOD OF ABRAHAM

Some readers may wonder why it is necessary to have a chapter on the religion of the Patriarchs. 'After all,' they may say, 'they were worshipping and serving God. We should not be much interested in them if they were not.' But we do need to ask what they believed about God, and in what ways they thought they should serve Him. It took the whole period covered by the Old Testament for God to prepare the hearts and minds of men to receive the truth revealed in Jesus Christ. Even then many of the Jews misunderstood Him. Abraham himself was very wise and very close to God, but he would not have understood all the truth if Christ had been born in his day.

Any teacher will understand this problem. It is never enough simply to tell people the facts of a subject which we want to teach to them. Those who are learning need to see how the new ideas are related to ideas which they already accept as true. Until the student knows and understands some ideas, other ideas will have little or no meaning for him. He will fail to fit them into the pattern of his thoughts, and so will fail to understand or remember them.

God had many things to teach mankind about Himself, and about the world and man's place in it. But God had greater skill and wisdom than the best of human teachers. He had to begin at the beginning and lead men on stage by stage in their thinking, until some at least were ready to receive the fullest revelation in the life, death, and resurrection of Jesus Christ. The questions we shall consider in this section are:

1. How much of God's truth did the Patriarchs understand? .
2. Where did they begin in their thinking?
3. How far forward was God able to lead them in the period of the history of Israel which we are studying?

But before we try to answer these questions we must note two other facts in the situation.

(a) We have already considered the religion of the Patriarchs. In general they all shared the same faith and practices. But they did not all have the same spiritual insight; some had a fuller grasp of God's truth than others. We cannot say that those who lived earliest knew the least, and those who lived latest knew the most. Each man had to grasp and make use of the knowledge which was available to him, and some did this more successfully than others. This explains why Abraham was a much more devout man than Jacob, even though Jacob was Abraham's grandson.

(b) The second difficulty which we face in trying to understand the religion of the Patriarchs comes from the fact that all that we know about them is contained in legends. We have already seen that for hundreds of years these stories were preserved by memory, and passed on by word of mouth. The story-tellers understood the things which they taught in the light of their own knowledge of God, and of their own insight into spiritual matters. As a result they interpreted the stories in such a way that they put their own thoughts and understanding into the hearts and actions of the people whom they mentioned as they told the stories of the Patriarchs.

We can see how this happened if we consider the ways in which different writers used the divine name *Yahweh*. (This name is printed in the RSV Bible as 'the LORD', using capital letters all the way through the word. We must notice the difference between this name and the word 'Lord', printed in small letters, which is used to translate a different Hebrew word.)

For example, in Exodus 6.2f we read, 'God said to Moses "I am the LORD. I appeared to Abraham, to Isaac, and to Jacob as God Almighty, but by my name the LORD I did not make myself known to them".' Yet in one of the earliest chapters of Genesis which refers to the Patriarchs we read about Abraham arriving at Bethel, 'and there he built an altar to the LORD and called on the name of the LORD'. (Gen. 12.8.) How could Abraham have called on the name of Yahweh, if that name had not yet been revealed to him? We may ask the same question about Genesis 14.22, 15.7, and 16.2.

The answer each time is probably that Abraham himself did not actually use the name Yahweh. But a later story-teller knew that Abraham had served the same God whom Israel was serving, so he put that same name for God on the lips of Abraham, or used it in his account of God's revelation to Abraham. The story-teller did not realize that God had not then revealed the name Yahweh, for it was a different story-teller who recorded this information in the book of Exodus. He was certainly right in supposing that Abraham's God, and the God of Israel, were one and the same God. His only mistake was in supposing that Abraham knew and used the name Yahweh.

This shows the sort of difficulties which are likely to arise when legends are the only source of information we have about the religion of the Patriarchs. In general we can be more sure about those things described as belonging to the religion of the Patriarchs which were *not* also part of the religion of the story-tellers. The story-tellers give detailed descriptions of many things which we know did not belong to their own religion. These things can only have been memories handed down from a much earlier time.

BEFORE GOD CALLED

According to Genesis, Abraham's ancestors were associated first with the city of Ur, and later with the city of Haran. We have seen that in Mesopotamia each city had its own god. The interesting thing is that the people of Ur and those of Haran worshipped the same god: the moon god, known by the name 'Sin'. At Ur the temple of this god can still be seen. It is a three-tiered *ziggurat*, or tower, built of brick. One huge platform of bricks stands on another, with a third platform on top. There is a great stairway by which the priest of the religion approached the shrine of the god at the top level. We must remember that Abraham's ancestors were not inhabitants of Ur, but were connected with the city through trade. Yet it is difficult to explain why this nomadic people moved from Ur to Haran where the same god could be worshipped, unless they had religious reasons for doing so. Also the names of several of Abraham's family, e.g. Terah, Laban, Sarah, and Milcah, are names which scholars know to be connected with the cult of the moon god.

THE GOD OF ABRAHAM

We have seen that Abraham did not know the divine name Yahweh.

'Abraham's family moved from Ur to Haran. . . . The people of both cities worshipped the same god: the moon god Sin' (pp. 33 and 35).
1.3   Remains of the three-tiered *ziggurat*, or tower, of the temple of the moon god at Ur can still be seen there today.

1.4   A stone seal discovered at Ur and probably made about 2500 BC shows a city governor being led by two goddesses to worship the king, Ur-nammu, under the moon god's symbol.

According to Exodus 6.3 the Patriarchs used the title *El Shaddai*, i.e. God Almighty. This name is used six times in Genesis, at least once in connection with each of the Patriarchs (Gen. 17.1; 28.3; 43.14; 49.25). The original meaning of this name is now lost to us, but in the Greek Old Testament, the Septuagint, it is translated as 'the sufficient One', 'the Almighty'. The first part of the name, *El*, is the usual word for God among the nomadic peoples of the ancient Near East, and is found in other names used by the Patriarchs: *El Elyon* (Gen. 14.22), i.e. 'God Most High'; *El Olam* (Gen. 21.33), i.e. 'the Everlasting God'; *El Roi* (Gen. 16.13), i.e. 'God of seeing'; and *El Bethel* (Gen. 31.13), i.e. 'God of Bethel'. We can safely assume that the Patriarchs normally used the name *El* (or its plural *Elohim*) as a form of respect when talking of God.

THE COVENANT

The peoples of the ancient world who lived a settled life, depending on agriculture and living in cities, usually thought of the gods whom they worshipped as belonging to a particular *place*. They also thought that the gods depended on human victories to spread their authority more widely. Perhaps Abraham's family moved from Ur to Haran because of this kind of belief. But Abraham's departure from Haran seems to have been for a different reason. He and his family believed that God was active both in Haran (Gen. 12.1f) and in Palestine (Gen. 12.7), and even as far away as Egypt (Gen. 12.17). But they believed that it was God's will that they should serve Him in Palestine. It seems that Jacob did not fully understand this. It came to him as a new revelation that although he was leaving Beersheba and Palestine, and returning to Mesopotamia, God would be with him all the way. It was only through a dream that this became clear to him (Gen. 28.10–17).

The Patriarchs regarded God as a God of *people*, rather than a God of places. Only once is He called 'God of Bethel', and then to remind Jacob that God had promised to be with him everywhere (Gen. 31.13). But this sort of religion was not entirely new with Abraham. It is easy to understand why nomadic peoples, who are continually moving about, usually think of their gods as being related to particular people rather than to places. In this sort of religion the relationship between the god and his people often takes the form of a Covenant, that is, an agreement in which the people promise certain forms of obedience and loyalty, in return for the blessing and protection which they believe that the god will give them. The relationship between God and Abraham was of this sort (Gen. 12.1–3). God frequently renewed His Covenant with Abraham (Gen. 15.1–6; 15.12–21), and later with Isaac (Gen. 26.23–25), and with Jacob (Gen. 28.13–15). In the story of Joseph, dreams seem to have formed the basis of his relationship with God (Gen. 37.5–11).

CIRCUMCISION

Those who inherited the Covenant which God made with Abraham became heirs by circumcision. This was a widespread custom in the time of the Patriarchs, and was normally part of the initiation ceremony by which a young man was accepted as an adult member of his tribe. But among the Hebrews there was an important difference: they were circumcised soon after birth. Genesis 17.9–14 and 17.24–27 suggest that Abraham adopted the custom when he settled in Palestine. At the time when Abraham adopted the custom Isaac was a baby, but Ishmael was a teenager. Perhaps this story was used at a later time to explain the difference between Jewish and Arabic custom.

ALTARS AND SACRIFICE

Every religion must have some form of ceremony or ritual through which the worshipper approaches his god. In the stories of the Patriarchs there is a strong emphasis on the fact that it is God who approaches His people. Altars are often mentioned—but they seem to have been set up to commemorate God's dealings with His chosen people, rather than as places where the people could approach God. In the legends preserved in Genesis, Abraham is in some way associated with all the places where altars were erected (Gen. 12.6, 8; 13.18; 21.33). Probably one of the story-tellers wanted to honour Abraham above the other Patriarchs by showing that Abraham possessed special insight into the matter of where God could best be worshipped.

Yet in each case there is another story in which God reveals Himself at a significant moment, and unexpectedly, to one or other of the Patriarchs: at Shechem to Abraham on his arrival in the promised land (Gen. 12.6f), at Mamre to Abraham where he was despairing of ever having a true heir (Gen. 18.1–15), at Bethel to Jacob when he was escaping from his brother's wrath (Gen. 28.10–22), and at Beersheba to Isaac when his security was threatened by the people of Gerar (Gen. 26.23–25), and also to Jacob prior to his departure into Egypt (Gen. 46.1–4).

In later ages the Israelites rejected these places of worship because they had been used for pagan worship. Even so, the story-teller remembered that these places had played an important part in the religion of the Patriarchs. This shows that the traditions about them are well founded. These were places where God had made Himself known to the Patriarchs.

According to the story of Jacob, the sort of altar erected by the Patriarchs was a single stone pillar. Worship consisted of pouring oil over the top of the stone (Gen. 28.18; 35.14). At the same time, those who worshipped called for a response from God (Gen. 12.8). No detailed rules for sacrifice at this time are known to us. No special priests were appointed. The leader of the tribe made offerings on behalf of his people.

ETHICS

No special rules of conduct were adopted by the Patriarchs, only such customs as were generally accepted by peoples of the time. Some of their customs would be judged as wrong by Christian standards, and even by the standards which the Israelites themselves accepted later. But a foundation was being laid for the development of Hebrew ideas of right and wrong. People already understood that the highest virtue was to do God's Will, and to serve Him. No doubt in later ages the stories of the Patriarchs were used to teach people how to serve God. The Patriarchs were greatly respected for the standard of their obedience (see for example Deuteronomy 9.27, and Nehemiah 9.7f). Yet the story-tellers recognized that the Patriarchs lived at a time when ideas of morality were only beginning to be formed. They did not attempt to describe the Patriarchs as living up to the standards of behaviour which were developed at a later time.

STUDY SUGGESTIONS

WORDS

1. What is or was a *ziggurat*?
2. (i) Explain the difference between the two names for God used by the Israelites, *Yahweh* and *El*.
   (ii) In what way is the difference between these two names shown in the English RSV of the Bible?
   (iii) Which name was used in each of the following passages?
   (a) Gen. 12.8   (c) Gen. 22.14
   (b) Gen. 14.19   (d) Gen. 31.13

REVIEW OF CONTENT

3. Which of the following statements are true and which are untrue?
   (a) All that we know about the religion of the Patriarchs is contained in legends.
   (b) Those of the Patriarchs who lived earliest knew least about God's truths.
   (c) The story-tellers who handed down stories about the Patriarchs put their own thoughts and understanding into the hearts and actions of the people they described.
   (d) Some of the customs practised by the Patriarchs would be judged as wrong by Christian standards.
   (e) Human sacrifice was common among the Patriarchs.

(f) The custom of circumcision was used by other peoples than the Israelites, but for these other peoples it did not have the same meaning.

4. (a) In what ways was the religion of the people of Ur like that of the people of Haran?

(b) What did the following names of members of Abraham's family have in common?

Terah   Laban   Sarah   Micah

5. Give *four* different names for God used by the Patriarchs, with their meanings in English.

6. What new truth about God's will for him did Jacob learn from the dream which he had at Bethel?

7. (a) For what chief purpose were altars most often set up by the Patriarchs?

(b) For what chief reason were some of these altars rejected by Israelites at a later date?

(c) Describe the sort of altar most usually set up by the Patriarchs, and how people worshipped there.

8. For what qualities did the Israelites of later times chiefly respect the Patriarchs?

BIBLE

9. Read Gen. 11.31—12.1; 12.6, 7; 12.10, 17.

What can we learn from these three passages about Abraham's belief about God?

10. Read (a) Gen. 12.1–3   (b) 13.14–17   (c) 17.1–8   (d) 26.23–25 (e) 35.11–15.

(i) What sort of relationship between God and man is described in each of these passages?

(ii) Name the man with whom God was relating in each case.

11. 'What happened at Sodom and Gomorrah that was worse than events in Judah?' (p. xi).

Read Genesis 18.22—19.29 and then answer this question, and say also which of the Patriarchs were involved in these events.

FURTHER STUDY AND DISCUSSION

12. 'God is a God of people, rather than a God of places' (p. 35).

(a) What difference does it make to a man if he believes in a god who belongs to a place rather than a god who belongs to a particular people?

(b) Which of these two sorts of God is worshipped in the traditional religion or religions of your country?

(c) Does God in whom Christians believe belong to a particular place or people? Give reasons for your answer.

13. 'Every religion must have some form of ritual through which the worshipper approaches his god' (p. 36).
Do you agree with this statement? Give reasons for your answer.

14. The altars at Shechem, Mamre, Bethel, and Beersheba were later rejected because they had been used for false worship, though they were places where God had made Himself known to the Patriarchs. What if anything can we learn from these facts about the importance —or unimportance—of church buildings?

15. 'We cannot say that the Patriarchs who lived latest . . . had a fuller grasp of God's truth' (p. 32). 'The Patriarchs lived at a time when ideas of morality were only beginning to be formed' (p. 37).
(a) Do people have a 'fuller grasp of God's truth' today than in the time of the Patriarchs?
(b) Are people's 'ideas of morality' better today than at the time of the Patriarchs? If so, how far do they live up to these ideas? Give your reasons, and examples from everyday life, in support of your answers.

16. Write a prayer that might have been used by Jacob after he was reconciled to Esau.

CHAPTER 2

The Exodus

1. WHAT IS THE EVIDENCE?

The Jews have always thought of the Exodus as the most important event in their whole history. The books of Exodus, Leviticus, Numbers, and Deuteronomy all refer again and again to the fact that God brought Israel out of the land of Egypt. The people who wrote the later history of Israel in the books of Joshua, Judges, 1 and 2 Samuel, and 1 and 2 Kings, often mention the event which had turned the descendants of the Patriarchs into a nation. All the major prophets (Isaiah, Jeremiah, and Ezekiel) reminded their hearers of the event, and many of the minor prophets did too. Several of the Psalmists sang praises to God for what He did at the Exodus.

Yet the Egyptian records from those times make no mention of the Exodus at all. To the Egyptians it was probably a very small event. The Israelites were not the only slaves in Egypt, and their escape would not have caused any great excitement. The description of Pharaoh and all his army pursuing the slaves was probably created out of the Israelite's memory of their terror at that time (Ex. 14.5–9). When people are afraid they always think that circumstances are worse than they really are. Probably Pharaoh did send a small band of troops after the Israelites. Afterwards he would have been annoyed at their failure to capture the escaping slaves, but no court record would be kept of the event. Certainly there is no record that a Pharaoh died by drowning in the Red Sea.

The lack of any Egyptian record makes it very difficult for us to be sure exactly when the Exodus took place. Scholars differ in their interpretation of the information which is available. In fact some scholars believe that the stories of the Exodus are based on several quite separate events in the life of the Israelites. For example, Martin Noth is convinced that the events at Sinai were quite separate, and not related to the Exodus, or to the entry to the promised land. Such scholars believe that we ought to look for separate dates for the separate parts of the story.

We cannot here go into the details of their reasoning, nor can we give all the reasons for rejecting their theory. We shall in this book accept the traditional view which puts together in history the Exodus, the happenings at Sinai, the Israelites' time of living in the wilderness, and their entry into the promised land, as one series of events, because it is difficult to see what else could have led up to the events at Sinai, except the

40

Exodus. The whole story of what happened at Sinai depends upon the celebration of a great act of deliverance in which God had set His people free. It is also difficult to see how Moses became associated in the memory of the people of Israel with both the Exodus and the events at Sinai, unless he was associated with them in actual fact.

When we try to see the connection between the events recorded in the Bible and the things which were happening in the world around at the same time, we find that we must try to answer the following questions:

1. When could Joseph have been so fully accepted in Egypt that he was promoted almost overnight from slavery to the position second only to Pharaoh? (See Gen. 41.44.)

2. What changes in the dynasties of Egypt would explain the slavery of Israel at a later date? (See Ex. 1.8–11.)

3. What evidence is there for the building of the two cities Pithom and Raamses?

4. When could Israel have met with the tribes which are named in the stories of their time in the Wilderness?

5. When was the situation in Palestine suitable for the arrival of the Israelites, as described in Joshua and Judges?

6. Is there any evidence of the widespread destruction of towns in Palestine at a time that can be related to the Israelite conquest?

7. Is there any evidence for the destruction of Jericho and Ai, as described in Joshua 6 and 8?

I. JOSEPH'S RISE TO POWER

Most scholars agree that Joseph's rise to power in Egypt is likely to have happened during the rule of the Hyksos kings. These kings were Semitic princes who first entered Egypt from south-west Asia about 1720 BC, and brought the whole country under their rule by about 1690 BC. They set up their own capital city at Avaris in the Nile Delta (see Map 2). From there they ruled a wide area of the ancient Near East, including Palestine and possibly reaching as far as Mesopotamia. They had the same tribal origins as the Israelites, and would naturally have welcomed Joseph as a new leader among them.

2. THE SLAVERY OF ISRAEL

The rule of the Hyksos lasted about a hundred years. Then the people of Upper Egypt broke free from their control, and eventually captured Avaris in about 1550 BC. The Hyksos were then driven out of Egypt. The ancient scholar Josephus thought that the Exodus took place at the same time. But that idea does not allow time for the oppression of the Israelites under 'a new king over Egypt, who did not know Joseph' (Ex. 1.8). Nor does it fit in well with the dates at which the other events in the Exodus story are likely to have happened. It seems probable that the

Israelites were in Egypt for much more than a hundred years—see Exodus 12.40. However, the overthrow of the Hyksos does explain why the Israelites, whom they had protected, were made slaves in Egypt.

3. CITIES BUILT

To discover how long the period of slavery lasted in Egypt, we must examine the evidence for the building of the store cities, Pithom and Raamses (Ex. 1.11). At Bethshan in Palestine there is a stele (a stele is an inscribed stone pillar) which refers to the reign of Raamses II (1290–1223 BC). It tells how a people of that time 'haul stones for the great fortress of the city of Raamses, the beloved of Amon'. Raamses II was in fact rebuilding Avaris, the ancient capital of the Hyksos kings, and he gave it his own name. He also built a city in Wadi Tumilat which was probably Pithom (see Map 2, p. 51). The map shows that Avaris and Pithom were situated one on each side of Goshen, where the Israelites are said to have lived (Ex. 8.22, etc.). Other evidence is provided by pictures preserved from ancient Egypt which show that the slaves of this period in Egypt included Semites: i.e. people of the same race as the Israelites—perhaps the Israelites themselves. All this suggests that the Exodus probably took place during the reign of Raamses II, in the middle of the thirteenth century BC.

4. TRIBES IN THE WILDERNESS

Moses met and married the daughter of Jethro, the priest of Midian (Ex. 3.1), who was also described as a Kenite (see Judges 1.16). The people of Israel fought against the Amalekites (Ex. 17.8–13) and had to make a detour round the land of the Moabites (Num. 21.21f). The Midianites and the Amalekites were both nomadic peoples. They travelled from place to place and left little that has survived to help archaeologists in their study of early history. We cannot expect to find clues to the date of the Exodus from any knowledge we have of these people. The Kenites seem to have been metal workers, and would quite naturally live in the Sinai peninsula where there were copper mines in the days of ancient Egypt. But again this gives little help in fixing the date of the Exodus, though it does support the traditional belief about the site of Mount Sinai. The Moabites did not become a settled people with a kingdom of their own east of the Dead Sea until the thirteenth century BC. But they had settled there by the time of the Exodus. This fact implies that the earliest possible time for the Exodus was the thirteenth century, and possibly in the reign of Raamses II.

5. PALESTINE OPEN TO SETTLERS

Throughout ancient history Palestine was a battleground. It lay between the major centres of civilization which then were in Egypt and Mesopo-

2.1 Joseph's rise to power probably happened under the Hyksos kings, when he 'stored up in every city grain in abundance' (Gen. 41.48, 49), and saved the Egyptians from starvation in time of famine. No doubt he directed the work of men like the high-ranking Superintendent of Granaries pictured in a wall-painting of the fifteenth century BC at Thebes.

tamia, and at later times included Asia Minor and Europe. Each kingdom which became powerful in the ancient Near East tried to gain control of Palestine. Palestine's position made it useful as a line of defence against enemy nations, or as a base from which to attack enemy countries. In the period which we are studying in this chapter, Egypt normally held control, but there were times when Egypt's internal political problems made this difficult. At these times life there became unsettled, and raids by nomads from beyond the Jordan were frequent. It seems likely that the Israelites conquered Palestine in such a time of weakness.

Much of the fourteenth century had been a period of Egyptian weakness. There is evidence for this in the Amarna tablets, which belong to that time. These were letters written to the Pharaohs by their officers in Palestine and Phoenicia, and even further away. They tell of uprisings against Egyptian control, and they refer to the 'Khapiru' as leaders of such revolts. Some scholars think that these 'Khapiru' were in fact the 'Hebrews', i.e. the Israelites. So they believe that the Israelites settled in Palestine at this earlier time. This belief does not fit in well with the evidence that the Exodus took place in the thirteenth century. But, as we shall see later, some of the tribes who eventually formed the people of Israel had probably not been in Egypt, were not involved in the Exodus, and were not brought into Palestine under the leadership of Joshua. These tribes were probably in Palestine from an earlier time, and may have been among the 'Khapiru' mentioned in the Amarna tablets. However, the term 'Khapiru' is *not* just an alternative spelling for the name of the 'Hebrews'. The Khapiru were far more widely spread over the ancient world than the Hebrews, and were simply a class of people with few rights who seem to have given little loyalty to the rulers of the lands in which they lived.

After the reign of Raamses II, Egypt went through another time of weakness. The new king Merneptah (1223–1211 BC) was elderly. He was unable to maintain proper control over Palestine, and so became involved in war. A stele which he erected at the end of the war records that Israel was among the enemies he defeated. It says, 'Israel lies desolate, its seed is no more.' The Pharaoh boasted, 'Everyone who was a nomad has been curbed by King Merneptah.' The importance of this stele is that it shows there were Israelites in Palestine by about 1220 BC. But their defeat must have had little effect on Israel because there is no mention of it in the Bible. It seems reasonable to suppose that the Israelites entered the promised land before the reign of Merneptah—perhaps about 1240 BC.

6. CITIES OF PALESTINE DESTROYED

As we have seen, much important information has been gathered from the tells which remain in Palestine (see p. 7). Archaeologists have discovered through their digging into tells that a number of towns were burnt down toward the end of the thirteenth century. This evidence seems to support the biblical records of the settlement in Palestine, for these towns include Debir (Josh. 10.38f), Lachish (Josh. 10.31f), Hazor (Josh. 11.10), and possibly also Eglon (Josh. 10.34f). If these towns were destroyed as the result of the attacks by Israel, this would support the date we have suggested for the Exodus, i.e. the thirteenth century.

7. JERICHO AND AI

The evidence from Jericho and Ai, however, is quite different. Although these towns are important in the story of the Israelites' settlement in Canaan, there is no evidence from the tells of these two towns to support the idea that they were destroyed by Israel in the thirteenth century.

Jericho seems to have been destroyed in the beginning of the fifteenth century, and again a little later than the middle of the fourteenth century. After that the site remained unoccupied until the ninth century (1 Kings 16.34). Perhaps the story of the destruction of Jericho was preserved by some of the people of Israel whose ancestors had entered Palestine before the Exodus. Then in later times the stories of the two periods of conquest may have become confused in people's minds. The story of the defeat of Jericho may have been combined with the stories of Joshua. The same kind of confusion arises today, when older people speak of important events in their history, and younger people are uncertain about when these things took place.

Ai had been destroyed even earlier, before the twentieth century BC, and had not been reoccupied. However, Bethel was little more than a mile away from Ai, and people could easily have confused the two places. Probably Joshua 6 refers to Bethel (compare with it Judges 1.22–26). We do know that Bethel was destroyed at about the same time as Debir, Lachish, and Hazor.

8. BIBLICAL DATING

So we see that much of the evidence suggests that the Exodus took place in the reign of Raamses II (1290–1223 BC). There are some items of evidence which do not support this view. But other suggestions for the date of the Exodus do not fit the known facts so well. The items of conflicting evidence suggest that some at least of the tribes which later formed Israel were in Palestine earlier than the time of Joshua.

The writers of the Bible themselves made two separate attempts to provide a date for the Exodus.

1. According to Exodus 12.40, it occurred '430 years' after the entry of Joseph and his family into Egypt. We have noticed that this was probably in the time of the Hyksos (1690–1550 BC). If this is true then the

Exodus happened somewhere between 1260 and 1120, which supports our view.

2. According to 1 Kings 6.1, the Exodus happened '480 years' before the founding of the Temple. The Temple was founded in about 958 BC, which would give a date for the Exodus of about 1438 BC. Such a date is too early. However, the '480 years' probably stand for twelve generations of forty years each. We know that the Israelites sometimes counted generations in this way. But in fact each generation was more likely to be twenty-five years. So twelve generations would cover a period of 300 years. If the writer of 1 Kings 6.1 was correct in speaking of twelve generations, the evidence that he gives places the Exodus at about 1258 BC. This also provides a date for the Exodus in the thirteenth century BC.

STUDY SUGGESTIONS

WORDS

1. What are the names given to the following?
   (a) A series of kings all belonging to one family.
   (b) People who wander from place to place, with no fixed home.
   (c) The land at the mouth of a river which divides into many channels and enters the sea at more than one place.
   (d) The study of things which remain from ancient civilizations.
   (e) The time it takes for children to grow up, marry, and have children of their own.
2. Who or what are or were:
   (a) The Pharaohs   (b) The Khapiru
   (c) The Hyksos   (d) Stele

REVIEW OF CONTENT

3. How can we account for the fact that Egyptian records do not mention the Exodus, although it is mentioned again and again in records of the history of Israel?
4. (a) Why is it difficult for scholars to know exactly when the Exodus took place?
   (b) Name four different events which can help scholars to discover approximately when it took place.
5. (a) What did the Hyksos kings and the Israelites have in common?
   (b) Where did the Hyksos come from?
   (c) When did they enter Egypt?
   (d) What was the name of their capital city?
   (e) For how long did they rule in Egypt?
6. Give two examples of historical evidence which suggests that Israelites were among the slaves who helped to rebuild the capital city of the Hyksos kings.

7. Name four different tribes with whom the Israelites came in contact during their travels in the wilderness.

8. (a) Is the Israelites' conquest of Palestine most likely to have happened in a time when Egypt's control of the land was strong, or when it was weak? Give reasons for your answer.
(b) What evidence for the date of the Israelites' entry into Palestine is provided by the stele erected by King Merneptah?

9. (a) Name three towns which the archaeologists have discovered were destroyed by fire during the thirteenth century BC.
(b) In what way is the archaeological evidence from these towns different from the evidence at Jericho and Ai?

10. (i) When did the Exodus happen, according to:
(a) Exodus 12.40? (b) 1 Kings 6.1?
(ii) What reasons can we give for the difference between these two accounts?

FURTHER STUDY AND DISCUSSION

11. Several different Pharaohs are mentioned in the Bible.
(a) Look up the verses listed under the word Pharaoh in a concordance. How many different Pharaohs are named, and which verses refer to each of them?
(b) Read the article in a Bible Dictionary under the word 'Pharaoh'. In what ways, if any, does your Bible dictionary differ from this Guide in what it says about the Pharaoh at the time of the Exodus? What reasons can you suggest for the differences?

12. The Hyksos were 'semitic' princes.
Use a dictionary and an encyclopaedia to discover:
(a) What is a Semite?
(b) Which were—and are—the 'semitic' languages?
(c) Are there any Semites today? If so, who are they and where do they live?

2. 'THE LORD BROUGHT THE PEOPLE OUT OF EGYPT'

The Exodus is the central fact of the Jewish faith. Jews remember always the time when God acted to save their ancestors the Israelites from slavery in Egypt. This fact of history confirms their belief that God chose the Jewish people to serve Him in a special way. They believe that the Laws of God were given to them at Mount Sinai. Today Jews still obey the many rules that have been preserved for them in the Old Testament.

The story of the Exodus has been told many times since the days when the Israelites came out of Egypt. There are no detailed written records preserved from the time of the Exodus. Many different legends were retained among the memories of the Israelites, and were eventually written into their history books, or used by the prophets and psalmists. When we look at the records in our Bibles today, we find that the story of the Exodus is not very easy to understand. The main events themselves are clear to us, but important details remain matters for thought and discussion. There are many questions we might like to ask, but there is nobody who can give us a clear answer which is full, and final, never to be questioned again. So we have to decide to follow one of the writers on the subject, or else attempt to discover for ourselves what is most likely to have been the truth.

I. THE CALL OF MOSES

The story of the early life of Moses appears clear and straightforward. He was born of an Israelite mother (Ex. 2.2), brought up in the Egyptian palace (Ex. 2.10), and exiled because he killed a man in uncontrolled anger (Ex. 2.11–15). So we see that by the time God called Moses to set the Israelites free, he had been influenced by an Israelite woman's piety, by the wisdom of the Egyptian court, and by the knowledge of desert life possessed by the Midianites.

In the desert Moses met God. The sign of His presence was a burning bush which was not destroyed by the flames (Ex. 3.2). People have tried to explain this in many different ways. Some have suggested that the bush was lit up by the rays of the setting sun, others that some sort of natural gas was escaping from the ground and was burning at too low a temperature to damage the bush. Perhaps the bush was part of a vision: something which happened in the mind and thought of Moses rather than actually existing in the physical world. We shall never know for certain what it was. It is enough to know that the experience led Moses into fellowship with God.

As a result, Moses believed that God told him to go to Pharaoh and to order Pharaoh to liberate the Israelite slaves. Moses felt that he needed some word of authority to encourage the Israelites and to convince Pharaoh. He was given a new name for God: 'I am who I am' (Ex. 3.14). The Hebrew form of the name 'Yahweh' became the most sacred name any Israelite could use when he wanted to speak of God. It was the name for God received by Moses at Mount Sinai. (Exodus 3.1 names the place Mount Horeb, but this is simply another name for Mount Sinai.)

Moses was also given signs to use to prove that he had authority from God: a rod that would become a serpent (Ex. 4.3), and a hand that would become leprous (Ex. 4.6). It is difficult to know how Moses produced these signs, but it is important to notice that the Egyptians knew the secret, and could do the same thing (Ex. 7.11). Moses may have decided such methods were useless to convince the Egyptians, for there is no record of his using the sign of leprosy. Moses was also given Aaron, to speak on his behalf (Ex. 4.14–16).

2. THE PLAGUES

Pharaoh was not at all willing to allow the Israelites to go free. The book of Exodus records ten plagues which were needed to persuade him to set them free. Even then he regretted his decision! Most scholars agree that the plagues described were natural disasters of the sort which occur in Egypt from time to time. The reason why these events seemed miraculous at the time when Moses went to Pharaoh was that so many plagues followed each other closely, and that Moses was able to foretell each before it came.

The Egyptians probably believed that such disasters were caused by angry gods, and that they could avoid them by finding a way to please the god that was angry. Moses told them that it was the God of the Israelite slaves who was angry, and that Pharaoh must set them free. Moses's ability to foresee each plague in turn seems to have convinced the Egyptians, at least for a time, that he was right. The accounts of the various plagues do not all come from the same source of information. None of the sources recognized by scholars list all ten plagues, but each adds evidence to support the idea that some natural disasters were used by Moses to convince Pharaoh.

One of the plagues was a disease which caused many children to die. It seems likely that as people told and retold the story, it grew into the legend about the death of all the Egyptians' first-born sons (Ex. 12.29). The Israelites may have escaped the disease because of their different diet, different eating habits, or even because they lived in separate communities, and away from the infected areas of Egypt. In later times the Israelites believed that the first Passover gave them immunity from this disaster sent by God (Ex. 12.27).

3. CROSSING THE RED SEA

According to Exodus 14, the escaping Israelite slaves became trapped between the Egyptian soldiers who were pursuing them, and the sea, and by a miracle the Israelites were saved and the Egyptians drowned. We find the earliest written record of the story in Exodus 15.21, which contains two lines from an ancient song which may have been written down in the time of Miriam. The longer poem in Exodus 15.1–18 does not come from such an early time.

In the English translation of the poem the stretch of water crossed by the slaves is named as the 'Red' Sea (v. 4). Yet in the Hebrew from which our Bibles are translated the name given to the water is the 'Reed' Sea. There are no reeds in the Red Sea. Almost certainly the Israelites crossed some other stretch of water than the Red Sea. The same name, Reed Sea, is used in later Hebrew records, i.e. Exodus 13.18 and 15.22. In Map 2 we see that there may have been water south-east of Pithom, or even due east, and that the crossing probably occurred there.

Exodus 14.21 records two separate accounts of what happened to make it possible for the Israelites to cross.

1. A strong east wind blew all night and drove the water back 'and made the sea dry land'. That was enough in itself, but the verse goes on to say that,

2. The 'waters were divided', and in the next verse the people are described as walking across, 'the waters being a wall to them on their right hand and on their left'.

The first is the more natural account of what happened in a place of fairly shallow water. The second describes an amazing miracle in which the wind kept the water standing on two sides, leaving a passage between. Many scholars think that the second account was written a long time after the event, and that it was expressed in poetic language which made the event seem more miraculous, as a way of giving honour to God. Today many people feel that it is more true to man's experience of God to say that 'He uses the forces of nature to fulfil His purposes', rather than that He breaks the laws of nature to do so. We shall discuss the question of miracles more thoroughly in volume 3 of this course.

Another suggestion about the crossing of the water is that earthquakes may have been happening at that time, and that the natural flow of the water was stopped for some hours by the rocks thrown into it by the earthquakes. Some people also explain 'the pillar of cloud' by day, and 'the pillar of fire' by night (Ex. 13.21) in this sort of way. They say that the smoke and flame from a volcano erupting in the distance would look like a 'pillar'.

4. FOOD AND WATER IN THE DESERT

Moses had spent some years in the desert, living as a shepherd with his father-in-law, Jethro. His knowledge of water holes and oases must have been useful to the Israelites as they travelled through the same regions. They remembered in later years that he had known how to purify bitter water (Ex. 15.23–25) and release water trapped in the rocks (Ex. 17.1–6). Moses was also able to show the Israelites that they could eat manna. The word *manna* means 'what is it' (Ex. 16.14f). It was probably a substance produced by insects that lived on tamarisk trees in the desert. And Moses was able to promise the Israelites meat from quail (Ex. 16.13; Num. 11.31f). These were almost certainly birds migrating from Europe to North Africa which had been blown off their route by gale-force winds, and which had arrived exhausted in the desert, where they were easily caught.

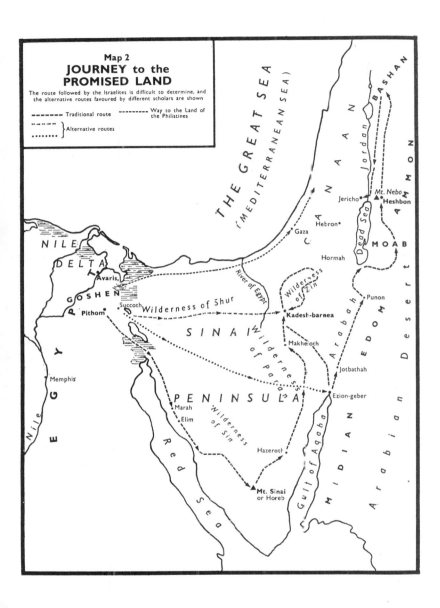

5. MOUNT SINAI

Moses led the people to the mountain where he had first met with God. There is considerable disagreement among scholars about the site of Mount Sinai.

By tradition Mount Sinai is believed to have been at the southern end of what today is called the Sinai Peninsula (see Map 2). But the tradition can only be traced back to the sixth century after Christ. There is a gap of over eighteen hundred years between the time of Moses, and the first historical evidence that men believed he came to this particular mountain.

(a) Some scholars think that this tradition about the site of Mount Sinai cannot be accepted, because the mountain it names was not a volcano. They say that such descriptions as Exodus 19.16 clearly indicate that Mount Sinai was a volcano. If it was, it must have been situated much further east, beyond Ezion-geber in the area traditionally associated with the Midianites. These scholars point out that Moses married a Midianite, who would probably have belonged to this land beyond Ezion-geber.

(b) Other scholars believe that Exodus 19.16 is a poetic description of a thunderstorm, which could easily have happened in any of the mountains of the Sinai Peninsula. They point out that the Midianites were nomadic people who were likely to move many miles from their tribal home in search of food for their animals, and who might easily have reached the Sinai Peninsula. The evidence seems fairly equal on both sides, and it is impossible to be certain of the truth.

There are three routes by which the Israelites may have travelled at the time of the Exodus (see Map 2). The route furthest to the south leads to the traditional site of Mount Sinai. The middle route leads to Ezion-geber and beyond. The route furthest north is suggested by those who believe that the people who came out of Egypt never went to Mount Sinai at all, but travelled directly to Kadesh-barnea. Noth believes that it was not the escaping slaves but a different group of people who were at Sinai (see p. 40).

6. THE COVENANT AT SINAI

The events at Sinai itself are the most difficult of all to clarify. A number of important questions cannot be answered with any certainty at all.

First, we may ask what Moses hoped to achieve at Mount Sinai. Why did he lead the people of Israel to the place where God spoke to him in the burning bush?

(a) Did he expect the Israelites to share directly in a similar experience? Exodus 19.10–11 and 19.17 together suggest that he did. But even if he did, the people refused to accept such a revelation (see Exodus

20.18–19). As a result of their fear, they were given laws instead, which made God's Will known to them indirectly through Moses.

(b) But there are two passages in the book of Exodus which suggest that Moses always expected to be the intermediary between God and the people: Exodus 19.9 and 19.20–21.

It seems that St Paul accepted the first of these alternatives as correct. In his letter to the Galatians he wrote about the Law as 'ordained by angels through an intermediary', as a first step only until something better were possible. Paul claimed that an intermediary, such as Moses, had been necessary only 'because of transgressions' (Gal. 3.19–20).

Probably the idea that Moses had a special relationship with God was pleasing to the Israelites, because it seemed to excuse the fact that most of them knew God by hearsay only. If they accepted that Moses had prepared the way for them to have a much more direct relationship with God, then they were guilty of turning away from that high calling. If they rejected this idea, they could claim that they fulfilled God's plans for them.

But it is not clear from the book of Exodus what kind of relationship there was between Moses himself and God. Nor is it clear whether this relationship was unique, or whether others shared Moses's experience of God. In Exodus 33.18 we find that Moses asked for a clear vision of God, 'I pray thee, show me thy glory.' The story goes on that he was given knowledge of the character of God, and as a special favour a vision of the back of God. But he was told quite firmly, 'You cannot see my face; for man shall not see me and live' (Ex. 33.20).

In contrast to this, we find in Exodus 33.11 that 'the Lord used to speak to Moses face to face, as a man speaks to his friend'. And according to Exodus 24.9–11 other leaders joined with Moses in having a vision of God: 'they beheld God, and ate and drank'. All we can say about this evidence is that some people who retold the story of Sinai believed that God could be known face to face by men, but others were not able to understand or accept this idea. Each writer described the events at Sinai in the way he believed that they happened. As a result, when their stories were combined in the book of Exodus there was no clear agreement.

Each of us will normally emphasize those parts of Exodus which fit in most clearly with his understanding of God, and of men's relationships with God. But this does not mean that we should ignore other points of view. We must study all the evidence carefully before reaching our own conclusions about these stories.

THE LAW AND THE COVENANT

When we study God's relationship with the whole people of Israel, as described in the book of Exodus, we find that two ideas are specially important: (1) the Law, and (2) the Covenant.

For many years now scholars have understood that the Laws recorded in the first five books of the Bible could not all have been prepared at the time of Sinai. Some of the laws are only suitable for a settled agricultural people, and not for the nomadic life which the Israelites were leading at that time in the wilderness. Some laws seem to belong to people whose ideas were those of a later period. And there are other differences. It seems therefore that the lawgivers of later times claimed the authority of Moses for rules which they themselves made. Many different codes of law have been put together in the Pentateuch.

It is fairly widely accepted that the Ten Commandments come from the days when the Israelites were at Mount Sinai. The version of the Commandments in Deuteronomy 5.6–21 differs from the version in Exodus 20.2–17, probably because it was recorded at a later time. Later writers were trying to express the basic laws in the way that the people of their own time would find most helpful.

Different writers gave different explanations of the origin of the stones (or 'tablets') on which the Ten Commandments were written. According to most accounts, God prepared these stones in a miraculous way. See Exodus 24.12; 31.18; and 32.16 for the first set of stones, and 34.1 for the stones which replaced the first set after Moses had broken them. Yet according to Exodus 34.28 it was Moses who cut the second set of stones, at God's command. There is evidence that 34.28 is an older record than the other passages, and so perhaps nearer to the actual facts of what happened. The Israelites treated the stones of the Commandments with great reverence. In later years this probably led men to suppose that they had come directly from the hand of God.

We have seen that Moses gave the Commandments as a means of making God's Will known to all the people of Israel. They were a necessary part of the Covenant between God and His people. The people promised, 'All that the Lord has spoken we will do' (Ex. 19.8 and 24.3). But there are different stories about this event also, and we cannot be sure exactly what happened at Sinai. According to Exodus 19.3–8 the people promised obedience before the laws had actually been given. According to Exodus 24.3–8 they made their promise after the Law had been made known. Probably the writers had different ideas about the significance of the Law. Some felt that the Law was the whole basis of the Covenant and that it was essential to Israel's relations with God. So they believed that the Law must have been given before the Covenant was established. Others felt that the Covenant came first, and that the Law was added later as an interpretation of what men must do if they are to serve God. Paul's attitude to the Law in his letter to the Galatians clearly suggests that he accepted the second of these ideas as being the truth. Paul reminds us that Abraham served God long before the Law was given (Gal. 3.17–18).

We shall look at the stories of Israel's entry to the promised land in the next chapter. The events at Sinai are a worthy climax to the story of Moses, and of the Exodus.

STUDY SUGGESTIONS

WORDS

1. What is the meaning of the Hebrew word *manna*?
2. (a) How do you understand the idea of God's 'face'?
   (b) From the verses containing the word 'face' as listed in a concordance, look up *five* which refer to the face of God. What have these verses to teach us about man's approach to God?
   (c) Read the article in a Bible dictionary under the heading 'Face'. Which of the following words could best be used instead of the word 'face' in the phrase 'the face of God'?
   Alertness   Beauty   Life   Presence   Sight

REVIEW OF CONTENT

3. (a) For what chief reason do Jewish people regard the Exodus as the central fact of their faith?
   (b) For what chief reason is the story of the Exodus difficult for us today to understand?
4. Name three different influences on Moses's early life.
5. Read Exodus 3 and 4.
   (a) What sort of word of authority did Moses receive from God which helped him to encourage the Israelites in Egypt?
   (b) What 'signs' did Moses use, to prove to the Egyptians that he had authority from God?
6. 'Most scholars agree that the plagues described (in the book of Exodus) were natural disasters . . .' (p. 49).
   (a) For what two reasons did these disasters seem 'miraculous' at the time of Moses?
   (b) What did the Egyptians at that time believe about disasters such as the plagues?
7. Read Exodus 13, 14, and 15.
   (a) What chief differences are there between the two accounts of the Israelites' escape from Egypt which you find recorded in chapter 14?
   (b) What are the reasons for these differences?
   (c) What natural happenings do some scholars suggest as explanations for the events described in Exodus 13.21 and 14.21?

8. How did Moses gain his knowledge about how to survive in the desert?
9. 'Did Moses expect the Israelites to share his direct experience of God, or did he expect to be the intermediary between God and the people?' (pp. 52 and 53).
   (i) What answers to this question do we find in each of the following passages?
      (a) Exod. 19.10–11 and Exod. 19.17   (b) Exod. 19.9
      (c) Exod. 19.20, 21   (d) Exod. 24.9–11
   (ii) Which of these answers did Paul accept?
   (iii) What is your own opinion? Give reasons for your answer.
   (iv) For what reason is the idea that Moses had a special relationship with God likely to have pleased the Israelites?
10. What two ideas about God's relationship with the Israelites as described in the book of Exodus are specially important?
11. For what two chief reasons do scholars today suggest that the first five books of the Bible were not all written at the time when Moses received the Law at Sinai?
12. Read Deut. 5.6–21 and Exod. 20.2–17.
   (a) List the variations between the two versions of the Commandments given in these two passages.
   (b) What difference, if any, do these variations make to your understanding of God's Law for His people?
13. Read Exod. 19.3–8, Exod. 24.3–8, and Gal. 3.17–18.
   (a) What is the chief difference between the people's response to God, as described in each of the two passages from Exodus?
   (b) Which version did Paul accept as the truth, and how did this affect his attitude to the Law?
   (c) What difference might acceptance of one version or the other make to our own attitude to the Law?

FURTHER STUDY AND DISCUSSION

14. 'It is more true to man's experience of God to say that "He uses the forces of nature to fulfil His purposes", rather than that He *breaks* the laws of nature to do so' (p. 50). What is your opinion?
   How does your opinion about this affect your understanding of:
   (a) The burning bush   (b) The plagues in Egypt
   (c) The crossing of the Reed Sea   (d) The gift of Manna
   (e) The writing of the tablets of the Law?
   (You may find it helpful to read an article on 'Miracle' in a Bible dictionary before answering this question.)
15. (a) What is the place of the Ten Commandments in the life of a Christian today?

(b) What was Jesus's attitude to the Law, according to Matthew 5.17–48?

(c) What value did Paul see in the Law (see Gal. 2.16; 3.2, 17, 23; 5.4)?

3. THE GOD OF MOSES

As a result of their experiences of the Exodus, the Israelites began to think about God, and about His relationship with men, in new ways. In the days of the Patriarchs people had thought of God as being concerned with individual men and women, and with their families. God's dealings with Abraham, Isaac, Jacob, and Jacob's twelve sons were personal and individual. And their response to God was as separate people, and as leaders of their families, though the *results* of their response were important for the people as a whole.

But in the days of the Exodus the Israelites saw that God was active in saving a whole multitude of people from slavery, and in helping them to become a well organized society. God chose Moses, not because he was the head of an important family, but in order that he should begin the work of making these people into a great nation.

THE COMMANDMENTS

The Ten Commandments (Ex. 20.2–17; Deut. 5.6–21) are central to the whole story. They show how the Israelites' ideas about God, and about His plan for mankind, had changed as a result of their experiences in the Exodus. Let us look at Exodus 20.2–17 to see what we can learn from this 'decalogue', as they are sometimes called (from the Greek *deka*, meaning 'ten', and *logos*, meaning 'word'.

v2. I am the LORD your God: We have already seen that in the RSV the word LORD in capital letters stands for the Hebrew name *Yahweh*, and that this special name for God was revealed for the first time to Moses at Mount Sinai, before he went back into Egypt to deliver the people of Israel from slavery. According to Exodus 3.14 the name means 'I am who I am', or as some translators suggest, 'I am what I am', or 'I will be what I will be' (see the footnotes to this verse in RSV). It is fairly certain that the name *Yahweh* does come from the Hebrew verb meaning 'to be'. But the tenses of the Hebrew verbs differ from those used in English, so it is difficult to translate the phrase exactly. According to the Concise Dictionary of the Bible, the name 'is probably intended to teach that God is active and that He Himself decides what He will do' (see article on Jehovah). Moses and his people came to understand the name as they saw what God did for them at the time of the Exodus.

Exodus 20.2 expresses the chief idea which the people of Israel always associated with the name *Yahweh*, i.e. that *Yahweh* is the God '*who brought you out of the land of Egypt, out of the house of bondage*'. Because God gave them freedom, when they knew that they could not free themselves, they knew that He was concerned for them, and for their good. At Sinai God gave them basic rules for behaviour, in their relationships both with Him, and with their fellow men. If they obeyed these laws, God's work of delivering them from slavery would be completed. His plan would be fulfilled by the establishment of a nation whose community life was based on peace and justice, in obedience to God.

v. 3. You shall have no other gods before me: These words can be understood in two different ways. Some people think they mean that there is no other god in existence. Others think they mean that Yahweh is the only God who is to be served. Later, some of the Israelites believed that there were other gods, and that Yahweh was simply the chief of all gods (see Ps. 89.5–7). The writer of Judges 11.24 had the idea that each nation has its own god, who is responsible for its life and prosperity: e.g. God on one side, Chemosh on another.

But we must remember that in every age some men have special spiritual insight, which others do not share. Probably Moses recognized the supremacy of Yahweh so clearly, that for him other gods were nothing. But many of his followers continued to believe that other gods had their own importance outside the community of Israel, even though they agreed that Yahweh should be given first place in their own lives. This explains the attitude of Jephthah in Judges 11.24.

v. 4. You shall not make yourself a graven image, or any likeness . . . : This command shows one way in which the Israelites were different from other peoples of their time. In every other religion in the days of Moses, idols were used to help the worshippers to think about their gods, and to understand them. The people of Israel had been living in Egypt where many such idols were worshipped, some with human bodies and animal heads.

Moses taught the people of Israel to think of God in a quite different way. For them the Ark of the Covenant probably provided a visible symbol of the presence of God in worship, instead of idols (see p. 61). Many people find it easier to worship if they have some object on which to concentrate their thoughts.

Aaron acted in response to the people's wishes when he collected gold from them and moulded a calf from it (Ex. 32.1–6). He seems to have wanted the people to regard the calf as a true representation of Yahweh. He suggested that the golden calf had been responsible for the delivery of the people of Israel from Egypt (Ex. 32.4), even though the calf itself had not existed at that time. Moses, however, saw great danger in such an object of worship, and acted quickly to destroy the

2.2   In the thirteenth century BC Egypt held control of Palestine. But the Pharaohs had to defend their empire from strong enemies to the north and east—like these Hittite warriors in their chariot, whom Raamses II defeated at Kadesh. A temple carving at Abydos records the battle.

2.3   Pictures from ancient Egypt—like this wall-painting in the tomb of Pharaoh Seti I—show that the slaves of this period in Egypt included Semites (2 at left in top row and 2 at right in bottom row): perhaps the Israelites themselves.

calf. Perhaps he recognized that an idol is under the control of men, whereas Yahweh certainly is not. The use of an idol can lead men into wrong ideas of their relationship with God. The Ark with its tablets of the Law was a continual reminder that it is God who is in control, and men who must serve Him.

v. 7. You shall not take the name of the Lord your God in vain: In ancient times, people thought that a name was powerful. They believed that by using a person's name they could influence or control its owner. Even today in some parts of the world men hide their real names for fear that they may be used to harm them. And by using the name of someone more important or more powerful than ourselves we can often persuade others to believe or even to obey us.

God had revealed His name to Moses, but this did not mean that Moses was to use it in order to control or direct God. Nor was it to be used as a way of exercising power over other people. God forbids people to use His name for their own schemes. It must not be used to work magic or cast spells. God's name should help us to think about Him properly, to honour Him for what He is, and to enjoy fellowship with Him. Later the Jews regarded the name Yahweh as so holy that it was too dangerous to be used at all, even in worship. From that time, whenever they read from their Scriptures they always said 'Adonai', which means 'Lord', when they found 'Yahweh' written.

v. 8. Remember the sabbath day, to keep it holy: The idea of setting aside one day in every seven for rest and for worship was not known before the time of Moses. This commandment started a new custom which in due time led to the Christian habit of observing Sunday as a special day. Jews still observe the seventh day, which is Saturday. In the early Church Jewish Christians continued to attend the synagogues on the sabbath, and special times of Christian worship seem to have been kept for the following day, Sunday, because this was the day of the Resurrection of Jesus. When the Church became largely Gentile in its membership, many of the Christians were not members of the synagogues, and could not worship there. Then the Lord's Resurrection day became the special day for Christian worship. And even in countries where Jews or Christians are a minority, many people value the use of the first day in every seven for regular rest and worship.

Notice that Exodus 20.11 and Deuteronomy 5.15 give different reasons for remembering the Sabbath. Probably both of these verses were added in later times by those who taught the Commandments to their own generations.

v. 12. Honour your father and your mother: This commandment stands between the first four, which concern our relationship with God, and the remaining five, which concern our duties to all our fellow men. Clearly father and mother are supremely important to their children. They have shared with God in the creation of their sons and daughters. They have taught their children to love and serve the Lord (Deut. 6.4–9). For these things they deserve honour, and care and protection in their old age.

vv. 13–17. You shall not—kill, commit adultery, steal, bear false witness, covet: These commandments are a firm foundation for all happy and peaceful relationships between men. All the later laws of conduct known in Israel are founded upon these ideas, and developed from them. Much of national and international law today has been built on the same foundations.

The Ten Commandments are the first attempt that we know of to describe in human words the will of God for mankind. Jesus confirmed their importance as a guide to mankind (Mk. 10.17–21). But He did more than just repeat their words and phrases. He Himself described the whole purpose and will of God more fully (Mk. 12.28–34). Laws can never take the place of a living knowledge of God, or of fellowship with Him. It seems that Moses himself recognized this truth. But the Israelites were not yet ready to understand it, so in God's name he gave them the Law until they were ready for a more personal relationship with God.

THE ARK OF THE COVENANT

The people of Israel responded to the revelation of God's will through the Ten Commandments by entering into the Covenant which He offered them. All that He had done for them, and all that He was planning to do for them, made them willing to serve and obey Him, and they made clear promises as a people that they would do so. The Ten Commandments were recorded on two stones, and these served as a constant reminder of the promises which the people had made. The 'Ark of the Covenant' was a wooden box made to contain these stones, so that the Israelites could carry them easily from place to place on their journeyings. Whenever they saw the Ark, the people of Israel remembered that they were the people of Yahweh, and that they must serve Him. They took the Ark with them wherever they went. When they had settled in Palestine they kept it at Shiloh, but sometimes they carried it into battle to encourage the fighting men (1 Sam. 4.3). David took the Ark to his new city capital of Jerusalem (2 Sam. 6.16f), where it was housed in the temple. It may have survived until the Babylonians destroyed Jerusalem, about six hundred years after the Exodus.

SACRIFICE AND WORSHIP

Jeremiah the prophet condemned the Israelites in later times for relying on sacrifice instead of on obedience. They seem to have believed that God would be satisfied with them if they made regular burnt offerings. Jeremiah said in God's name, 'in the day that I brought them out of the land of Egypt, I did not speak to your fathers or command them concerning burnt offerings and sacrifices. But this command I gave them, Obey my voice, and I will be your God, and you shall be my people' (Jer. 7.22f).

The Ten Commandments do not contain any instruction about sacrifice. If we set on one side all the laws in Exodus referring to the priests and to sacrifice which are known to belong to a later time, we find that the remaining references to this subject are very few. But some verses do give us an idea of what happened at Sinai. They show that there were no great changes from earlier times. The people still made altars of natural stones, and set them up as altars when needed (Ex. 20.25). The sacrifices which they presented at these altars were burnt offerings and peace offerings (Ex. 20.24; 24.5) which were widely known and used before the Israelites reached Sinai (Gen. 22.8; Ex. 18.12). The difference between these two sorts of sacrifice seems to have been that burnt offerings were completely destroyed by fire on the altars, but parts of the peace offerings were eaten by the people who made the sacrifice. Possibly burnt offerings were used to express honour and submission to God, and peace offerings to express fellowship with Him through a shared meal.

THE CULTIC DECALOGUE

Some scholars believe that Exodus 34.14–26 comes from the time when the Israelites were at Mount Sinai. They believe these verses give the original form of the Ten Commandments. They call these verses the 'Cultic Decalogue' because they are chiefly concerned with the 'cult', or ritual workings of God. These scholars believe that these verses were written earlier than the 'Ethical Decalogue' recorded in Exodus 20, which is chiefly concerned with people's behaviour toward God and one another. But other scholars point out that Exodus 34 describes practices which are more suitable for a settled agricultural community than for nomadic people travelling from place to place. They believe that these verses come from a later time, when the Israelites were settled in Palestine. We shall study them again in the next chapter. (See the section on the 'Three Festivals', p. 76.)

THE PASSOVER

This feast is celebrated among the Jews as a reminder that God rescued the people of Israel from slavery in Egypt. Probably the feast was already customary among the people of Israel before the time of the Exodus. The ceremony in which a lamb was sacrificed, and shared by each family, was similar to ceremonies carried out by other nomadic peoples. It was probably intended originally to obtain God's blessing on the people, and on their flocks, at the beginning of a new year. At the time of the Exodus this ceremony became associated with the departure from Egypt, which gave it a new meaning and importance. There are several different descriptions of the Passover in Exodus 12 and 13. They were all written long after the Exodus, and include details which were added to the ceremony in later times. Probably the use of unleavened bread was added to the Passover after the people of Israel had settled in Palestine.

STUDY SUGGESTIONS

WORDS

1. (a) Read the article under the heading 'covenant' in a Bible dictionary, and then write a single sentence to explain the meaning of the word as it is used in the Bible.
(b) Which *one* of the following words is most helpful in explaining the nature of a covenant?
contract agreement treaty bargain promise

REVIEW OF CONTENT

2. What was the chief difference between God's dealings with Abraham and his family, and His dealings with Moses and the Israelites at the time of the Exodus?
3. 'Moses and his people came to understand the name *Yahweh* as they saw what God did for them at the time of the Exodus' (p. 57).
(a) What chief idea did the people of Israel associate with the name Yahweh?
(b) What did the people learn about God Himself and about their relationship with Him, from the events of the Exodus?
4. In what way were the Israelites different from other peoples of their time as regards the use of idols?
5. Read Exodus 32.1–20.
What was the attitude of (a) Aaron, and (b) Moses, to the people's wish for visible 'gods'?
6. For what reason did the Jews use the word *Adonai* instead of *Yahweh* for the name of God, when reading from their Scriptures?
7. (a) All Ten Commandments are concerned with 'relationships'. With whom are these relationships in (i) the first four Commandments, (ii) the fifth Commandment, and (iii) the last five Commandments?
(b) Read Exodus 20.2–17 and 34.14–16. What names are given to these two passages?
8. In what way did the Israelites respond to God's revelation of His will for them through the Ten Commandments?
9. What was the 'Ark of the Covenant', and why was it given that name?

10. Read Exodus 12 and 13.
    (a) At what festival did the Israelites celebrate their rescue from slavery in Egypt?
    (b) What ceremonies took place at that festival?

11. What human relationships were used by the prophets and by Paul in each of the following passages to express the idea of 'covenant'?
    (a) Isa. 54.5–8 (b) Jer. 3.19 (c) Jer. 3.20 (d) Hos. 2.19, 20
    (e) Rom. 9.4 (RSV)

12. What ideas about God were expressed by the writers of the following passages?
    Exod. 15.11 Judges 11.24 Ps. 95.13 Ps. 97.9

13. In what way does the teaching of Jesus recorded in Mark 12.28–34 'confirm the importance' of the Ten Commandments, and in what way does it 'describe the purpose and will of God more fully' (p. 61)?

FURTHER STUDY AND DISCUSSION

14. The Israelites were forbidden to make idols to help them in their worship of God. But Christians often use pictures of Jesus, and some show His image in stained-glass windows or statues. Are they breaking the third commandment by doing this? If not, what is the difference?

15. How would you reply to someone who said, 'Christians today are no longer bound by the Law, so I do not need to keep the Sabbath'?

16. Give three examples from everyday life of ways in which a 'name' has power.

17. 'Jeremiah condemned the Israelites for relying on sacrifice instead of obedience' (p. 62, and see Jer. 7.22–29).
    In what ways do Christians today sometimes 'rely on sacrifice instead of obedience'?

CHAPTER 3

The Twelve Tribes

1. THE PROMISED LAND

Thus the Lord gave to Israel all the land which He swore to give to their fathers; and having taken possession of it, they settled there. (Josh. 21.43)

This verse sums up the subject of this chapter, i.e. the way in which the Israelites found a home for themselves in Palestine. Most of the biblical account of this period is found in the books of Joshua and Judges. We shall understand the events recorded in these two books much more easily if we know what was happening in Palestine and the surrounding nations in the years between 1250 and 1000 BC.

The land which we usually call Palestine was known as Canaan in the early years of this period. The Israelites gave two names to the peoples who had occupied this territory before they did: 'Canaanites' and 'Amorites'. Many of the story-tellers of Israel used these names without distinguishing clearly between them. But probably the real difference between the two peoples is that the Canaanites were the original inhabitants of the land, while the Amorites were those who entered it in biblical times. The population of Canaan was very mixed, and many different tribes seem to have lived there (see Josh. 3.10).

The people living in Canaan reached a fairly high level of civilization. Their cities were well built and strongly fortified, with some fine houses alongside the smaller dwelling-places. Most cities had their own over-lord, and their own small farming area nearby. Some of the city-dwellers were men of authority and power, while others were their servants. Trade was carried on with Egypt and Mesopotamia, and even with places as far away as the land we know today as Greece.

Perhaps the most remarkable fact about the Canaanites is that they invented the alphabet. Until that time, 'writing' had been made up of pictures of the objects or ideas written about, or else pictures represent-ing words or syllables in a less direct way. The development of signs to stand for sounds, rather than objects, led to the production of the first alphabet. As a result it became easier for ordinary people to learn to read and write.

The people of Canaan believed in a supreme god called El, but they worshipped Baal more fully, and more often. They believed that Baal, with a number of goddesses (Asherah, Astarte, Anat), was responsible

65

for the fertility of crops, herds, and human families. Baal was thought to die and rise again, and thus to cause the varying seasons. Canaanite worship was violently sexual in form. The Canaanites believed this would ensure the fertility of their farms and flocks, and of their own families.

Until about 1250 BC Egypt had often held control of the land of Canaan. The various Pharaohs had made the Canaanite city-lords their servants: taking taxes from them, and giving military support and protection in return.

Whenever Egypt had been weak the city overlords had been in trouble. Often they were unable to maintain their authority, and were frequently attacked by other city overlords, or by new groups of immigrants who wanted to settle in the land. By the time of the Israelite settlement Egypt had lost most of its ancient glory and power.

We have seen how Merneptah tried to regain control of Palestine, and was able to celebrate his victories by erecting a stele. But he had little time to enjoy his success, for Egypt itself was soon attacked by a new enemy: the Sea Peoples. These included the Philistines, who came to Egypt from Crete (Amos 9.7; Jer. 47.4).

The Egyptians had found it very difficult to prevent the Sea Peoples from invading their land. They could only do so by allowing them to settle in Canaan instead. The Philistines built five cities on the southern coastline of Canaan: Gaza, Ashkelon, Ashdod, Ekron, and Gath.

Other parts of the coast lands were also invaded by the Sea Peoples at this time. Egypt suffered repeated attacks by these people, and lost much of its power. The Philistines became strong, and gave their name to the coastal area of Canaan, Philistia. Much later the Romans used their name as the title for a wider area: 'Palestine' as we know it today.

Palestine went through a further time of unrest as a result of the weakness of Egypt. New groups of immigrants entered the country, taking over existing cities, or building new ones for their own use. The most densely populated areas were in the lowlands, where agriculture was easily developed; along the coastline; and in the plain of Esdraelon. Some cities were also built in the highlands: notably Shechem and Jerusalem.

Outside Palestine there were changes too. The Edomites and the Moabites were establishing kingdoms south east and east of the Dead Sea. Small Amorite states of Bashan and Heshbon existed east of the Jordan. The Ammonites were trying to gain possession of these same areas. And beyond the settled lands, in the desert regions, strong bands of nomads lived: for example the Amalekites and the Midianites.

None of the states of Mesopotamia were strong enough to have any lasting influence in this period, and the great Hittite nation to the north disappeared altogether.

3.1 'Perhaps the most remarkable thing about the Canaanites is that they invented the alphabet' (p. 65). The earliest known alphabetic inscription is on the tomb of King Ahiram of Byblos, who lived about 1250 BC. In this picture the inscription can be seen running along the lid of the tomb.

3.2 'At this time the Philistines became strong, and eventually their name was used as a title for the whole area we know as *Palestine*' (p. 66). Philistine soldiers can be recognized on Egyptian monuments by the high headdresses they wore.

STUDY SUGGESTIONS

REVIEW OF CONTENT

1. (a) What two peoples occupied the land we call Palestine before the Israelites settled there?
   (b) What was the chief difference between them?
2. (a) Describe in your own words how the Canaanites lived before the arrival of the Israelites.
   (b) For what invention were the Canaanites specially important, and what sort of influence did it give them over their neighbours?
3. All three names in each of the following groups belong to the same sort of person or place. What were they?
   (a) Asherah, Astarte, Anat
   (b) Ashkelon, Ashdod, Ekron
4. Are the following statements true or untrue?
   (a) Whenever Egypt was strong, the city overlords in Palestine were strong also and able to maintain their authority.
   (b) As the Philistines became strong, the power of Egypt became stronger still.
   (c) By the end of period 1250–1000 BC, the great Hittite nation had lost all its power.
5. Which areas of Palestine were the most densely populated in this period?
6. Draw a sketch map of the land of Palestine and mark on it the areas where the following tribes settled.
   (a) Amalekites   (b) Ammonites   (c) Canaanites   (d) Edomites
   (e) Midianites   (f) Moabites   (g) Philistines

BIBLE

7. Read Judges 6.7–10 and 25–32.
   (a) For what reasons do you think the people of Israel were tempted to worship the false gods of the Canaanites?
   (b) In what way did Gideon try to prevent them from doing so?

FURTHER STUDY AND DISCUSSION

8. Egypt was a weak nation in the period 1250–1000 BC. Yet Egypt is named at least seventeen times in the book of Joshua. Use a concordance to find out as many ways as you can in which Egypt continued to play a part in the life of Israel.
9. Read the section on the Philistines in a Bible dictionary.
   (a) Explain in your own words why this people became an important enemy of Israel.
   (b) When did the Israelites manage to destroy the power of the Philistines?

2. HOW DID THE TWELVE TRIBES SETTLE IN PALESTINE?

Map 3 (p. 71) shows the places where the twelve tribes were settled toward the end of the period 1250 to 1000 BC. How did the tribes come to settle in these places? The book of Joshua tells the main story of their settlement in Palestine, and the book of Judges tells what happened to the tribes after their arrival.

The book of Joshua tells how the Israelites crossed the Jordan under Joshua's leadership, and took the city of Jericho (Josh. 1—5). It describes their conquest of the hill country north of Jerusalem (Josh. 7—9), and south of Jerusalem (Josh. 10). It also describes their conquest of the northern part of Palestine, around Hazor (Josh. 11). We have already seen (p. 45) that archaeological evidence confirms that cities such as Debir, Lachish, and Hazor were destroyed in this period; and also Bethel—but not Ai. The biblical record in Joshua is based soundly on the memories preserved among the tribes of what happened at that time. It was preserved as an account of the way in which God gave the promised land to His people.

SHARING THE LAND

The last few chapters of the book of Joshua tell how the land was shared out between the twelve tribes. Some verses in these chapters suggest, however, that the Israelites did not conquer the whole of Palestine, and especially that many of the Canaanite cities remained independent even after the twelve tribes had settled in Palestine (Josh. 13.1–6, 13; 15.63; 16.10; 17.11–13). This is confirmed by the first chapter of Judges, which makes it quite clear that the twelve tribes did not conquer the whole of Palestine so completely that they could make it their own territory. See especially Judges 1.29–36.

In order to understand this period, we need to notice what the writer of the book of Joshua does *not* say.

1. He does *not* mention any battles in which the Israelites captured coastal areas of Palestine. The Sea Peoples were already settled there, and were too strong to be defeated (Josh. 13.2–3).

2. He does *not* describe the capture of the Plain of Esdraelon, along the valley of the Kishon. This area was too thickly populated by the Canaanites and Amorites for the twelve tribes to be able to gain land there.

3. He does *not* describe capture of Shiloh and Shechem in the centre of the country, even though these two places were important in the later history of the twelve tribes.

It seems, therefore, that:

(a) the Israelites settled in the south, centre, and north of Palestine, in the hill country where there were fewer established cities; and

(b) the tribal areas were divided into three groups, with strong Canaanite settlements between them in the area around Jerusalem, and in the Plain of Esdraelon.

So far as we know there were no political or legal ties between the tribes. All that joined them together was their shared service of the Lord, and their desire to obey Him. Each tribe had its own independent life and organization, but according to Joshua 24 they were bound together by their Covenant with God. Joshua had called the people together at Shechem. He had urged them to put away false gods, and to make public promises of obedience to the Lord. This religious unity held the tribes together, and gave them a sense of responsibility to each other. At a later time Shiloh became a centre for shared worship between the tribes.

Some scholars believe that the fact that the book of Joshua does not tell how Shechem and Shiloh came into the control of the twelve tribes, means that this part of Palestine was already held by Israelites *before* Joshua led his group into the land and began his conquest of Canaanite territory.

It is difficult to be sure who these Israelites were, who were in the land before Joshua came. But it is interesting to notice that although Reuben, Simeon, and Levi were the most important of the twelve sons of Jacob, the tribes who received their names played very little part in the history of Israel after the time of Joshua. Reuben is shown on our diagram east of the Dead Sea, where Moab held control for many centuries (see Map 3, p. 71). Simeon is shown as sharing land with Judah (see Josh. 19.1–9). These two tribes soon became united, with Judah taking the lead. Levi quickly became a religious community with no land of their own.

Some scholars suggest that these three tribes occupied land in Palestine before the time of Joshua, but that they had suffered severe defeats at the hands of an unknown enemy. This left them weak, but still in possession of the central highlands between Shechem and Shiloh. If this is true, the Covenant described in Joshua 24 helped to bring the two groups of tribes together as servants of the one Lord.

The book of Judges continues the story of the twelve tribes, and records the many difficulties which they faced in holding their position in Palestine. We have seen that the tribes were united by their worship of the one Lord. The writer of the book of Judges shows that the tribes were strong when they were obedient to God, and weak when they failed to serve Him.

THE WORK OF THE JUDGES

The Judges were men inspired by God to lead the tribes in battle against their enemies. They were rather like the chiefs of some warlike peoples

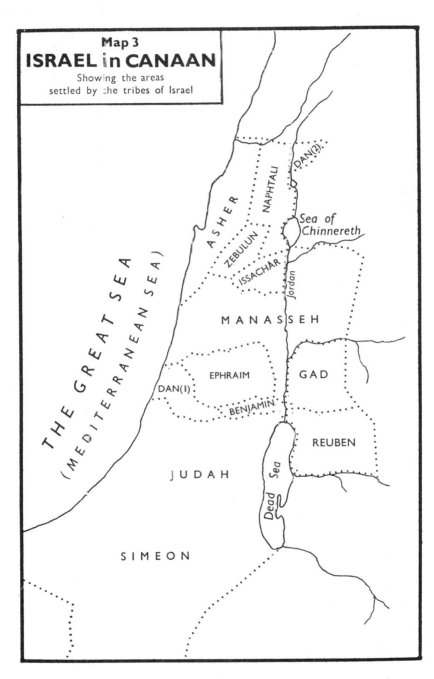

Map 3
ISRAEL in CANAAN
Showing the areas
settled by the tribes of Israel

DAN(2)

NAPHTALI

ASHER

Sea of
Chinnereth

ZEBULUN

ISSACHAR

Jordan

MANASSEH

THE GREAT SEA

(MEDITERRANEAN SEA)

EPHRAIM

DAN(1)

GAD

BENJAMIN

REUBEN

JUDAH

Dead Sea

SIMEON

71

in Africa and south-east Asia in recent times. Under the Judges' leadership the tribes regained their strength. They remembered that they owed service to the Lord, and so to one another, and they became stronger as their unity was thus restored. Judges 2.16–23 gives a general summary of the history of this period, describing the way in which the Judges drew the people together in time of conflict.

We must not suppose, however, that all twelve tribes always came together in times of danger. The book of Judges makes it clear that the tribes often fought alone or in small groups. This was usually enough, under good leadership, to enable them to defeat their enemies. It was not until later that they felt the need for a king who could command the obedience of them all.

We have already seen that the twelve tribes failed to gain control of the whole of Palestine. On the sea coast were the Sea Peoples including the Philistines, and inland many Canaanite cities remained independent. There were Aramaic-speaking tribes forming their own kingdoms east of the Jordan. These tribes occupied territory between the Jordan and the desert, and as their numbers grew they tried to get more land across the Jordan in Palestine. And there were nomadic people living in the desert regions who were tempted to steal from the settled communities in Palestine. The book of Judges tells how the tribes of Israel had to deal with these enemies during this period, in order to keep enough land for themselves, and to make progress as settled communities.

ENEMIES OF ISRAEL

1. *The Philistines.* Two Judges are described as working against the Philistines: *Shamgar* in about 1150 BC (Judges 3.31), and *Samson* about fifty years later (Judges 13.1—16.31). Both seem to have acted on their own, working as guerrillas rather than as leaders of armies. They were quite unable to destroy the power of the Philistines, but they did cause serious damage at places inside Philistine territory.

2. *The Canaanites.* Deborah was responsible for stirring up the Israelite tribes of the centre and north of Palestine to fight against the Canaanites in the Plain of Esdraelon. The Israelites seem to have had a considerable victory in about 1125 BC. The book of Judges records two accounts: one in prose (Judges 4), and the other in poetry (Judges 5). The Israelites won because the Canaanites depended on chariots in their fighting, and the Israelites attacked just when a severe flood of the river Kishon made these horse-drawn carts difficult to use. It is unlikely that this victory gave Israel permanent control of the Plain of Esdraelon.

3. *The Aramaic-speaking tribes.* All three major kingdoms east of Jordan were at war with Israel during this period.

(a) *Othniel* defeated the king of Edom in about 1200 BC (Judges 3.7–11). (The RSV says 'king of Mesopotamia', where the Hebrew text gives 'Aram'. Only one small mark needs to be added to the Hebrew word for it to read 'Edom'. It is unlikely that a king of Mesopotamia was at war with Israel at this time, but very probable that a king of Edom was.)

(b) *Ehud* killed the king of Moab in about 1175 BC, and so ended a long period in which the Moabites had forced some of the tribes of Israel to pay tribute to their king (Judges 3.12–30).

In about 1050 BC *Jephthah* led an army against the Ammonites, who were trying to gain power over Israelite territory east of the Jordan (Judges 10.6—12.7). He was able to prevent them, and 'the Ammonites were subdued before the people of Israel' (Judges 11.33).

4. *The nomadic raiders. Gideon* led a small band of Israelites against the Midianites and the Amalekites, who had frequently raided the Israelites' territory and stolen their crops. In about 1100 BC he was able to drive the raiders out of Palestine, and thus relieve the sufferings of the tribes involved. See Judges 6.1—8.35.

The book of Judges shows that the twelve tribes were able to defend themselves fairly well against most of their enemies, and at times to gain important victories. But the Philistines remained too powerful for them. This probably explains why the tribe of Dan moved, as shown on Map 3 (p. 71). They tried first to gain territory on the sea coast, but when this failed they had to retreat to the far north. See Joshua 19.40–48, and Judges 18.1

STUDY SUGGESTIONS

REVIEW OF CONTENT

1. In each of the following groups of names, *three* have something in common which the fourth does not share. In each group:
    (i) Say what the three have in common,
    (ii) Mark the one which is different from the others.
        (a) Benjamin, Levi, Reuben, Simeon.
        (b) Amorites, Canaanites, Danites, Philistines.
        (c) Ammonites, Edomites, Ephraimites, Moabites.
        (d) Asher, Judah, Naphtali, Zebulun.
        (e) Deborah, Gideon, Jephthah, Samson.
2. For what reason or reasons were the Israelites at first apparently unable to capture:
    (a) The coastal areas of Palestine?
    (b) The valley of the river Kishon in the Plain of Esdraelon?
    (c) The cities of Shiloh and Shechem?
3. Read Joshua 13.1–6, 13; 15.63; 16.10; and 17.11–13.
    (a) Name the Canaanite cities listed in these passages which were *not* captured by the Israelites.

(b) Compare your list with the account in Judges 1.29–36, and note which cities are included in *both* books, as remaining independent even after the Twelve Tribes had settled in Palestine.

4. (a) What political or legal ties were there, if any, between the Israelite tribes at this time?

(b) What was the *chief* tie which held the twelve tribes together?

(c) Which city later became a centre where the tribes shared in worship together?

BIBLE

5. What language was spoken at this period by the kingdoms east of Jordan?

6. Read Joshua 4 and Joshua 5 through once or twice.

(a) What event do the two chapters both describe?

(b) What chief differences are there between these two accounts of the event,

(i) as regards *what* is described,

(ii) as regards the *way* in which it is described?

FURTHER STUDY AND DISCUSSION

7. Read Judges 6.33–5, and 7.2–25.

(a) What sort of people were the Midianites?

(b) For what reason did they attack the Israelites?

(c) Which of the twelve tribes were involved in this battle?

(d) Why did Gideon cut down the size of his army from 32,000 to 300?

(e) How did trumpets and torches help the Israelites to defeat the Midianites?

8. Summarize in your own words the attitude of the people toward their leaders as described in Judges 2.16–23.

9. How would you answer somebody who said: 'It was wrong for the twelve tribes to rob other people of their land, and to kill their enemies'?

10. Are there any stories of past tribal conflicts in your own country which help you to understand the attitudes and actions of the Israelites at this time in their history?

11. How does the attitude of the Israelites to the Judges compare with people's attitude toward the political and military leaders in your country today?

3. THE LORD OF HOSTS

The twelve tribes knew that they belonged together because they accepted and worshipped the same God, Yahweh, the LORD. They made a Covenant together at Shechem to serve only Him (Josh. 24). Probably some of the people who shared in the Covenant had only known the name 'El' before that time, but under Joshua's leadership they all agreed that God should rightly be called the LORD (*Yahweh*). Notice how many times the name LORD is used in Joshua 24.14–28.

Three things were specially important in the religion of the twelve tribes: The Ark of the Covenant, the Book of the Covenant, and their Festivals.

1. THE ARK OF THE COVENANT

The Ark became the centre for the united worship of the LORD. Perhaps in the earliest days of the settlement it was kept at Gilgal (Josh. 4.15–24). Later it was kept at Bethel (Judges 20.27). In the early days of Samuel it was kept at Shiloh (1 Sam. 3.3). The Israelites believed that the Ark itself possessed power because it was closely linked with the LORD. In times of battle it seems to have been carried in front of the army to encourage those who were fighting for God (1 Sam. 4.5–9). The Israelites seem to have held some form of ceremony in which their leaders asked God in the presence of the Ark whether He wanted them to go into battle or not (Judges 20.27–28). They used a new name for God in connection with the Ark: *Yahweh Sabaoth* or 'LORD of Hosts'. This name was used to remind the Israelites that God was their leader in warfare (1 Sam. 4.4).

2. THE BOOK OF THE COVENANT

When the Israelites settled in Palestine they began a new way of life. They ceased to be nomads, and became farmers. They saw the Canaanites worshipping gods of fertility, and following rules and customs suitable for an agricultural community. Quite naturally the Israelites wanted to know how far they could copy the Canaanites, while still serving the LORD. The Ten Commandments were still important, but new rules were needed for their new way of life. The leaders in Israel probably met this need by introducing the instructions which are found today in Exodus 20.22—23.33 (see Vol. 2). These chapters of Exodus are often called the Book of the Covenant.

Some of the laws contained in these chapters of Exodus are very similar to the laws of other settled peoples in the ancient world. They normally took the pattern 'If a man . . ., he shall . . .', i.e. they showed how people should behave in various circumstances (see for example Ex. 22.14, etc.). The leaders of Israel may have copied the ideas contained in these laws from the codes of law belonging to other peoples. But there are other laws in the Book of the Covenant which are similar in form to the Ten Commandments ('You shall . . .', 'You shall not . . .'). These seem to have been completely new, both in form, and in what they said. They show us how Israel differed from other nations.

The Book of the Covenant states clearly that the Israelites must serve only God, and that they had no duty to worship the Canaanite gods and goddesses (Ex. 22.20; 23.13). Archaeologists have never found images of the pagan goddess Astarte among the remains of early Israelite settlements.

Some of the laws seem to warn the Israelites against following Canaanite customs in their worship of God (Ex. 22.18; 23.18, 19b), e.g. the instructions about the building of altars: Exodus 20.24–26. No Israelite altar was to be made of carved stones, or to have steps for the priest to approach the altar. Canaanite forms of altar were not to be used for the worship of the LORD.

Other laws encourage compassion for people likely to need help: i.e. strangers (Ex. 22.21; 23.9), widows and orphans (Ex. 22.22), the poor (Ex. 22.25–27; 23.3), and slaves (Ex. 21.1–11).

3. THE THREE FESTIVALS

The Book of the Covenant tells of three festivals to be held annually in Israel (Ex. 23.14–17). A similar list is given in Exodus 34.18–23. Two of these festivals, the Feasts of Unleavened Bread, and of Harvest, were to be held in the spring, at the beginning and the ending of the corn harvest. The other festival, the Feast of In-gathering, was for the autumn, at the end of the fruit-gathering season. These three feasts were suitable for a farming community, where corn and fruit were regularly grown.

The Israelites began to celebrate these festivals as a way of worshipping God when they settled in Palestine, and took up agriculture for themselves. Their Feast of Passover was held at the same time as that of Unleavened Bread, and the two became one major festival in Israel. Thus the Exodus story became connected in Israelite thought with the Feast of Unleavened Bread. Later, the other two festivals became connected with historical events. The Feast of Harvest became Pentecost, which commemorated the giving of the Law at Sinai. The Feast of In-gathering became the Feast of Booths (or tents) which commemorated the Israelites' wanderings in the wilderness. So these agricultural festivals came to be times for remembering how God had set Israel free from slavery in Egypt, and how He had made the Israelites His own special people. The autumn festival may have become the time of an annual gathering of the tribes at Shiloh where the Ark was kept. This would have been a time for renewing the Covenant which kept the tribes together as servants of the one LORD (Deut. 31.9–13; I Sam. 1.3).

STUDY SUGGESTIONS

WORDS

1. In what chief ways was the work of the 'Judges' in Israel different from the work of 'Judges' in most countries today?
2. What is meant by the Hebrew name *Yahweh Sabaoth*?

REVIEW OF CONTENT

3. 'The Israelites believed that the Ark itself possessed power because it was closely linked to the Lord' (p. 75).
   In what way was the Ark of the Covenant 'linked to the Lord'?
4. What was the 'new way of life' (p. 75) which the Israelites began when they settled in Palestine, and in what ways did it differ from the sort of life they had led before that time?
5. (a) Why is the name 'the Book of the Covenant' sometimes given to Exodus 20.22—23.33?
   (b) In what ways were the Laws recorded in these chapters different from the Commandments received by Moses at Sinai and recorded in Exodus 19.1–9 and 20.1–17?
6. (a) What evidence is there in Exodus 20.22—23.33 which suggests that the leaders of Israel may have copied some of these laws from codes of law already followed by other peoples?
   (b) In what chief way did the Israelites' laws about worship differ from those of the pagan Canaanites?
7. What were the three chief festivals which the Israelites began to celebrate each year? What did each celebrate, and at what times of year were they held?
8. Which of the following things and ideas were only known among the Israelites *after* they had settled in Palestine?
   (a) The Ten Commandments   (b) The Book of the Covenant
   (c) The Ark of the Covenant   (d) The Name 'Lord of Hosts'
   (e) The name 'El'   (f) The Feast of Passover
   (g) The Feast of In-gathering   (h) Burnt Offerings
   (i) An altar at Gilgal   (j) An altar at Bethel

BIBLE

9. Read Exodus 22.5–9. Name five things mentioned in these verses which suggest that these laws were meant for a time when the Israelites had ceased to live a nomadic life and had settled down and become an agricultural people, with land and farms of their own.

FURTHER STUDY AND DISCUSSION

10. A student once said: 'When I read the words of Jesus recorded in Matthew 25.31–46, I think I can understand what He meant when

77

He said "I have come not to abolish the law and the prophets but to fulfil them".'

What *additional* teaching do you think the student found in that passage from Matthew's Gospel, which is not contained in the 'law' as recorded, for example, in Exodus 22.21–27?

11. (a) What Christian festivals, if any, have taken the place of those celebrated each year by the Israelites?

(b) In what ways are such Christian festivals (i) like and (ii) unlike the Israelite festivals?

CHAPTER 4

The First Kings

1. THE HAND OF THE PHILISTINE

Despite all the efforts of the Judges, the Israelites had failed to gain full control of the land of Palestine. They had settled where they could, and had left many parts of the land in the possession of other peoples. We must now study the way in which Israel became a powerful nation, able to rule over neighbouring tribes and peoples. There were strong enemies to be defeated before the Israelites could call the land their own.

For more than 100 years Egypt and Assyria lacked strong leadership and were unable to play any important part in international affairs. But other enemies of Israel were still active. The desert nomads had to be overcome before the Israelites could live in peace. The Aramaic-speaking tribes east of the Jordan went on fighting to gain more land for their own kingdoms. But the Israelites' most dangerous enemies were the Philistines and other Sea Peoples.

The Philistines had settled on the southern coastal plain of Palestine. They occupied five cities there: Gaza, Ashkelon, Ashdod, Gath, and Ekron. The sites of the first three of these cities have been dug up by archaeologists in recent years. The Philistines seem to have taken over cities which belonged to the Canaanites in earlier times.

Each city was ruled by its own lord, but they acted together in times of war. There was a central shrine for their chief god Dagon at Ashdod. They were probably sea traders, which may have helped to make them strong and prosperous, even though there were no natural harbours along the coast where they lived.

The Philistines were the first people in Palestine to learn how to use iron to make tools and weapons. Before that time men had used bronze (a mixture of copper and tin) which was softer and more easily moulded, but quickly blunted. The iron weapons were stronger and more effective than bronze weapons and so helped the Philistines to win.

They also learned to use horse-drawn chariots to carry their warriors into battle. The Israelites could not use chariots in the hill country where they lived.

Shortly before 1000 BC the Philistines began to seek control of larger areas of Palestine. The activities of Shamgar and Samson had done little to prepare the Israelites for war with the Philistines. 1 Samuel 4 describes the first big battle between them. Aphek was on the edge of the coastal plain and at the foot of the central highlands, between the territories of the two peoples.

In the first attack the Philistines were victorious. Then the Ark of the Covenant was brought out to the battlefield, to encourage the Israelites with the idea that the LORD was with them. At first this frightened the Philistines, but again they were victorious, and this time the Israelites fled to their homes. The Philistines captured the Ark, and killed the sons of Eli who were responsible for the Ark. Probably the Philistines went on to destroy the shrine at Shiloh, where the Ark was usually kept. We do know that Eli died of shock at the news of all that had happened.

These were the most disastrous things that could have happened to the Israelites at that time. The Israelites had believed that the Ark represented the power of the LORD among His people, but it had been captured by people who worshipped other gods. The LORD had promised the land of Palestine to Abraham and his descendants, but it had been seized from them by foreign people. The twelve tribes had been united by the Covenant which they renewed each year at Shiloh, but Shiloh was destroyed.

Even so there was a leader left in Israel who had been called by God. He was Samuel. He had begun his service of God at Shiloh, and God had chosen him to rebuke Eli and Eli's sons for their false ways (see 1 Sam. 3.10–14). After Shiloh was destroyed Samuel moved to his family home at Ramah. From there he went out year by year to act as Judge among the twelve tribes, settling cases and keeping peace between the people (1 Sam. 7.15–17). The future of Israel was in his hands, but for a long time he was content to leave things as they were. When the time was right he became the king-maker in Israel.

STUDY SUGGESTIONS

REVIEW OF CONTENT

1. The Israelites settled in Palestine at a time when Assyria and Egypt were weak.
   (a) What *three* other sorts of enemies did the Israelites face at that time, and where did each come from?
   (b) Which of these three were the most dangerous?
2. At about what date did the Philistines start to attack other tribes in order to gain more land?
3. List three things which helped to give the Philistines an advantage over the Israelites in battle?
4. Read 1 Samuel 4.
   (a) Where did the first big battle between the Israelites and the Philistines take place?

(b) After their first defeat, what did the Israelites do, and what was the immediate effect of their action on the Philistines?

(c) What was its effect on the final result of the battle?

5. The capture of the Ark by the Philistines and the destruction of Shiloh, were 'the most disastrous things that could have happened to the Israelites at that time' (p. 80).

For what *three* chief reasons did these events seem disastrous to the Israelites?

6. Name the leader who remained as a Judge among the Israelites after their defeat by the Philistines.

7. Look up Ashdod in a Bible dictionary, concordance, and atlas.
   (a) What god was worshipped at Ashdod?
   (b) Why were the Philistines afraid to keep the Ark there?
   (c) What did King Uzziah do to the city of Ashdod?
   (d) Why did Amos preach against Ashdod?
   (e) What was the Greek name for this city?
   (f) What else have you found out about this city?

8. Read 1 Samuel 5.1–6; 1 Samuel 6.1–16; John 3.1, 2; Mark 15.33–39; John 20.1–8 and 24–28.

   In what ways were the events described in the two Old Testament passages (i) like and (ii) unlike those described in the four Gospel passages?

9. (a) What does the story of the capture of the Ark teach us about the importance of the things which we use in worship?

   (b) In what ways, if any, do you think that the work of God in Israel was either hindered or helped by the loss of the Ark?

2. KINGS IN ISRAEL

The Israelites chose their first kings to lead them into battle against the Philistines. Only a highly organized and well disciplined army could hope to defeat this enemy. It was not enough to gather volunteers from the various tribes immediately before a battle, as the Judges had done. The Israelites needed to find a leader who could maintain a permanent army and train them for battle. Samuel played an important part in choosing a leader for the Israelites.

1. SAUL

The story of Saul's appointment is recorded in 1 Samuel 8—12, and the story of his rule is told in the remaining chapters of that book. 1 Samuel 9.1—10.16 tells how Samuel anointed Saul. The Egyptians had a custom of anointing men as court officials in Egypt and in Palestine who would be responsible to the Pharaoh. Samuel seems to have copied the custom in order to appoint a leader in Israel who would be responsible to God. 1 Samuel 8 and 10.17–27 show that Samuel had doubts about the appointment of a king. The reason given for his reluctance to appoint a human king was that God was already King of Israel (1 Sam. 8.7; 10.19). Samuel feared that the king would misuse the powers given to him by God, and would rule the people in selfish and violent ways (1 Sam. 8.11–18).

Saul's authority in Israel was fully accepted, however, when he proved that he could be an effective leader in warfare. The Ammonites tried to capture an Israelite town east of the Jordan, and Saul gathered the tribes to fight them, and to rescue the town from their attack (1 Sam. 11). In doing this Saul was acting very much like a Judge. The Israelites understood and accepted this kind of authority, and they were now willing to give their leader more permanent authority, and recognized him as king in Israel.

Soon afterwards Saul had his first conflict with the Philistines (1 Sam. 13 and 14). He had formed a permanent army (1 Sam. 13.2), and had placed Jonathan, his son, in command of part of it. Jonathan gained a victory over some of the Philistines who had camped at Geba, to the north of Jerusalem. The Philistines then came out in battle against the Israelites, intending to punish them for Jonathan's attack. But Jonathan's great courage and careful planning helped the Israelites to defeat the Philistines, and to drive them right out of the hill country of Palestine, back to the coastal plain.

Yet this victory was not enough to bring peace to Israel. The whole of Saul's reign was a time of warfare. The Philistines were a continual trouble, and Israel's other enemies were very active in Palestine. 1 Samuel 15 describes a battle with the Amalekites, one of the tribes of desert nomads. Saul had to be constantly leading his soldiers into battle. Probably the physical and emotional strain of this situation was too hard for him. He began to give way to moods of deep depression (1 Sam. 16.14–23), and came into conflict with Samuel, who rebuked him for acting too independently. Saul seems to have claimed the right to make sacrifices before battle (1 Sam. 13.8–9), and to decide for himself what to do with people, animals, and property taken in warfare (1 Sam. 15.9), instead of obeying God's will as interpreted by Samuel. Samuel felt that his doubts about appointing a king in Israel had proved to be right. Saul was failing to serve God as he ought (1 Sam. 15.22–23), and Samuel declared that Saul had lost God's favour (1 Sam. 13.14; 15.11, 18).

Perhaps Saul's greatest fault was that he became bitterly jealous of David. Instead of working hard to overcome Israel's enemies, Saul turned his attention to pursuing David, and eventually drove him out of

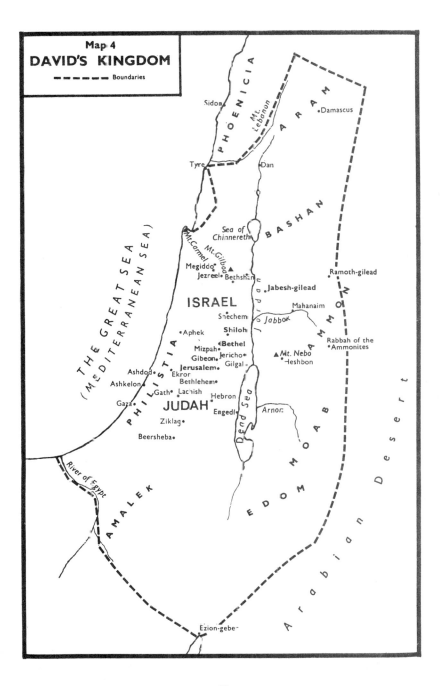

Map 4
DAVID'S KINGDOM
━ ━ ━ ━ ━ Boundaries

Sidon

PHOENICIA

Mt. Lebanon

ARAM

•Damascus

Tyre

Dan

BASHAN

THE GREAT SEA
(MEDITERRANEAN SEA)

Mt. Carmel

Mt. Gilboa

Sea of
Chinnereth

Megiddo
Jezreel• •Bethshan

Ramoth-gilead

Jabesh-gilead

ISRAEL

Shechem

Mahanaim

Jordan

Jabbok

AMMON

•Aphek

Shiloh

Mizpah

Bethel

Gibeon• Jericho•
Gilgal•

Rabbah of the
•Ammonites

PHILISTIA

Ashdod•

Ekron•

Jerusalem•

Bethlehem•

▲Mt. Nebo
Heshbon

Ashkelon•

Gath• Lachish•

Hebron•

Gaza•

JUDAH

Engedi•

Ziklag•

Dead Sea

Arnon

MOAB

Beersheba•

River of Egypt

EDOM

AMALEK

Arabian Desert

Ezion-geber

83

the territory he ruled (1 Sam. 27.1). David honoured the fact that Saul had been anointed king over Israel, and avoided open conflict with him (1 Sam. 24.10; 26.9).

Saul's reign came to an end when the Philistines once more set out to conquer Israel. They marched from Aphek northward to the plain of Esdraelon. Saul gathered his army at Mount Gilboa. He had little hope of victory, and even tried to contact the spirit of the dead Samuel to gain some comfort from him (1 Sam. 28.8–19). The battle was fierce. Saul's three sons were killed (1 Sam. 31.2), and Saul took his own life (1 Sam. 31.3–4). The Philistines gained control of the whole of Palestine, and may even have had power over land east of the Jordan as well.

2. DAVID

When Saul died, Israel needed a new king. David was the sensible choice. He had already been chosen by Samuel to succeed Saul (1 Sam. 16.1–13), and had already become well known among the tribes of Israel. He had killed Goliath, a Philistine leader (1 Sam. 17.48–49), and had himself been a successful leader in Saul's army (1 Sam. 18.12–16). He had shown himself an honourable man in his attitude to Saul the king (1 Sam. 24.10; 26.9). He had gathered a large band of men around him and had trained them as an effective army (1 Sam. 22.2). He had gained the approval of the Philistines, without betraying his loyalty to his own people (1 Sam. 27.8–12). All these things made David a suitable choice as the next king in Israel. The second book of Samuel tells the story of David's reign.

The people of Judah welcomed David as their new king (2 Sam. 2.1–4). They had anointed him at Hebron, a place which reminded them of Abraham (Gen. 13.18).

The Philistines also seem to have approved the appointment of David. They were strong enough to have prevented him from becoming king if they had wanted to. But his appointment probably seemed to them a good thing because it divided the Israelite tribes' loyalty. Saul's army commander, Abner, had declared Eshbaal, a son of Saul, to be the new king of Israel, rather than David (2 Sam. 2.8–10). This took place east of Jordan at Mahanaim, a place connected with Jacob (Gen. 32.1–2). In the book of Samuel Eshbaal is called *Ishbosheth*, which means 'Man of Shame'. But the book of Chronicles (1 Chron. 8.33; 9.39) makes it clear that he was really Eshbaal, which means 'Baal exists'. This name means that he was a worshipper of the Canaanite god Baal.

Eshbaal may only have been king for a few months, for when Bible writers said that a king 'reigned two years', they often counted the year in which he began to reign as one year, and the year in which he ceased to be king as another year. Counting this way he may have begun to reign at the end of one year, and ceased at the beginning of the next. But some of the writers used a different method of counting.

It is clear that Eshbaal was a weak man, and that he was dominated by his army commander, Abner. When Eshbaal quarrelled with Abner he could not prevent Abner from giving his support to David instead (2 Sam. 3.6–11). Joab, David's commander, disliked Abner, and may have feared that Abner would take over his authority over the army. So Joab killed Abner (2 Sam. 3.23–27); and in revenge two men killed Eshbaal (2 Sam. 4.7–8). David denied that he had any part in these murders, and punished those who had committed them. But these events made it possible for David to be king over the whole of Israel (2 Sam. 5.1–3). This did not please the Philistines, and they immediately attacked David (2 Sam. 5.17–25) in the valley of Rephaim and at Baal-perazim, both in the region of Jerusalem. The Philistines wanted to prevent the two groups of Israelite tribes from joining together, and they tried to do this by keeping control of the land between them. But David defeated the Philistines in both places, and they fled.

David was determined to do all he could to unite the people of Judah with the other tribes of Israel, and make one nation of them. He decided to make Jerusalem the capital city of his kingdom. Jerusalem had never been a city of Judah, nor of the Israelites. David's own private army captured it for him, so that it became his own personal property: 'the City of David' (2 Sam. 5.7). It lay between Israel and Judah and was a suitable centre for national life. David brought the Ark of the Covenant to Jerusalem (2 Sam. 6.12–15). The Ark had been the old symbol of tribal unity, and emblem of the presence of God. David was very wise to make Jerusalem the new home for the Ark.

When David defeated the Philistines, he seems to have gone on to break their power altogether. Very little is recorded in the Bible about this, but the Philistines are listed among those whom David subdued (2 Sam. 8.12). The Canaanite cities which had been independent of Israel up to this time probably became part of David's kingdom too. The Bible contains no record of Canaanite kings later than this.

The land of Palestine west of Jordan was thus fully under David's control. He also gained victories over the Aramaic-speaking tribes east of the Jordan: the Ammonites, Moabites, and Edomites (2 Sam. 8.12). The story of David's battles with the Ammonites is told in some detail in 2 Samuel 10.1–14, and 12.26–31. It was during this period of his reign that David committed adultery with Bathsheba, the wife of Uriah the Hittite, and Nathan rebuked him (2 Sam. 11—12). David eventually became king of Ammon (2 Sam. 12.30). He also fought the tribes living north of Ammon, and captured Damascus (2 Sam. 8.3–10).

The result of all this fighting was that David became king over a wide area of the Near East. Israel was more powerful in his reign than at any

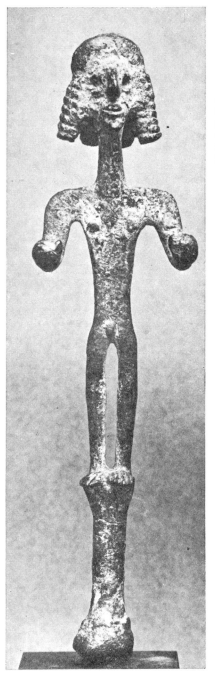

4.1 The Ark of the Covenant had been captured by people who worshipped other gods (p. 80). The Philistines and other pagan peoples made idols of wood or metal, like this bronze Phoenician Baal.

other time before or after, and was able to rule over neighbouring tribes and peoples. David was the most popular and most successful of all the kings of Israel.

David's reign ended with a long period of trouble. Like many powerful rulers throughout history, he delayed choosing who should be king after him. Each of his sons was anxious to win this honour for himself. Probably David's oldest son expected to be made king, but the situation was confused by the fact that David had several wives. 2 Samuel 3.2–5 lists the order in which some of his sons were born: Amnon, Chileab, Absalom, Adonijah, Shephatiah, Ithream.

Amnon was murdered by Absalom because he had raped Absalom's sister (2 Sam. 13.1–29). Nothing is said about Chileab; perhaps he died while he was still young. Absalom escaped into exile after he had killed Amnon. He returned after three years, but may have believed that David would pass him by when choosing his successor. He led a rebellion against David, and marched with an army against Jerusalem. David fled, but when the rebels pursued him they were defeated and Absalom was killed (2 Sam. 14–18).

When David was dying, Adonijah, his fourth son, claimed the right to be king (1 Kings 1.5). He was supported by Joab, the army commander, and by Abiathar, one of the two chief priests in Jerusalem (1 Kings 1.5).

But Nathan the prophet and Zadok the other priest, and also some of David's fighting men, all preferred Solomon. Bathsheba persuaded David to proclaim Solomon to be the new king, by making Adonijah's activities seem like yet another rebellion, and by reminding David of a private promise he had made to her because she was his favourite wife (1 Kings 1.15–31). So Solomon became the new king at David's command.

3. SOLOMON

Solomon became the ruler of Israel at a time when it was a powerful kingdom with few enemies. The story of his reign is told in 1 Kings 1—11. He prevented any division within the kingdom by quickly ordering the death of his rival Adonijah (1 Kings 2.19–25), and also of Joab who had supported Adonijah (1 Kings 2.28–35). Solomon also sent away the priest Abiathar who had approved Adonijah's appointment (1 Kings 2.26–27).

Solomon strengthened the kingdom by fortifying cities which were likely to be attacked (1 Kings 9.15–17). He introduced the use of chariots into Israel (1 Kings 4.26). He made agreements with kings of neighbouring countries, and strengthened these ties by marrying daughters of the kings concerned (1 Kings 11.1–2).

All this was possible partly because Egypt was so weak at that time that the Pharaoh had to accept a treaty with Israel, and gave Solomon one of his daughters in marriage. Even so, Solomon was unable to maintain rule over all the territory that had belonged to David. He lost control of Damascus, and some parts of Edom also (1 Kings 11.14–25).

Ezion-geber (Map 2, p. 51), in the southern part of Edom, remained fully in Solomon's control. Archaeologists have discovered evidence that this town became an important centre for the copper industry. Copper was mined in the Arabah (Map 2), and was brought to Ezion-geber for smelting. Solomon probably exported the copper, and we know that he carried on overseas trade from the port of Ezion-geber (1 Kings 9.26–28; 10.11,12, 22). It is difficult to be sure where Solomon's ships travelled when they went to Ophir. The things which they brought back after trading could have come from India, but more probably from the land of the Somali. There was silver, rare woods, jewels, ivory, and monkeys.

Solomon's sea trading probably became a serious rival to the over-land trading done by Arabs in those days. The Queen of Sheba seems to have come from the eastern part of Yemen to make some kind of trade agreement with Solomon (1 Kings 10.1–13). The wealth of her country may have come from taxes paid by the Arab traders on their way to and from East Africa. Possibly too Solomon was able to control the northern end of the same trade routes, and could hinder the over-land trade if he wished. It is said that he received taxes from the Arabian kings (1 Kings 10.15). There was real advantage for both Solomon and the Queen of Sheba in coming to some proper agreement together.

Solomon also carried on a profitable trade in horses and chariots. He bought chariots from Egypt, and horses from Kue (Cilicia), and sold them to the small states in central and northern Syria (1 Kings 10.28–29).

Solomon spent much of the money which he gained from trade in very large building schemes. We have already seen that he fortified a number of important cities, and developed the port of Ezion-geber, but his most important building projects were in Jerusalem. 1 Kings 6 describes how he built the Temple there. It was begun in about 959 BC, and completed in seven years (1 Kings 6.37).

But this was only a small part of the development of Jerusalem in his reign. Another building of about the same size, called 'the House of the Forest of Lebanon', seems to have been used as a store for weapons (1 Kings 7.2; 10.16f). There was the Hall of Pillars, which may have been the store house for the king's treasures (1 Kings 7.6), and the Hall of Judgement where the king sat to settle disputes (1 Kings 7.7). There were also two great palaces, one for the king, and the other for his wife, the daughter of Pharaoh (1 Kings 7.8). Solomon even built temples for the foreign gods that his wives worshipped (1 Kings 11.7–8). The wealth and the glory of Jerusalem in those days is described in 1 Kings 10.14–22.

Solomon became extremely ambitious. Only the best things and only the greatest wealth and glory could satisfy him. He attempted to do too much, and he spent more than he could afford, even though the foreign trade brought so many riches to Israel. He imposed heavy taxes on his people to raise the money he needed. He divided the land into twelve areas, different from the old tribal districts, and including the Canaanite towns which he controlled, and appointed officers over these twelve areas to collect food from the people for use at the King's court (1 Kings 4.7–19).

Besides all this, Solomon demanded that the men should work on his building projects, serve in his army, and help with the work of the court (1 Kings 9.15–22). At first the rougher tasks were given to the Canaanites, but gradually as Solomon's plans grew bigger he began to use the Israelites too. This was so unpopular that one of Solomon's officers, Jeroboam, believed he could lead a revolt. Ahijah, a prophet, encouraged him, but Solomon was too powerful, and Jeroboam fled (1 Kings 11.28–40). Solomon got into debt, and he found it difficult to settle his account with Hiram, the king of Tyre. Eventually he gave Hiram twenty villages in Galilee in payment of the debt (1 Kings 9.10–14).

Solomon did all the things which Samuel had described when he warned the Israelites of the dangers of having a king (1 Sam. 8.10–17), and the people gradually became more and more discontented with the way in which Solomon was ruling. But he was a strong king, and the people remembered that he was David's son. When Solomon died, however, there was open rebellion against his son.

STUDY SUGGESTIONS

WORDS

1. According to the book of Samuel the son of Saul whom Abner declared King in Israel was called *Ishbosheth*. According to the book of Chronicles he was called *Eshbaal*.
   What does each of the two names mean, and what reason can you suggest for the difference between the two accounts?

REVIEW OF CONTENT

2. (a) For what special qualities of leadership did the Israelites choose their first kings?
   (by Why were these qualities necessary at that time?
3. (a) What possible failings in a king made Samuel doubt the wisdom of appointing one?
   (b) What Egyptian custom did Samuel follow when he made Saul the first king over Israel?
   (c) What qualities did Saul show which made him acceptable to the people?

4. (a) What effect did the strain of continued warfare have on Saul?
   (b) For what failings did Samuel rebuke him?
5. What events led to the end of Saul's reign?
6. (a) List five reasons why David was a suitable choice as the second king to be appointed in Israel.
   (b) For what reason did the Philistines also approve David's appointment as king in Israel?
7. (a) For what special reason did the Philistines choose Rephaim and Baal-perazim as the place for an attack on the Israelites under David? What was the result of the attack?
   (b) In what way was Jerusalem different at that time from other cities in Palestine?
8. 'Israel was more powerful than at any other time, and was able to rule over neighbouring tribes and people' (pp. 85 and 87). Which of the following peoples were *not* at any time directly ruled by the kings of united Israel:
   Amalekites Ammonites Assyrians Babylonians Canaanites
   Egyptians Moabites Philistines Phoenicians Syrians
9. (a) What was the cause of the 'long period of trouble' with which David's reign ended?
   (b) In what way, if any, might this 'trouble' have been avoided?
10. (a) Give two examples of ways in which Solomon strengthened the kingdom after he became king.
    (b) Give two examples of territories which Solomon lost after he became king.
    (c) Give two examples of building projects which show Solomon's ambition.
11. (a) What did David mean when he called Saul 'the Lord's anointed' (1 Sam. 24.6)?
    (b) Were David and Solomon also anointed before they ruled over Israel? (Give chapter and verse references for your answer.)
    (c) How did it come about that David was anointed three times?

FURTHER STUDY AND DISCUSSION

12. The first three kings of Israel were all men who were capable of great sin. For each of them mention, if you can, a sin which did harm to their work as leaders in Israel.
13. David's delay in naming his successor led to much rebellion and violence in Israel.
    (a) What rulers of our own of recent times can you name whose failure to appoint a successor has led to unrest in their countries, or seems likely to do so in the future?
    (b) What reasons can you suggest for the frequent unwillingness of powerful rulers to nominate anyone as their successor.

(c) Do you think this unwillingness is an argument in favour of 'hereditary' systems of government? Give reasons for your answer.

3. KINGS, PROPHETS, AND PRIESTS

When the first kings were appointed Israel became a nation, in which religion became far more highly organized than it had been in the past. We shall understand the way in which religious thought developed if we look carefully at the three sorts of religious leader in the united kingdom of Israel at this time: (1) the King, (2) the Prophets, and (3) the Priests.

I. THE KING

The first kings appointed in Israel had political responsibilities. Their work was to unite the twelve tribes, and make them strong enough to overcome Israel's enemies. But their work had religious purposes also. The Israelites believed that God had given them the land of Palestine, and that He intended them to have freedom to live there in peace. When the Judges failed to gain permanent victory over their enemies, the Israelites were willing to choose a king, in the hope that he might be more successful. He would be working to achieve God's purposes in Israel, so must have God's approval as a leader.

Samuel became king-maker because the Israelites knew that he had often spoken in the name of God, and they believed that he would do so again. They accepted his choice of a king. The kings were anointed as a sign that they were God's servants, and their success in battle was accepted as proof that they were truly chosen and appointed by God.

David's many victories showed that he had God's special favour. He was a man of whom God approved (1 Sam. 13.14), and it is recorded that God made a special covenant with him. By this covenant God promised that David's family would continue to rule in Israel: 'And your house and your kingdom shall be made sure for ever before me, your throne shall be established for ever' (2 Sam. 7.16). The Psalm which is written in 2 Samuel 23.1–7 probably comes originally from the hand of David himself. Similar ideas are expressed in such Psalms as: 2, 21, 72, 144.

Some scholars believe that there was a New Year festival in which the king took a leading part, representing the renewal of God's rule over creation. But there is not much evidence of such a festival in the Bible. The ideas associated with it are so clearly pagan that it is doubtful whether it would have been readily accepted among the Israelites.

2. THE PROPHETS

The Hebrew word for prophet seems to have been used to describe several different sorts of men, who played different parts in the religious life of Israel; i.e. the seers and the prophets, both in bands and individuals.

(a) *The seers:* The first of these groups to appear in Israel were the seers. These were men who could 'see' and interpret the truth about the past, present, or future more fully than other people. These seers were often employed for a fee (Num. 22.7; 1 Sam. 9.6–8). They were expected to have answers for everyday problems, and especially to foretell the future. But sometimes they gave important messages about God's purposes for Israel (Num. 23.22–24; 1 Sam. 10.1). There is no evidence that they looked for signs of God's will in the physical universe. They did not cast lots, or seek omens. Their special insight was a gift from God (1 Sam. 3.15). At times there were no seers, and the Israelites believed this was a sign of God's displeasure with them (1 Sam. 3.1; 28.6). The seers who received their revelation from God felt bound to pass on the truth to their fellow men (1 Sam. 3.19–21). Because people found that the seers' words were true, they became respected in Israel.

(b) *The bands of prophets:* These were groups of men who lived together, often, but not always, at the usual places of worship like Gilgal and Gibeah (see 2 Kings 4.38; 1 Sam. 10.10; 2 Kings 2.5). They shared together in fits of ecstasy stimulated by music (1 Sam. 10.5f). Among pagans it was usual for such prophets to inflict injuries on themselves (1 Kings 18.28f), but we do not read of this among the Israelites. These bands of prophets (or 'sons of the prophets' as they were sometimes called) claimed to be able to present a message from God which they all accepted as the truth (1 Kings 22.6).

Such men were not always highly respected (2 Kings 9.11). Some scholars believe that Saul's friends were disgusted when he joined a band of prophets (1 Sam. 10.11), and at a later time Amos refused to be regarded as one of them (Amos 7.14). At their best these prophets were truly used by God, and were only able to prophesy when inspired by Him. Then their message was usually of national importance, and was often expressed in poetic form. Some scholars believe that the Psalms which contain a message from God come from these men (e.g. Ps. 12.5; 14.4; 50; 81.6–15; 82.2–7; 95.8–11). But often these bands of prophets joined in a corrupt form of ecstasy and prophecy without true inspiration, chiefly in order to please people and to obtain payment for their work (Isa. 28.7; Jer. 5.31; 6.13; see Deut. 18.20).

(c) *The individual prophets:* These are the men for whom the title 'prophet' or 'prophet of God' is most often used: such people as Nathan, Elijah, Isaiah, Ezekiel, Haggai, and Malachi. It is important to notice that they first came to a prominent position in Israel when kings had been appointed. The kings were chosen to lead Israel in the service of God, but very often they turned aside from doing His will, and used their authority for their own pleasure and gain. The prophets were men who spoke up in God's name at such times, to rebuke the kings and to point out the way in which God wanted them to go. They were also guides and counsellors to the king, when he wished to know what God wanted him to do.

Nathan is a good example. When David wanted to build a temple he first consulted with Nathan, and when Nathan warned him that he should not build a temple, he obeyed (2 Sam. 7.1–7). Later, when David committed adultery with Bathsheba, Nathan rebuked him for his sin (2 Sam. 12.1–15). Nathan also helped Solomon to gain the right to rule after David (1 Kings 1.11–14), and shared in making him king (1 Kings 1.38–40).

The early prophets were spokesmen for God, and people remembered only those parts of their work which affected the history of Israel. The words of later prophets were recorded for them by their disciples, and some actually wrote books themselves. But always their function was to learn God's will for His nation, and to warn or encourage the people of their time accordingly.

3. THE PRIESTS

The duty of a priest is to lead people in the worship of God, and to ensure that they worship in a suitable and orderly manner. In Israel the most important part of worship was sacrifice. But the priest was not the only one who could offer sacrifice (Judges 5.22–24; 13.19, etc.). His duty was to learn and interpret the regulations governing sacrifice, and to advise and instruct others about it.

Notice how the priests were condemned, in such passages as Hosea 4.6, Jeremiah 2 8, and Ezekiel 7.26, for not knowing 'the Law'. Very early in the history of Israel this priestly duty became the special responsibility of the Levites, i.e. the tribe or family of Levi (Deut. 33.8–10). Detailed knowledge of the regulations for worship was passed on from generation to generation within that family. The *Thummim* and the *Urim* seem to have been objects which were used to cast lots in order to answer questions arising in the conduct of worship (Num. 27.21; 1 Sam. 14.41).

When the temple was established in Jerusalem a separate line of priests were appointed there, known as the Zadokites. Earlier, they had worked alongside the family of Abiathar in Jerusalem (2 Sam. 8.17). But in Solomon's time Abiathar was discredited and Zadok took his place (1 Kings 1.5–8; 2.35). It has been suggested that Zadok was priest in Jerusalem before David captured the city, and that he continued his work there under David's rule. If so, the priests of the family of Abiathar were the original Levites, and Zadok's family only became regarded as Levites at a later time.

The traditional priests continued to carry on their work in other parts of the territory, because even when the temple was built in Jerusalem, some people continued to worship at the old shrines. After the country became divided into two kingdoms several of the old places of worship such as Dan and Bethel became important again, especially for the people of the Northern Kingdom (see 1 Kings 12.28).

STUDY SUGGESTIONS

REVIEW OF CONTENT

1. There were three sorts of leader in Israel at this time: 'kings', 'prophets', and 'priests'.
   (a) Describe briefly the place and function of each in the life of the nation.
   (b) Of which sort was each of the following?
   Abiathar   Ahijah   David   Eli   Eshbaal   Nathan   Saul
   Solomon   Zadok

2. (a) What were the chief differences between the 'seers' and the 'sons of the prophets'?
   (b) What were the chief differences between the 'seers' and the 'prophets of the Lord'?

3. Who or what were:
   (a) the 'Zadokites'.   (b) the 'Levites'.

4. Which of the following statements are true, and which are untrue?
   (a) Success in battle was accepted as proof that kings in Israel were appointed by God.
   (b) The 'Sons of the Prophets' in Israel were not always highly respected.
   (c) All the prophets of God actually wrote the books which bear their names in the Bible.
   (d) The priests in Israel were the only people who could offer sacrifice.

BIBLE

5. Which of the following Psalms contain the same message as 2 Samuel 7, 12–16? Give verse references to support your answer.
   Psalms 13, 18, 67, 89, 118, 130, 132

FURTHER STUDY AND DISCUSSION

6. For what reason do you think that Amos refused to be regarded as belonging to the 'Sons of the Prophets'?

7. Rule by a king or queen is only one among many different sorts of government. It is called monarchy, meaning 'rule by one'. Look up the following sorts of government in a dictionary:

aristocracy bureaucracy plutocracy democracy theocracy

(a) Give one example of each, if you can, from among the nations today.

(b) What sort of government has your own country?

(c) What is your opinion of the following statement; does it mean that we should accept anarchy? 'There is no perfect system of government, because whoever has power can use it unwisely and selfishly.'

8. According to 1 Peter 2.9, the Church is 'a royal priesthood'.

(a) What are the priestly responsibilities of all Christians today?

(b) Compare the special duties of the priests in Israel with those of priests in the Christian Church.

9. Read Hosea 4.6; Jeremiah 2.8; Ezekiel 7.26.

When Christians today criticize the 'establishment' in their Churches, is it usually for the same reasons as those for which these prophets rebuked the priests in Israel? Give examples to support your answer.

CHAPTER 5
The Two Kingdoms

1. A TIME OF SMALL NATIONS

In the reigns of David and Solomon, Israel dominated Palestine and the land beyond the Jordan for more than half a century. The great nations of Egypt and Mesopotamia were too weak to interfere. The smaller nations close to Israel surrendered to the power of the united Israelites. But when Solomon died, the situation changed. The Israelite nation was split by revolution into two unequal parts. The northern territory continued to use the name Israel, but the southern territory became known as the kingdom of Judah. Because of this division, the Israelites, after Solomon's time, were unable to maintain their rule over neighbouring countries.

Nations which had been dominated by Israel gained their independence. The Philistines regained their freedom, and the nations east of Jordan: Ammon, Moab, and part at least of Edom, probably did so also. Damascus had already broken free in Solomon's time, and its king undoubtedly gained control of more territory after Solomon's death. Perhaps because the city of Damascus became the centre of a powerful and well organized state, we find the kingdom there described at this time as 'Syria'. This name had already been used in a much more general way to describe the Aramaic-speaking tribes who lived across the Jordan. Two kingdoms to the north, Phoenicia and Hamath, had probably kept their freedom in the days of the united Israel, and remained independent in the time following Solomon's death.

None of these nations was powerful enough to gain mastery over the others. So there began a period of small nations, with constant border disputes, and conflict over the control of towns in the border areas. From time to time groups of nations banded together to fight a common enemy. But those who helped each other for a time soon broke apart again and fought one another instead. Alliances were made and broken time after time.

Unity among the nations was greatest at times when the whole of Palestine, and the area across the Jordan, was threatened by invasion from outside.

I. EGYPT

Egypt was the first outside power to launch a widespread attack on the small nations. In 918 BC Pharaoh Shishak I set out to gain mastery over

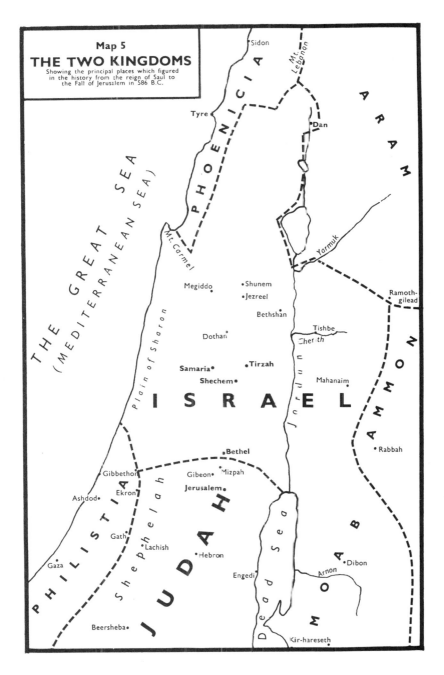

Map 5
THE TWO KINGDOMS
Showing the principal places which figured
in the history from the reign of Saul to
the Fall of Jerusalem in 586 B.C.

Sidon

Mt. Lebanon

PHOENICIA

ARAM

Tyre

Dan

THE GREAT SEA
(MEDITERRANEAN SEA)

Mt. Carmel

Yarmuk

Megiddo

Shunem

Jezreel

Ramoth-gilead

Bethshan

Plain of Sharon

Dothan

Tishbe

Cherith

Samaria

Tirzah

Shechem

Mahanaim

AMMON

ISRAEL

Jordan

Bethel

Rabbah

Gibbethon

Gibeon

Mizpah

Jerusalem

Ashdod

Ekron

PHILISTIA

Shephelah

Gath

Lachish

Hebron

Gaza

JUDAH

Engedi

Dead Sea

Arnon

Dibon

MOAB

Beersheba

Kir-hareseth

97

Palestine. The king of Judah, Rehoboam, paid a very large sum in tribute to the Pharaoh, and so saved Jerusalem from further attack (1 Kings 14.25–28). But the Pharaoh invaded Israel with great energy. He left an inscription listing 150 towns in and around Palestine which he attacked, including Bethshan and Megiddo. There is evidence to suggest that he also attacked Shechem, which was at that time the capital of northern Israel. The town Penuel was perhaps adopted as capital in place of Shechem as a result (1 Kings 12.25). Pharaoh Shishak had acted too quickly for the small nations to set up organized resistance against him. Equally quickly he withdrew from Palestine again. After that Egypt played no important part in the history of this area for over a century.

2. ASSYRIA

Assyria first played a part in the life of Palestine and the lands across the Jordan at this time. It was a nation with a long and varied history, and was gathering strength in preparation for the period of its greatest power. Several times under different kings the Assyrians made bold and successful attacks on the nations to their west and south-west.

One of these kings, Ashur-nasir-pal II, who reigned 883–859 BC, attacked Syria and several of the Phoenician cities on the Mediterranean coast. His son Shalmaneser III (859–824 BC) attacked the small nations several times. The kings of Israel, Syria, and Hamath joined their armies together to defend themselves, and fought a battle against Shalmaneser at Qarqar in 853 BC. The Assyrian king claimed a great victory, but was not able to maintain control of the nations he had conquered. Several times he fought against Hamath and Syria, but we do not know how far Israel was involved on these later occasions.

In 802 BC another Assyrian king, Adadnirari, fought against the Syrians, and forced their king to submit. After this the Syrians were no longer strong enough to influence events in Palestine, and for a time the Assyrians did not attempt to interfere in Israel and Judah.

STUDY SUGGESTIONS

REVIEW OF CONTENT

1. Explain the chief differences between:
   (a) The nation called 'Israel' in Solomon's time, and the nation of that name in the time of the kings who followed him.
   (b) The Syrians and the Assyrians.
2. Which of the outside powers was the first to launch a widespread attack on the small nations of Palestine at this time?
3. Pharaoh Shishak I seems to have attacked Israel and its capital Shechem with great vigour, but he spared Jerusalem. Why?

4. (a) Which nations joined together to defend themselves against the Assyrians under Shalmaneser III?
   (b) Which side won at Qarqar and in what year?
   (c) What was the chief result of the Assyrian victory over Syria in 802 BC?
5. 'So there began a period of small nations' (p. 96).
   (a) At what times during this period was unity among the nations greatest, and for what reason?
   (b) Give an example from recent times, if you can, of nations uniting for a similar reason.

FURTHER STUDY AND DISCUSSION

6. Use a Bible dictionary, concordance, and atlas to find out all you can about the history of the city of Damascus, which became the capital of a state called Syria at this time. Set out the information in proper order of time, beginning with the earliest details you can discover.
7. Use a concordance and Bible dictionary to find out which of the Assyrian kings mentioned in this chapter are named in the Bible. Where do you think that scholars found their information about the other kings mentioned?

2. ISRAEL AND JUDAH

We shall now trace the events which affected the people of Israel and Judah between the death of Solomon (922 BC) and the end of Syria's strength as a nation (802 BC). We shall find most of the information in the books of Kings, but there are additional details in the books of Chronicles. Time chart 3 (p. 101) shows the kings of the two kingdoms, and when they reigned.

I. THE REVOLUTION (I Kings 12.1–20)

The heavy taxes and forced labour which Solomon imposed had been very unpopular. Ahijah the prophet had encouraged Jeroboam to lead a revolt during Solomon's lifetime, but this had failed. When Solomon died, his son Rehoboam was accepted as king in Jerusalem and among the people of the south. But Rehoboam had to claim his right to rule over all the tribes by holding a national gathering at Shechem. The people of the north were eager to see taxes reduced and life made more easy for them, and they challenged Rehoboam to introduce these changes. His young court advisers urged him not to yield, and he followed their advice. Meantime Jeroboam had returned from exile, and the northern tribes chose him to be their king instead of Rehoboam.

2. THE INFLUENCE OF THE PROPHETS

We have seen that Ahijah supported Jeroboam's claim to be king.

Another prophet warned Rehoboam not to attempt to enforce his rule over the northern tribes (1 Kings 12.21–24). Thus the prophets began to influence the affairs of the northern kingdom of Israel.

Very few of the prophets of this period were concerned with events in Judah. Only much later, at the time when Israel was facing its final destruction at the hands of the Assyrians, did the prophets turn their full attention to Judah. The reason for this is clear. All the kings who reigned in Judah at that time were direct descendants of David. Each was appointed because he could claim the right to inherit David's kingdom (2 Sam. 7.12–16). The people of Judah accepted the right of a son to follow his father as king, so there was little dispute over the succession.

In Israel the situation was quite different. No one family there could claim the right to rule in successive generations. The first king, Jeroboam, had been chosen by a prophet, Ahijah. He could only rule because the people of Israel believed that he had been chosen by God in this way. Each king who followed him had to gain the support of the prophets in order to prove his right to rule, and the people expected the prophets to know whom they should accept as king.

3. THE NEW KINGDOM OF ISRAEL

Judah was smaller than Israel. But Judah had the old capital city, the Temple, and David's family as hereditary rulers. It was fairly easy for Rehoboam and his successors to maintain the life of the state in Judah.

Jeroboam's task was much more difficult: he needed to select a suitable capital city. At first he ruled from Shechem (1 Kings 12.25), where Joshua had established a Covenant between God and the twelve tribes at an earlier time. When Pharaoh Shishak attacked Palestine in 918 BC, Jeroboam seems to have moved his court to safety across the Jordan at Penuel (1 Kings 12.25). Later he moved again to Tirzah (1 Kings 14.17), and it was not until the reign of Omri that the court was finally established in Samaria (1 Kings 16.24, 29).

National worship was another problem for Jeroboam. The Ark was housed in the temple in Jerusalem, and the people of Israel were accustomed to making pilgrimages to worship there. But Jerusalem was also the capital of Judah, and the city where kings of David's line reigned. Jeroboam in the northern kingdom could not allow his people to make Jerusalem the centre of their worship. So he introduced new cults in Israel, at places where for a long time there had been shrines for the worship of God.

He chose Bethel and Dan, and set up golden calves there (1 Kings 12.26–33). It seems that these calves were not at first meant to be images of God, but foundation stones for His throne. They probably served the same purpose as the golden Cherubim in the temple at

TIME CHART 3: The Two Kingdoms

Year BC	JUDAH	ISRAEL
925		
920	Rehoboam 1 Kings 14.21−31	Jeroboam 1 Kings 13.33−14.20
915	Abijah 1 Kings 15.1−8	
	Asa 1 Kings 15.9−24	
910		
905		
900		Nadab 1 Kings 15.25−31
		Baasha 1 Kings 15.32−16.7
895		
890		
885		
880		
		Elah 1 Kings 16.8−10
875		Zimri 1 Kings 16.11−20
		Omri 1 Kings 16.21−28
870	Jehoshaphat 1 Kings 22.41−50	
		Ahab 1 Kings 16.29−22.40
865		
860		
855		(2 Kings 1.18
		Ahaziah 1 Kings 22.51−
850	Jehoram 2 Kings 8.16−24	Jehoram 2 Kings 3.1−10.29
845		
	Ahaziah 2 Kings 8.25−9.28	
	Athaliah 2 Kings 11.1−16	Jehu 2 Kings 10.30−36
840		
835	Joash 2 Kings 12.1−21	
830		
825		
820		
815		Jehoahaz 2 Kings 13.1−9

Jerusalem (1 Kings 6.23). But the people seem to have associated them with the pagan fertility cults that were widespread in Palestine in those days. Many of the people were descendants of the Canaanites (see p. 66), who had practised this sort of worship. The writer of the book of Kings repeatedly blames Jeroboam for making these calves, and so encouraging the people to share in false ways of worship (1 Kings 13.34; 15.30, 34; 2 Kings 10.29; 13.6; 14.24; 17.22). The prophet Ahijah also, who had chosen Jeroboam as king, finally rejected him (1 Kings 14.1–16).

4. DISPUTES BETWEEN JUDAH AND ISRAEL

Map 5 shows that Jerusalem is close to the border between Judah and Israel. David had chosen this town as his capital city because it lay between the two groups of tribes that he ruled.

But when Israel broke free from the control of David's family, Jerusalem was in danger because it was too close to the border, and could easily be attacked. Rehoboam seems to have seized the territory of the tribe of Benjamin, which traditionally belonged to the northern tribes. The Bible contains different traditions about the tribes which remained loyal to the house of David. 1 Kings 12.20 names only Judah. 2 Chronicles 11.12 adds Benjamin. 1 Kings 11.31–32 tells of ten tribes for Israel, and only one for Judah.

The two kingdoms seem to have been continually quarrelling about the right to rule over Benjamin (1 Kings 14.30). Jeroboam's son Nadab ruled in the north for a very brief time, and was murdered by Baasha who took his place as king (1 Kings 15.27f). Baasha tried to free the tribe of Benjamin from the rule of the king of Judah, who was at that time Asa. Baasha captured the town of Ramah, and used it as a troop-centre from which he could interfere with Judah's foreign trade. Asa bribed the king of Syria to attack some of the towns in the northern part of the kingdom of Israel, so that Baasha's troops would be needed there, and so would leave Ramah. Then Asa fortified Geba and Mizpah in Benjamin to protect Jerusalem from further interference (1 Kings 15.16–22). The next king of Israel, however, tried to make peace with Judah.

5. THE RULE OF THE FAMILY OF OMRI

(a) *Omri.* Baasha's son, called Elah, was murdered by Zimri (1 Kings 16.8–10). But Zimri himself committed suicide when one of his commanders, Omri, led a revolution against him (1 Kings 16.15–18). The book of Kings does not record very much about Omri, though he was one of the most important kings of Israel (1 Kings 16.23–28). Omri chose Samaria as the new capital for Israel, and worked for peaceful relationships with neighbouring countries. He arranged the marriage of his son

Ahab to Jezebel, a princess of Phoenicia (1 Kings 16.31), and he may have helped to arrange the marriage of Ahab's daughter (Athaliah) to the son of the king of Judah (2 Chron. 18.1; 2 Kings 8.18).

Across the Jordan Omri gained control over Moab. Mesha, a king of Moab, left a stone inscription which states that 'Omri, king of Israel, afflicted Moab many years, because Kemosh was angry with his land.' Kemosh, or Chemosh, was the god of the Moabites (see p. 58). The inscription goes on to tell how Moab broke free from Israelite control in the reign of Ahab.

(b) *Ahab.* Ahab became king in Israel because he was Omri's son (1 Kings 16.28). His father had ruled well, and Ahab inherited the goodwill of the people. His marriage with Jezebel, daughter of the king of Phoenicia, made him tolerant of those who wanted to take part in the fertility cults. The people in his kingdom who were descendants of the Canaanites were happy under his rule, and worship of the Baalim became very popular. This was why God called Elijah to rebuke the people for worshipping false gods: 'How long will you go limping with two different opinions? If the Lord is God, follow Him; but if Baal, then follow him' (1 Kings 18.21). The full story of Elijah's challenge to Ahab, and to the people of Israel can be found in 1 Kings 17—21.

(c) *Omri's family lose their authority.* Toward the end of his life, Ahab became involved in a conflict with Syria. Benhadad, the king of Syria, had seized Ramoth-Gilead in the north of Israel. Ahab led an army against Banhadad, and Jehoshaphat king of Judah helped with his army. Ahab was killed in the battle (1 Kings 22.29–36). Ahab's son, Ahaziah, then ruled for a short time, but he died as the result of an accident (2 Kings 1.2). Another son of Ahab, Jehoram, then became king.

Jehoram's reign was a time of war; he tried to enforce Israel's control over Moab, and failed. He also continued the war with Syria, and was seriously wounded in battle. Elisha the prophet saw this as an opportunity to break the power of Omri's family in Israel, and arranged that one of the army commanders, Jehu, should be anointed king. Jehu killed Jehoram, and became king.

6. JUDAH AND THE FAMILY OF OMRI

We have seen that the first three kings of Judah were in conflict with the kings of Israel and fought for control of the land of Benjamin. But Omri and his family wanted peace with Judah, and Ahab's daughter Athaliah was married to Jehoshaphat's son, another Jehoram, as a sign of the new relationship between the two countries. Jehoshaphat helped Ahab in his battles with the Syrians. Jehoshaphat's son was influenced by his wife, Athaliah, in much the same way as Ahab was influenced by Jezebel. Jehoram encouraged worship of the Baalim, even in Jerusalem.

But because he was descended from David (2 Kings 8.17–19), the prophets did not oppose him so fiercely as they opposed Ahab.

While Israel was troubled by revolt in Moab, Judah faced similar trouble in Edom (2 Kings 8.20). When Jehoram died, his son, Ahaziah, became king. But Ahaziah ruled over Judah for only a few months. When Jehu revolted against the king of Israel and killed him, he also killed Ahaziah (2 Kings 9.27f). This murder brought renewed conflict between Judah and Israel, for Ahab's daughter Athaliah, who was Ahaziah's mother, seized power in Judah. She took control by killing all the members of the royal family who might have better claim to inherit the kingdom (2 Kings 11.1).

Ahaziah's son Joash, however, was rescued by his aunt, who arranged for him to be hidden in the Temple. When Joash was seven years old he was made the centre of a revolt against Athaliah. She was seized and executed, and the boy Joash was proclaimed king (2 Kings 11.2–21). He reigned under the influence of the priests who had brought him up. Probably he put an end to the pagan rites in Jerusalem. Certainly he arranged for repairs to the house of the LORD (2 Kings 12), but later he turned against the priests, and murdered their spokesman (2 Chron. 24.17–22).

7. A TIME OF WEAKNESS

Jehu's revolt broke the power of Omri's family, but it also destroyed the peace which the nations had enjoyed while they ruled. We have already seen why Judah broke alliance with Israel. Phoenicia also turned against Israel, because Jehu had murdered Jezebel, a Phoenician princess (2 Kings 9.30–34). The Assyrians made one of their many raids into Palestine at that time, and forced Israel to pay tribute. When Assyria withdrew, the new king of Syria, Hazael, was free to trouble Israel, and Jehu lost control of all the territory which Israel had claimed across the Jordan (2 Kings 10.32f).

The situation in Judah was not much better. Syria was so powerful that her armies were able to attack Gath, on the far side of Judah from their homeland. They then attacked Jerusalem, and only departed when they were given large gifts of gold (2 Kings 12.17f; 2 Chron. 24.23f). Joash was wounded in the fighting, and then murdered by his own servants (2 Chron. 24.25). Until the power of Syria was broken, the people of both Judah and Israel went through a time of great difficulty.

STUDY SUGGESTIONS

REVIEW OF CONTENT

1. In which books of the Bible do we find most of the information about Israel and Judah between 922 and 802 BC?

(Study the time-chart on p. 101 before answering the following questions 2–5.)

2. (a) Which kings were reigning in Judah and in Israel when Pharaoh Shishak I attacked Palestine in 918 BC?
   (b) What treasure did this Pharaoh take from Jerusalem?
3. (a) Which king of Judah ruled for the longest time during this period?
   (b) The Bible says he 'did what was right in the eyes of the Lord'. What did he do?
4. Which king of Israel reigned for the longest time during this period?
   (a) Was he a good king?
   (b) Was he a successful king?
   (c) For what action was he famous in Israel?
5. Which kings, if any, ruled over *both* Judah and Israel during this period?
6. In Israel, when rulers were killed in battle or revolution, *different* families seized power. In Judah, though Ahaziah and Athaliah were both killed in revolts, the *same* family continued to reign.
   (a) What was the reason for this?
   (b) In what way did it affect the activity of prophets in the two kingdoms?
7. Each of the following pairs of kings reigned at the same time: one in Judah, the other in Israel. Were they friends or enemies?
   (a) Rehoboam and Jeroboam   (b) Asa and Baasha
   (c) Jehoshaphat and Ahab   (d) The two Jehorams
   (e) Athaliah and Jehu
8. (a) Describe in your own words the situation and events which led to the division of Israel into two kingdoms after Solomon's death.
   (b) Why was Jerusalem in danger after the division of the kingdom of Israel?
   (c) Which tribe was a special cause of territorial dispute between Israel and Judah?
9. (a) Give three reasons why it was fairly easy for Rehoboam to maintain the life of the state in Judah after its separation from Israel.
   (b) Describe two special problems which Jeroboam faced in Israel, and how he solved them.
10. (a) What was it that brought the power of Omri's family to an end?
    (b) Why did Phoenicia become the enemy of Israel?
11. Kings Nadab, Elah, and the Jehoram mentioned in 2 Kings 3.1, all died violent deaths.
    (a) Which of the two kingdoms did each belong to?

(b) What, if anything, can you deduce from these murders about the monarchy in that kingdom?

BIBLE

12. Jeroboam I and Aaron were both rebuked by prophets, and for similar reasons.
    (a) What was the reason in each case?
    (b) Who was the prophet in each case?
    Give chapter and verse references from the Bible for your answers.
13. In what way were Elijah's words in rebuking the Israelites, as recorded in 1 Kings 18.21, like the words of Jesus in His sermon on the mountain, as recorded in Matthew 6.24?

FURTHER STUDY AND DISCUSSION

14. (a) Which of the following prophets did their work in the years covered by this chapter (i.e. 922–802 BC)?
    (b) Which of the two kingdoms was the centre for their activities?
    Ahijah   Amos   Elisha   Nathan
    If necessary use a Bible dictionary.
15. Read 1 Kings 17—21. Which *four* of the following words would you use to describe the character of Elijah as shown in those chapters:
    Abusive   Censorious   Confident   Courageous   Dogmatic
    Faithful   Impudent   Obedient   Timid   Violent
16. (a) List any modern nations in which princes or other leaders have committed murder in order to become either king or leader of the state.
    (b) Do you think that murder in such circumstances can ever be justified? Give reasons for your answer.

3. THREE PROBLEMS FOR GOD'S PEOPLE

I. THE PROBLEM OF THE KINGS

Among the Israelites the appointing of kings was a religious matter. The function of the king was to do God's will, and to lead the people in obeying God. Samuel had anointed both Saul and later David to be king. Nathan had promised in God's name that children of David's family would rule after him, and had helped Solomon to become king. Israel had been ruled by three kings, Saul, David, and Solomon, who were accepted by the people as men chosen by God to rule over them. But none of them had ruled with complete justice and wisdom. Even David had faults.

After Solomon's death, the people were anxious to have a king who would rule well. They wanted a king who would be pleasing to God. But how could they know whom God had chosen? Rehoboam claimed the right to rule because he belonged to the family of David. Jeroboam claimed the right to rule because he had been chosen by a prophet. Each could point to earlier kings of Israel who had been chosen for similar reasons. The division of the kingdom was at least partly the result of a theological dispute. Each side gave a different answer to the question: how does God choose men to rule His people?

In *Judah* people believed that one duty of a king was to bear a son who would rule after him. They believed that belonging to a particular family gave a man the right to rule, and that kings were born with the necessary qualities and abilities for their work.

In *Israel* people believed that a man should be chosen as king when he was mature. There the prophet's responsibility was to recognize the man with the qualities needed to rule in God's kingdom.

Israelites in both kingdoms were struggling with the problem: *what makes a man?* Is it mainly a matter of inborn gifts and abilities? Or is it a matter of what a man becomes as a result of the life he lives? Today we might ask which is the more important, the influence of heredity, or the influence of environment? The stories recorded in the book of Kings show clearly that *both* influences were regarded as important, but that neither by itself could produce the perfect king. A man *born* to be king in Judah could become an evil influence: for example, Jehoram (2 Kings 8.18). A man *chosen* by a prophet in Israel because he had character and ability could turn out to be a disappointment: for example Jehu (2 Kings 10.30–31).

The writers of these stories recognized also the importance of free will. On the one hand a man's development is not wholly controlled by the influences and experiences through which he lives his life. On the other hand, his response to life is not completely governed by the qualities and abilities which he received at birth. There is a third element in man's personality which can best be described as the development of his character in response to God: either by obedience, or by defiance. Later, the writers of the books of Kings recorded what each king did 'in the sight of the LORD'. Sometimes a king did 'right' (1 Kings 15.11; 22.43) in God's sight, and sometimes a king did 'evil' (1 Kings 15.34; 2 Kings 8.18.)

The fact that Judah survived whilst Israel was destroyed led the writer of the book of Kings to suppose that heredity was the stronger influence for good in the life of a king, and to emphasize that the kings of Judah were better men than the kings of Israel. The family of David continued to be important throughout the later history of Israel. Even so, the writer was aware that his attitude to the kings of Judah and of Israel was not in all cases supported by the facts. Some kings in Judah ruled badly, and some in Israel ruled well.

The Assyrian king Shalmaneser III attacked the small nations of Israel, Syria, and Hamath several times, and forced the Israelites under their leader Jehu to pay tribute.

5.1 A panel on the 'Black Obelisk' at Nimrud (see pp. 10 and 98) records some of Shalmaneser's victories, and shows 'Jehu, son of Omri' kneeling to him as a sign of submission.

5.2 The gates of Shalmaneser's palace were decorated with scenes from his military campaigns. In the panel shown, Shalmaneser, seated, watches the battle as his soldiers attack two Syrian towns.

2. THE PROBLEM OF THE BAALIM

The most serious religious conflict of this period was concerned with the worship of the Baalim. It reached a crisis in the reign of Ahab in Israel, but was felt in Judah too. Elijah is given an important place in the book of Kings because he rejected the worship of the Baalim so thoroughly and so fearlessly. This sort of worship was inherited from the people who lived in Palestine before the Israelites settled there. Those people in the two kingdoms who were descendants of the Canaanites approved of it. Jezebel, wife of Ahab, openly encouraged it because it was the religion of her own people, the Phoenicians.

'Baalim' (plural of the Hebrew word *baal*, meaning 'lord' or 'owner') was the name given to fertility gods, who were thought to have control over crops, herds, and men. They came to be regarded as the appearances in each area of the god Baal. The worshippers of the Baalim believed that the god died each spring, and then rose again from the dead in the autumn. This was a way of explaining why vegetation died off in the heat of summer, and then appeared with renewed strength in the autumn. There were different accounts of how Baal died and rose again. Many people believed that he was killed by another god called Mot, and that his body was found and brought back to life by a goddess called Anat. In some places Anat was believed to be the wife of Baal, and she was also known as Asherah or Ashtoreth.

For the Israelites, there were two dangers in this worship:

(a) It could turn them away from serving the LORD only, or at least lead them to suppose that the LORD was merely one of the appearances of Baal.

(b) It could also encourage them in disobedience, as the worship of the Baalim included temple prostitution, and other forms of sexual behaviour which conflicted with the Law which God had given to the Israelites. Many of the ordinary people felt compelled to worship the Baalim, because they believed these gods brought fertility to their crops, herds, and even their families.

Elijah did everything he could to prove that the Baalim were powerless, and that the LORD alone can say when a drought will come, or when rain is on its way. The 'fire from heaven' mentioned in the story of Elijah on Mount Carmel probably means lightning. Whoever can produce lightning when He wants to, can equally well provide rain (1 Kings 18.24). Elijah showed the power of the LORD, but was then faced by the anger and opposition of Jezebel. Her position in the kingdom was far more powerful than Elijah's, and he was forced to escape.

Then came Elijah's experience on Mount Sinai. The presence of God is to be seen most clearly in the 'still small voice' (1 Kings 19.11–12).

Those who respond to the inward voice of God will know His power to achieve all His purposes. In the end not even Jezebel could win against the LORD. This is part at least of the answer to the problem that evil men sometimes have great authority and cause great trouble for their fellow men.

3. THE PROBLEM OF HISTORY

So far, we have used twelve of the first thirteen books of the Old Testament in order to study the history of Israel. But we need to remember that none of them were written at the time when the events which they record actually happened. In fact none of these books were available even to the people of the period we are now studying. Many of the stories which they contain were already known and remembered, but nobody had tried to set these stories down in writing as a connected record of the history of Israel.

Some books were in existence in the period we are now studying, but these were rather like diaries. The writers simply recorded important events in the life of the two kingdoms, without showing their place in the whole history of the Israelites. There may have been a record of the building of the Temple in Jerusalem, and it is fairly certain that somebody recorded information about Elijah, either during his lifetime, or very soon afterwards. But this writer also was simply concerned to record the facts about a great religious disagreement, and about Elijah as the central character in the story.

The first attempt to outline the whole story of God's dealings with the Israelites was made in this period. Many scholars describe a document which they call J, because it was prepared in Judah, and uses the name Yahweh (Jehovah) for God. Although this book or document no longer exists, we know that parts of it were later used by the writers of several of the books of the Old Testament. We shall study the theories about J in the second volume of this course. R. H. Pfeiffer in his *Introduction to the Old Testament* has suggested that J provided a connected record of the history of Israel from the time of Abraham through to the conquest of Palestine, to show how the promises which God made to Abraham were fulfilled in the later history of the Israelites.

Probably the writer of J was encouraged to write because he knew how glorious Israel had been in the reign of David, and he must have seen the great wealth of buildings and culture left from Solomon's time. Yet here was a problem: Israel had been great, but in the time of J the kingdom was split, and its glory had faded. God had done so much for and through Israel, but what was His purpose now? The writer of J does not try to answer this question, but his book must have raised it, and he must have made people realize that they did not know what God's plan was for their own age. Later preachers and writers had to

110

think about God's continuing plans for the Israelites: why had God brought His people into being, and given them the promised land?

STUDY SUGGESTIONS

REVIEW OF CONTENT

1. 'The division of the kingdom was partly the result of a dispute about the question, "How does God choose men to rule His people?"' (p. 107).
   (a) What answers were given by (i) people in Judah and (ii) people in Israel?
   (b) What answer is suggested by the stories recorded in the book of Kings?
2. (a) For what reason did Queen Jezebel encourage worship of the Baalim in Israel?
   (b) What two chief dangers for the Israelites could result from worship of the Baalim?
3. 'None of the first twelve books of the Old Testament were written at the time when the events which they record actually happened' (p. 110).
   (a) When were these books written?
   (b) From what document or documents did later writers gain their knowledge of the time of the first kings in Israel.
   (c) From what other chief source did the writers gain their knowledge of the early history of Israel?
4. Which book or books in the Old Testament record the following events in the history of the Israelites?
   (a) The Israelites entered Palestine to settle there.
   (b) David made Jerusalem capital city of Israel.
   (c) Elijah opposed the worship of the Baalim.
   (d) Saul was chosen as first king over the Israelites.
   (e) Gideon defeated the Midianites.
   (f) The descendants of Abraham went to live in Egypt.
   (g) The Israelite kingdom was split into two parts.
   (h) Moses led the Israelites to Mount Sinai.

FURTHER STUDY AND DISCUSSION

5. (a) What part, if any, does heredity play in the choice of rulers in our own age?
   (b) Do you think a man is more likely to govern well if he believes himself born to be a king or leader? Give reasons for your answer.
6. What similarities, if any, are there between the worship of the Baalim and the traditional religion of your own people? What importance, if any, does the story of Elijah have for your people?

7. Do you believe that God is working His purposes out in the life of your own nation? If so, what do you think His special purpose is for your people?

8. Find out, if you can, in what countries today the appointing and function of the monarch is a religious matter.

CHAPTER 6

The Assyrian Empire

1. WHO WERE THE ASSYRIANS?

The Assyrians were one of the peoples who had lived for many centuries in Mesopotamia Their capital city was Asshur, on the west bank of the river Tigris. Archaeologists digging into the ruins of this city have found the remains of palaces, temples, walls, and gates which were first built at about the time of Abraham. Twice already in the centuries which followed the first building of Asshur, Assyria had become a strong and independent nation. This happened first at the time of the Patriarchs, and then near to the time of the Exodus. But at those times Assyria did not become powerful enough to influence events in Palestine and Egypt.

We have already mentioned (p. 98) Assyria's raids on Palestine in the ninth century BC. For a third time Assyria was becoming strong and independent, and was reaching the period of its greatest strength. In the eighth and seventh centuries BC events there deeply affected the life of all the peoples spread across the ancient middle east, including the Israelites and even the Egyptians.

Assyria was not always powerful in those two hundred years; but when it was, many of the small nations were forced to submit, and when it was not, they tried to gain their independence. Their history became a repeated story of submission to the Assyrians and rebellion against them.

The Assyrians kept records of their kings and princes, and of the wars they fought and the tribute money they received from the nations which they defeated. These records still exist, and help us to understand the history of the Israelites also. The Assyrians maintained control over the countries they conquered, by reorganizing the areas of government. They did away with old national boundaries, and established new provinces, with new capital cities. If the people continued to be rebellious they were deported from their homes and resettled in other parts of the Assyrian Empire. Only a few nations who submitted to Assyria were allowed to retain their own political systems, and then only under rulers chosen by the Assyrians.

The most important kings of Assyria were the following:

Tiglath-Pileser III	745–727	BC
Shalmaneser V	727–722	BC

Sargon II	722–705 BC
Sennacherib	705–681 BC
Esarhaddon	681–669 BC
Ashurbanipal	669–631 BC

Tiglath-Pileser III established Assyrian rule over the area shown in Map 6, except for Egypt which they did not conquer until the time of Esarhaddon and Ashurbanipal, and then not for long. Each of the Assyrian kings who followed Tiglath-Pileser III had to prove his power to control this Empire. Some were more successful than others, but most rebellions took place at times when a new king came to the throne. The Assyrians' rule was harsh and violent, and the people whom they ruled hated their masters, and took every opportunity to break free.

Apart from Egypt, Assyria's most dangerous enemies were nearby in Mesopotamia. Assyria and Babylonia had always been rivals. Media and Elam were also trouble-makers for Assyria. Ashurbanipal was followed as king by two of his sons, one after the other. Neither of them was powerful enough to maintain Assyria's hold on its Empire. The Medes attacked and captured Asshur in 614 BC. And in 612 BC the armies of Media and Babylonia together attacked and destroyed Nineveh, which had become the Assyrian capital city in the reign of Sennacherib. The remaining Assyrians tried to maintain their independence in Haran, but were defeated there in 610 BC. Even help from Egypt did not save the Assyrians from final destruction.

ASSYRIAN RELIGION

The Assyrians believed in many different gods, and each city had its own god. Ashur was god of the capital city Asshur, and thus was regarded as the 'king of all the gods'. Ishtar was goddess of Nineveh. The kings believed that it was the gods, and especially Ashur, who gave them the victories which they gained over enemy nations. The Assyrians regarded their enemies as rebels against the gods, to be punished for their failure to serve them. Sargon II in one place recorded, 'By decree of the god Ashur, my lord, I inflicted a defeat upon them.' Sennacherib took up the same idea, 'On the help of Ashur, my lord, I clashed and effected their defeat.'

STUDY SUGGESTIONS

REVIEW OF CONTENT

1. The Assyrians were a *powerful* people. What part did each of the following 'powers' play in the history of this period?
   (a) Powerful gods (b) Powerful leaders (c) Powerful armies
   (d) Powerful government

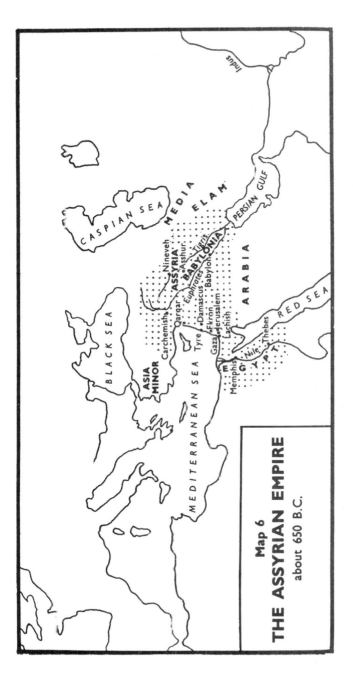

Map 6

THE ASSYRIAN EMPIRE

about 650 B.C.

2. Describe the ways in which the Assyrians treated the peoples whom they conquered.
3. (a) At what three periods in history, approximately, were the Assyrians powerful and independent?
(b) In which of the three did they influence events in Palestine and Egypt?
4. Which countries were Assyria's most dangerous enemies?
5. In what chief ways was the religion of the Assyrians (a) like and (b) unlike the religion of the Israelites?

FURTHER STUDY AND DISCUSSION

6. Use a concordance to discover:
(a) Which of the kings of Assyria listed in this chapter are mentioned in the Bible.
(b) In which book or books of the Bible each is named.
(c) Which of these kings belong to the period of history we are studying?
7. Use a Bible dictionary or Bible atlas to find out all you can about the city of Nineveh.
8. What peoples of today do you know of, if any, who believe that there is a god who specially protects their nation, and gives them victory in war? What is your opinion of their belief?
9. (a) Give examples, if you can, of modern nations who have conquered their less powerful neighbours, as the Assyrians did.
(b) In what ways has their treatment of conquered nations been like that of the Assyrians?
(c) In what ways has it been *un*like?
10. In Time chart 3 (p. 101) a Bible reference is given for each king listed, to show where a passage containing evidence for his reign is to be found.
Use a concordance to find a similar reference for each of the kings of Judah and Israel listed in Time chart 4 (p. 118), and insert them in the chart.

2. ASSYRIAN POWER IN JUDAH AND ISRAEL

We shall more easily understand events in Judah and Israel in the following two hundred years, 800–600 BC, if we remember that Assyria was the most powerful nation during this period. Each Israelite king had to decide his foreign policy, and even some matters inside his own country, in the light of events in Assyria. It will be useful to study the period in sections, according to the reigns of the various kings of Assyria (see Time chart 4, p. 118).

I. A TIME OF ASSYRIAN WEAKNESS (800–745 BC)

We have seen that the Assyrians broke the power of Syria in 802 BC. But they had too many enemies among neighbouring nations at that time to be able to attempt the conquest of Judah and Israel. So the Israelites were free from interference from more powerful nations for more than half a century. The kings of Judah and Israel set out to regain the control which Solomon had exercised over the other small nations of Palestine and across the Jordan.

In the northern kingdom of Israel, Jehoash recaptured the cities which had been seized by Syria in his father's time (2 Kings 13.25). His son Jeroboam II gained control over territory east of Jordan as far north as the kingdom of Hamath, including even Damascus. Jeroboam II seems to have had some power over the Moabites and Ammonites as well. The writers of the books of Kings and Chronicles did not record these victories: our information comes from Amos 6.14.

In Judah Amaziah attacked Edom and captured a town fifty miles south of the Dead Sea (2 Kings 14.7). He also fought against Israel, and was severely defeated (2 Kings 14.8–14). His son Uzziah, also known as Azariah, rebuilt Jerusalem (2 Chron. 26.9, 15), and extended Judah's power over Edom, reopening the port at Ezion-geber on the gulf of Aqaba. Uzziah defeated the Philistines, forced the Ammonites to pay tribute, and also gained some control over the tribes of the Arabian Desert (2 Chron. 26.6–8). As a result of these victories, Judah and Israel shared between them almost as much power as Solomon had held.

A time of peace and prosperity followed, with no enemies to trouble the two kingdoms. The people of the northern kingdom of Israel began to believe that God was pleased with their service, and that He had blessed them with wealth and strength. Yet at the time of their triumph two prophets started preaching judgement and punishment for their sins. These were Amos and Hosea. They firmly declared that God was not satisfied with Israel, because the people were competing with each other for wealth and honour, and those who were rich and strong were behaving very unjustly to those who were poor. Money-lenders were gaining power over the small farmers, and selling them and their property when they were unable to pay their debts. Judges in the law courts were accepting bribes, and were failing to give the people justice. Pagan forms of religion were being widely adopted, especially the fertility cults. Even some men who claimed to be prophets were speaking what people wanted to hear, rather than the truth.

Amos declared: 'Therefore thus says the Lord God: "An adversary shall surround the land, and bring down your defences from you, and your strongholds shall be plundered"' (Amos 3.11). Hosea repeated the warning 'therefore the tumult of war shall arise among your

TIME CHART 4: The Assyrian Empire

Year BC	JUDAH	ISRAEL	ASSYRIA
800	Amaziah	Jehoash	Adad-nirari III
790			
780	Uzziah (Azariah)	Jeroboam II	
770			Time of weakness
760			
750	Jotham		
740		Zechariah Shallum Menahem	Tiglath-pileser III
	Ahaz	Pekah	
730		Hoshea Assyrian	Shalmaneser V
		Governor	Sargon II
720		End of Israel	
	Hezekiah		
710			
			Sennacherib
700			
690			
	Manasseh		
680			Esarhaddon
670			Ashurbanipal
660			
650			
	Amon		
640	Josiah		
630			
620			Time of weakness
610	Jehoahaz Jehoiakim		End of Assyria
600			

118

people and all your fortresses shall be destroyed' (Hosea 10.14). Both prophets recognized the growing power of Assyria, and they saw that Israel was weak in face of this danger because the nation was divided against itself. They saw Assyria bringing God's punishment on His people. We shall study the work of these two men in more detail in volume 2.

2. TIGLATH-PILESER III (745–727 BC)

This Assyrian king successfully led his armies against Babylonia, Urartu, and Media. He made Assyria strong enough to try to gain control over the small nations of Palestine and across the Jordan. At first, several of these nations joined their armies together to fight Tiglath-Pileser, under the leadership of Uzziah of Judah. But within five years Assyria had forced most of the states of the northern part of this area to pay tribute, including Hamath, Tyre, Byblos, Damascus, and Israel. Uzziah, who had leprosy, died before Judah was forced to pay tribute, but Jotham, his son, submitted to Assyria.

Later, Pekah of Israel formed an alliance with Rezin, king of Damascus, in order to break free from the Assyrians' control. The two kings invited Jotham to join them, but he refused to do so. So Israel and Syria attacked Judah in order to compel him to join the alliance (2 Kings 15.37). At the same moment the Edomites revolted against control by Judah (2 Kings 16.6), and the Philistines attacked the southern parts of the land (2 Chron. 28.18).

At this moment of crisis Jotham died, and Ahaz became king of Judah. He looked to Assyria for help against these enemies (2 Kings 16.7f). The prophet Isaiah warned Ahaz against this policy (Isa. 7.17), but his warnings were ignored, and Tiglath-Pileser III came with full force against the nations that had rebelled. He attacked the Philistines, and built a fort at the River of Egypt (see Map 2). Then he attacked Israel, and destroyed a number of cities there; the ruins of Megiddo and Hazor show evidence of being burnt at that time. Pekah, the king of Israel, was assassinated, and Hoshea became king. He submitted to Assyrian authority (2 Kings 15.30).

Tiglath-Pileser created three new Assyrian Provinces out of the lands of Israel: two with capitals at Megiddo and Dor, and one in Gilead beyond the Jordan, while Israel itself remained as a tiny state in the hills of Ephraim. Tiglath-Pileser went on to capture Damascus in 732 BC.

The Assyrians had dealt with the enemies of Judah. But they expected Ahaz to show his gratitude for their help. Tiglath-Pileser called him to Damascus, and forced him to adopt Assyrian ways of worship. A special form of altar was set up in the temple at Jerusalem, for the worship of the Assyrian god Ashur, in place of the altar of the LORD (2 Kings 16.10–16).

6.1 The Assyrians believed in many gods. This marble relief of about 885 BC is of a benevolent deity, believed to protect people from accident or disease.

6.2 The Assyrians also believed that each city had its own god who helped the citizens in war. There is evidence for this belief in a relief at Nimrud, showing the king Ashurnasirpal besieging an enemy town. A winged figure of Ashur, god of the Assyrian capital city, is shown shooting his bow to help the besiegers (top left-hand corner).

120

3. SHALMANESER V (727–722 BC)

When Tiglath-Pileser III died, Hoshea of Israel tried to break free from Assyrian rule. He asked for aid from Egypt, but Egypt was too weak and divided in loyalty to be able to help. Shalmaneser besieged Samaria, and put Hoshea in prison (2 Kings 17.1–4).

4. SARGON II (722–705 BC)

Shalmaneser's successor continued the attack on Samaria. He captured the city in 721 BC, and took 27,290 of the leading people into Exile (2 Kings 17.5–6). This was the final end of the northern kingdom, for the exiles intermarried in the lands to which they were taken, and lost their separate identity as a nation. Sargon also brought foreigners to live in Israel (2 Kings 17.24). These people were taught to worship the LORD, but they simply added His name to those of the other gods they worshipped (2 Kings 17.41). They intermarried with the remnants of the people of Israel who had been left in Palestine, and their descendants became the people called Samaritans.

Judah escaped destruction at this time because Ahaz had submitted to the Assyrians. When Hezekiah became king in 715 BC he planned to break free from Assyrian control, but he was prepared to wait for the right moment. Already Egypt was growing stronger under good leadership, and was encouraging the small nations of Palestine to revolt against Assyria. In 713 BC Ashdod did revolt, with the help of other Philistine city-states, and of Edom and Moab. Judah was invited to join the revolt, but Isaiah opposed this (Isa. 14.29–32). Probably Hezekiah accepted Isaiah's warning, and did not join the revolt, for Sargon did not fight with Judah at this time. The Philistines were severely beaten by the Assyrians, and Egypt failed to give them help.

5. SENNACHERIB (705–681 BC)

When Sargon died, many of the nations revolted against Assyria. Hezekiah seems to have thought that the time was now right for Judah to join the revolution. He began to reform religion, and started by forbidding the Israelites to worship the Assyrian gods. He also introduced some changes in the traditional patterns of worship in Judah (2 Kings 18.4, 22). Hezekiah refused to pay tribute to Assyria, and formed alliances with Babylonia (2 Kings 20.12–13) and with Egypt too.

The prophet Isaiah, however, rebuked Hezekiah for relying on foreign aid. He told him that Egyptian help was 'worthless and empty' (Isa. 30.1–7; 31.1–3), and that Babylonia would one day rule over Judah (Isa. 39.5–7). Hezekiah expected to be attacked by Assyria, and made preparations to defend Jerusalem. He built a tunnel to bring water from the spring Gihon outside Jerusalem into the Pool of Siloam inside the city, and left an inscription telling how his men dug from each end until they met at the middle. This required great skill in engineering.

In 701 Sargon's son and successor, Sennacherib, launched an attack on the rebelling nations, both within Palestine and across the Jordan. He defeated Tyre, and Byblos, Arvad, Ashdod, Moab, Edom, and Ammon all submitted to him. He attacked Ashkelon and Ekron, and drove off help from Egypt. Judah suffered severely. Sennacherib had the story of his attack on Judah inscribed on a stone prism, which is now in the British Museum. Part of the inscription says: 'And Hezekiah of Judah, who had not bowed beneath my yoke, forty of his cities and numberless small towns in their neighbourhood I besieged and took; 200,150 people, young and old, male and female horses, beasts of burden, sheep, camels, cattle and flocks without number I took from them and accounted as spoil.'

We can read the Bible record of these events in 2 Kings 18.13–16. According to this passage, Hezekiah stripped the Temple of its treasures to provide the tribute which Sennacherib demanded.

2 Kings 18.17—19.37 probably describes another revolt led by Hezekiah and put down by Sennacherib, in about 691 BC. Several times in the years that followed 701 BC, Babylonia revolted against the rule of Assyria, and in 691 BC Sennacherib was severely defeated by a group of nations in Mesopotamia. There was a new ruler in Egypt, and Hezekiah probably felt the time had come for another attempt to break free from Assyrian power. However, Sennacherib was able to reconquer Babylonia in 689 BC, and probably marched into Palestine in the following year. He tried to defeat Judah before Egypt could send help, but Hezekiah continued to defy him.

Suddenly and without warning the besieging Assyrian army disappeared from outside Jerusalem. Perhaps there was an epidemic of plague among the soldiers (see 2 Kings 19.35), or perhaps troubles at home made the Assyrians withdraw (2 Kings 19.7). Whatever the cause, the people of Judah thanked God for their release and took it as a sign that He would always protect His people in Jerusalem (2 Kings 19.32–34).

6. ASSYRIA AND EGYPT

The next two kings of Assyria, Esarhaddon and Ashurbanipal, set about the task of conquering Egypt, a country which had continuously stirred up trouble for Assyria among the small nations of Palestine. Esarhaddon captured Memphis in 671 BC, and gained control of the delta region of Egypt. Ashurbanipal went further and captured and destroyed Thebes in 663 BC (see Nahum 3.8–10). Assyria's power was then at its greatest, but only for a short period.

For most of this time, Manasseh was king in Judah (687–642 BC). The Bible record of his reign is found in 2 Kings 21.1–18, where the writer tells us that Manasseh encouraged all kinds of 'abominable practices', leading the people to worship pagan gods, and to use magic. Manasseh was subject to the rule of the Assyrians, who compelled him to worship their gods. But he seems to have taken a delight in doing so, and to have encouraged other forms of false religion that did not come from Assyria. Manasseh's son, Amon, followed him as king (642–640 BC) and carried on the same policies as his father: submitting to Assyria, and encouraging pagan forms of religion.

7. THE FINAL YEARS OF ASSYRIA

While Manasseh was still king in Judah, Assyria faced more trouble. Babylonia rebelled again in 652 BC, and was only brought under control after a fierce struggle. In the midst of the struggle, Egypt too rebelled, and broke free from Assyrian control.

This was the beginning of the end of Assyrian power. We have already seen how the Assyrians were finally defeated. When Josiah became king of Judah he took advantage of Assyria's growing weakness and tried to gain independence for Judah. Perhaps he even hoped to rule over the old territory of Israel as well. Josiah carried out a thorough reform of the religious life of Judah, and was encouraged by the discovery of a scroll in the Temple which set out in detail the way in which Israelites should serve the LORD (2 Kings 22.3—23.25). This book was almost certainly an earlier version of the book we now call Deuteronomy. Assyria was unable to prevent Judah from claiming its independence. When Pharaoh Neco of Egypt went to the aid of the shattered Assyrians, Josiah opposed him and was killed at Megiddo in 609 BC (2 Kings 23.29).

STUDY SUGGESTIONS

WORDS

1. What is a co-regent? Why do you think Jotham had to act as a co-regent?

REVIEW OF CONTENT

Study the time-chart on p. 118 before you answer questions 2–4.
2. Which of the following kings rebelled against the authority of Assyria:
   Ahaz   Hezekiah   Manasseh   Amon   Josiah
3. (a) Who was ruling in Judah when the Assyrians finally destroyed Israel?
   (b) What was his attitude to the Assyrians?
4. (a) Who were the kings of Judah in the times when Assyria went through a period of weakness?
   (b) Did they go into battle against Assyria?

5. (a) From which book of the Bible do we learn of the victories of Kings Jehoash and Jeroboam II of Israel?
   (b) What peoples did they conquer?
6. What peoples did Kings Amaziah and Uzziah conquer?
7. (a) In what ways did the Assyrians expect King Ahaz to show his gratitude for their help against the northern kingdom of Israel?
   (b) What happened to the northern kingdom after it had been conquered by Tiglath-Pileser III?
   (c) Explain the statement, 'This was the final end of the northern kingdom' (p. 121).
   (d) What made it possible for Judah to escape a similar 'end'?
8. Read 2 Kings 18 and 19.
   (a) Which king of Judah finally decided to join the revolt against Assyria in about 705 BC?
   (b) To which foreign power did he turn for help?
   (c) What preparations did he make for defending Jerusalem against attack?
   (d) Who was the Assyrian leader at that time?
9. What were the two chief differences between Hezekiah and his successor Manasseh?
10. Which two nations by their rebellion caused the gradual end of Assyria's power?
11. Distinguish between the two men Hosea and Hoshea. Were they both alive at the same time? (See Hosea 1.1.)

BIBLE

12. Amos was a prophet in Israel. Which king was ruling there in his time? Roughly what dates can you give for the work of this prophet? (See Amos 1.1.)
13. Read Amos 2.4–8 and Hosea 4.1–3; 6.4–10; 9.1–7.
    (a) For what sorts of behaviour did Hosea and Amos rebuke the Israelites?
    (b) What sort of punishment did each foresee?

FURTHER STUDY AND DISCUSSION

14. Find out what you can about Josiah from a Bible dictionary and concordance. Write an account of the major events in his reign over Judah.
15. Use a Bible dictionary to find out what you can about the book of Deuteronomy. Which of the following words best describe the Laws which it contains?
    Compassionate   Easy   Harsh   Practical   Social
16. 'The besieging Assyrian army disappeared . . . the people of Judah took it as a sign that God would always protect His people in

Jerusalem' (p. 122). Armies going into battle today often pray to God for victory.

(a) In what way, if any, were the battles between the people of Judah and the Assyrians different from battles between modern nations? Do you think God 'protected' the people of Judah in a special way?

(b) Do you think that God protects one nation against another today?

Give reasons for your answers.

3. 'THE ROD OF MY ANGER'

The Israelites suffered a new and unpleasant experience in this period of their history; conquest by a much more powerful nation, Assyria. The prophets of the time foresaw Israel's defeat, and trouble for Judah. They thought deeply on the question which the Israelites were certain to ask: 'Why has the LORD allowed foreigners to conquer His own people?' As a result they gave fresh emphasis to some ideas, and developed new thoughts on other matters which the Israelites had not faced before. The bitterness of this experience gave them a deeper understanding of God, and of His ways in the world and with His people.

1. THE LORD AND ASHUR

In those days most people believed that each nation had its own chief god, and that victories gained in warfare were the work of the god of the winning nation. We have seen already that the Assyrians believed that they gained their victories through the power of Ashur (see p. 114). The Assyrian officer known as the Rabshakeh made use of this idea when he appealed to the people of Jerusalem to surrender (see 2 Kings 18.33–35). He claimed that none of the gods had been able to protect other peoples against the attack of Assyria, and so why should the Israelites expect the LORD to do so.

This was after the Assyrians had defeated and destroyed the northern kingdom Israel. So it really did seem that the LORD was unable to deliver His people. But long before that time the prophets had foretold Israel's defeat. They believed that the LORD Himself had planned destruction and exile for the Israelites. See for example Amos 3.11; 5.27; Hosea 10.14; 11.5–6; and Isaiah 5.13.

These prophets believed that God was simply using Assyria to punish His people (see for example Isaiah 7.17–20). It was true that the Assyrians did not know that they were being used by the LORD (Isa. 10.5–11). But when the Assyrians became proud of their victory, and went on to use more violence than the LORD intended, the time would come for Him to punish them. And the Assyrians would know that it was the LORD who punished them (see for example Isaiah 10.12, 24–27; 30.31;

6.3 The Assyrian king Tiglath-Pileser III successfully led his armies against many nations (see p. 119). This carving of about 750 BC shows him in his chariot.

6.4 'In 701 BC Sennacherib attacked the rebelling nations . . . Judah suffered severely (p. 122). A carving at Nineveh shows Sennacherib's archers attacking the town of Lachish, which he made his headquarters for a time.

126

31.8). The prophets believed that the LORD controlled every event. Although the Assyrians had freedom to choose their actions, God was able to use what they did to fulfil His own purposes, and He had power to keep their victories within limits which could serve His will.

2. THE LORD AND THE ISRAELITES

The prophets stated clearly why the LORD gave victory to the Assyrians. The LORD had shown His own people how to be righteous, but instead they had done much that was evil, and so deserved punishment (see for example Amos 2.4–8; 3.10; Hosea 10.13; 11.7). The Israelites had no right to claim the LORD's protection while they failed to do His will. They had failed in matters of worship, and in matters of social justice.

Amos pointed out to them how wrong they were to think that the LORD would accept formal worship in place of fair and just dealings with their fellow men (Amos 5.21–24: compare Isa. 1.10–17). Hosea rebuked the people for following pagan ways of worship, including customs adopted from the Assyrians when they had power over the Israelites (Hos. 4.11–14; compare Isa. 17.7–11).

But above all the prophets attacked again and again the Israelites' selfishness, pride, and greed (see for example Amos 6.4–7; Hos. 10.11; Isa. 5.20–23). According to the prophets, Israel and Judah richly deserved all that they suffered from the Assyrians.

3. THE ONLY HOPE

When the Israelites found that God would not protect them, they turned from Him to look for human help in their times of trouble. This meant either seeking the favour of the Assyrians, or making alliances with other nations who had reason to hate the Assyrians. Much that happened in this period resulted from the kings choosing one or other of these alternatives.

But Isaiah continually warned the Israelites against making human alliances: these would not help them. Isaiah warned Ahaz not to seek Assyrian help, because the Assyrians would then insist on Ahaz submitting to their rule (Isa. 7). Isaiah also warned Hezekiah that Egyptian help would be useless (Isa. 19).

The one hope that Isaiah could offer to the kings of Judah was that they should trust in God (Isa. 7.9b, 26.3–4). God's justice and God's judgements, he preached, would be worked out in the pattern of history, and would not be hindered. The kings should lead the people in placing their trust in the LORD and in Him alone.

4. THE LORD'S JUSTICE

In this period four ideas became important which helped to express the idea of the establishment of God's justice on earth:

(a) *Belief in the Day of the Lord.* Many of the Israelites seem to have had the idea that a day would come when God would deliver His people from all their enemies, and give them peace and prosperity. But Amos rejected this idea of a day of deliverance: 'Woe to you who desire the day of the LORD. . . . It is darkness, and not light' (Amos 5.18). And according to Isaiah it would be a time of judgement (Isa. 2.12; 13.9), when all evil-doers would be punished (Isa. 10.3; 24.21; compare Amos 3.14; 8.3; Hos. 5.9). God would use Assyria to carry out His judgements (Isa. 7.18–20), and because of their disobedience the people of Israel would be defeated (Isa. 17.4). But it would also be a day when those who repented would be restored (Isa. 12.1–2, 17.7). There was hope even for the Egyptians if they would repent (Isa. 19.21). Prosperity would depend upon penitence (Isa. 30.19–26; compare Hos. 2.14–23).

(b) *Belief in a righteous king.* The idea that God would send a new king to rule over His people in righteousness is expressed in Isaiah 9.6–7, and 11.1–9. Scholars disagree about the date of these two prophecies. Some think that they belong to a much later time, and were added by the writers who preserved the records of Isaiah's preaching.

But already in the eighth and seventh centuries the prophet had shown disapproval of Israel's rulers (see for example Hos. 7.7; 8.4; Isa. 7.9). In Hosea 3.4–5 we find clearly expressed the idea of a new king who would take the place of those who had failed. The two prophecies from Isaiah probably belong to the same period. They express the faith that although other kings had failed, God would raise up a leader in Judah who would rule with justice, and who would establish righteousness on earth.

(c) *Belief in a righteous 'remnant'.* The prophets condemned the Israelites for their disobedience so forcefully that it would have been easy for the people to think that God had finished with them altogether, and that they could have no further place in His plans for the world and for men. But the prophets believed that at least a few who were repentant would remain to serve God.

This did not give anybody the right to feel that they were safe, for the survivors would be a very few (Amos 3.12; Isa. 1.9). It was only because the LORD was gracious and willing to pardon that He would save this 'remnant' to serve Him (Isa. 11.11; Micah 2.12; 7.18). The few people to be saved would prosper (Isa. 37.31). They would put their trust in the LORD and would serve Him, loving good and establishing justice (Isa. 10.20–3; Micah 4.7; Amos 4.15).

(d) *Belief in the Holy City.* It was in this period that the Israelites came to recognize Jerusalem's special place in God's plans. It had always been important, because it was the city of David, where the royal court met, and where the Ark of the Covenant was kept. But in the time of the Assyrians a new importance was attached to God's plans for the city. The Assyrians had captured and destroyed Samaria, but despite several attacks they had never captured Jerusalem. So the people gradually came to believe that Jerusalem would never be captured, and that it would eventually become the centre of God's rule on earth. In several of his prophecies Isaiah expressed his belief that Jerusalem would be saved (e.g. Isa. 24.32; 29.5–8; 31.4–5).

The idea of Jerusalem as the centre of God's kingdom on earth is found in a prophecy which is included in both Isaiah 2.2–4, and Micah 4.1–3. The prophets recognized that Jerusalem was not a perfect city in their day. Amos spoke about God's punishment coming on Jerusalem (Amos 2.4–5). Isaiah spoke about the corrupt behaviour of people in the city, and about the cleansing that would be needed before it would become 'the city of righteousness' (Isa. 1.21–26).

Perhaps it was the influence of these two prophets which drove the two kings, Hezekiah and Josiah, to cleanse the city by destroying the pagan cults which had been allowed to continue there. Clearly there were also political reasons for this action. The reforms which these kings carried out included the destruction of objects used in the pagan cults which had been introduced into Judah after the kings had submitted to Assyria. Such an act of destruction was a clear sign of rebellion against Assyria, and could only have taken place at a time when there was some hope of breaking free from Assyrian control.

But perhaps the lessening of Assyrian power encouraged the kings to believe that the day of the LORD was near, and that they should prepare for it. The kings could fairly easily control religious activities in Jerusalem, and ensure they conformed with the ways of worship that were acceptable to the LORD. It was more difficult for them to keep a check upon religious activities in other centres of worship. This was probably the reason for the change of custom introduced in the time of Josiah, when the whole worship of the Israelites became centred in Jerusalem, and many of the old places of worship were destroyed. Josiah gained his authority for this change from the book found in the Temple during repairs, the book of Deuteronomy, or part of it (see Deut. 12.10–14). Josiah was determined to make the land a place where people served the LORD by following the ways that the prophets had shown to Israel.

STUDY SUGGESTIONS

WORDS

1. *Remnant* is an important term often used by the prophets of the eighth and seventh centuries BC.
   Which three of the following words have the same or nearly the same meaning as the word remnant as it is used by the prophets:

Dregs   Refuse   Remainder   Residue   Ruins   Surplus
Survivors

2. (a) Who or what is capable of being righteous, or of having righteousness?

(b) Read the following verses in Isaiah: 1.21, 26; 3.10; 5.16; 10.22; 11.4; 26.2, 9; 24.16; 32.1; 33.5

List the people or things described in these verses as righteous, and say in what way they possessed this quality.

REVIEW OF CONTENT

3. (a) What would you reply to someone who said: 'If the Israelites were God's chosen people, why did He allow foreigners like the Assyrians to conquer them?'

(b) What would you reply to someone who said: 'If God used Assyria to punish His people, I cannot believe in Him. Why should hundreds of Assyrians die in battle just because the Israelites had been disobedient?'

4. In what chief ways had the Israelites failed to do God's will?

5. 'In this period four ideas became important, which helped to express the idea of the establishment of God's justice on earth' (p. 127).

(a) What were these four ideas?

(b) In what special way did each give hope to the Israelites?

6. For what chief reasons did Jerusalem become the centre for the whole worship of the Israelites?

BIBLE

7. Hosea declared: 'You shall know the LORD' (Hos. 2.20), and in other parts of his book he gave details of what can be known about the LORD. Read Hosea 2.8; 6.3; 11.3; 13.4, and 14.9, and write a paragraph describing what men can know of the LORD, according to these verses.

8. (a) What idea expressed in Isaiah 2.2–4 is also expressed in Micah 4.1–3?

(b) What idea expressed in Isaiah 1.21–26 is also expressed in Amos 2.4–5?

FURTHER STUDY AND DISCUSSION

9. (a) What other cities besides Jerusalem have been considered 'holy' at different times and by different peoples, and for what reasons?

(b) Find out all you can about the situation in Jerusalem today.

Do you think it deserves to be called 'the city of righteousness'?

(c) What special reason do Christians have for regarding Jerusalem as the Holy City?

CHAPTER 7
The Babylonian Empire

1. A TIME OF GREAT NATIONS

The kings of Assyria never ruled over the whole of the ancient Near East. The countries which did come under their control often rebelled. When the Assyrians captured Egypt it meant spreading their authority too far from home, and they could not keep proper control over their empire. While they were busy dealing with a revolt in Babylonia near their home country, they lost cont ol of Egypt. Then the armies of Media and Babylonia moved in and destroyed the Assyrian homeland. These are the broad details of a period of Assyrian history which we have studied already. We recall them now because they show us where power lay after the Assyrian empire was overthrown. Egypt, Media, and Babylonia were all strong and influential in the period which followed. Maps 6 and 7 help us to understand what happened in each of these countries.

I. EGYPT

Pharaoh Neco II of Egypt was afraid of the growing power of Media and Babylonia. He supported the Assyrians when they were close to defeat. When this failed, he tried himself to gain control of Palestine and the lands across the Jordan, but in 605 BC Nebuchadnezzar led the Babylonian army in battle against the Egyptians at Carchemish (see Map 7), and severely defeated them (Jer. 46.2). Babylonian records describe an even greater victory over the Egyptians of Hamath, further south, and by these victories the Babylonians gained control of Palestine.

The Egyptians repeatedly promised to help the smaller nations of that area if they would rebel against Babylonia. But often when the time came Egypt failed to give the promised help. However, Egypt itself remained independent of Babylonian rule for another thirty-six years, and became a home for refugees escaping from the anger of the Babylonian rulers of Palestine.

2. MEDIA

When Assyria was first defeated by the united armies of Babylonia and Media, these two kingdoms shared out the Assyrian empire between them. The Medes took the Assyrian homelands, and the territory to the north and east, while Babylonia ruled over the southern part of

131

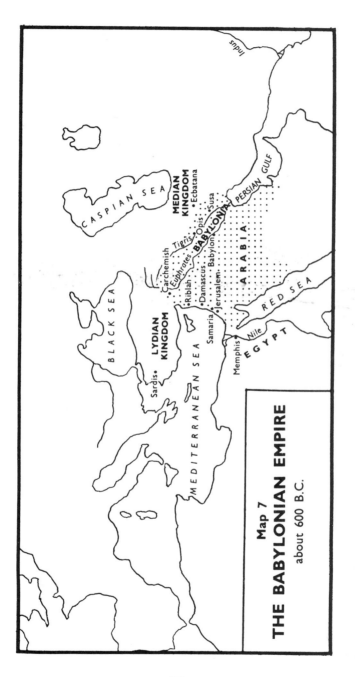

Map 7

THE BABYLONIAN EMPIRE

about 600 B.C.

Mesopotamia, including Babylon itself. And as we have seen, the Babylonians also took control of Palestine, and land across the Jordan.

For about seventy years there was peace between the Medes and the Babylonians. Throughout this time the kings of Media were extending their control over the northern parts of the Near East, and thus preparing the way for the establishment of the Persian Empire, as we shall see in the next chapter.

3. BABYLONIA

The nation which had greatest influence over the people of Judah in the eighth and seventh centuries BC was Babylonia. We need to look back at the earlier history of this nation in order to understand the part it was able to play.

The ancient kingdom of Babylon had been destroyed about one thousand years earlier. In more recent times the Assyrians had control over the city and its peoples, who were known as Chaldeans. Assyrian rulers had been appointed to direct the life of the city and its surrounding countryside. In 625 BC, one of the Chaldeans, Nabopolassar, seized power in the city. Later he led the armies which attacked and destroyed Nineveh with the help of Media. Nabopolassar's son Nebuchadnezzar was the most powerful of the Chaldean kings of Babylon.

Nebuchadnezzar led the armies which defeated the Egyptians at Carchemish and at Hamath. He delayed his attack on Egypt itself for thirty-six years, perhaps because he remembered the disasters which the Assyrians had suffered when they had tried to maintain rule over far-away Egypt. However, there did come a time when Nebuchadnezzar decided to conquer Egypt. In 570 BC there was a revolution in Egypt, in which Pharaoh Apries was overthrown, and Pharaoh Amasis claimed control. While the matter was still unsettled, Nebuchadnezzar attacked (Jer. 46.13–26). Perhaps he meant to persuade Pharaoh Amasis not to interfere in the affairs of the Babylonian empire, but whatever the reason, there was peace between the two nations after that time.

The kings who followed Nebuchadnezzar in Babylon were far less successful than he had been, and the rule of the empire passed quickly from one to another, sometimes with violence. Eventually Nabonidus became king. He showed great interest in ancient cults, and little concern for the rule of his empire. For a long period during his reign he allowed Belshazzar his son to rule in his place, as regent.

Nabonidus angered many of his people by neglecting the worship of their chief god, Marduk. At about the same time, Media came under the rule of a king called Cyrus, who declared himself willing to serve the god Marduk. As a result, the people of Babylon surrendered the rule of their empire to Cyrus without any great effort to retain their independence (see chapter 8).

THE RELIGION OF BABYLON

Marduk (or Merodach, as the name is spelt in the Bible) was the ancient god of the city of Babylon. The Babylonians thought he was an appearance of the Sun-god. They gave him the title 'Bel', which means 'Lord', and he is mentioned by this name in the Bible in Isaiah 46.1, Jeremiah 50.2, and 51.44. According to the Babylonian story of creation which is preserved on ancient tablets, Marduk was given the work of overcoming the forces of chaos. In the story (or myth, see p. 6) Tiamat was the champion of these forces. Marduk killed Tiamat, and from her body he created the sky and the earth. In reward for his victory Marduk was made ruler over all things:

'For unspecified time shall thy word stand inviolate,
To promote and to abase lie both in thy power;
Thine utterance shall be law, thy command uncontrovertible,
None among the gods shall dispute thy decree . . . (IV 7)

According to the story, Marduk then created Babylon as the place where the gods would assemble year by year to his court, and where the great gods would dwell permanently. He created men to serve these great gods, and so released the lesser gods from permanent service. There was to be an annual assembly at the time of the New Year.

There is evidence that this ancient story influenced the thought of later peoples in Babylon. Even Sargon, the Assyrian, included Marduk among the gods which he honoured. Nebuchadnezzar wrote an inscription about an attack which he made on the Lebanon in order to gain timber for the temple of 'Marduk my king'. Nabonidus records a vision which he received from Marduk at the beginning of his reign, prophesying the rise to power of Cyrus.

Scholars have suggested that the most important ritual which the Babylonians observed was the New Year festival. This seems to have been related to the idea of the annual assembly of the gods before Marduk in Babylon. The festival involved the renewal of the appointment of the human king of Babylonia. There was a symbolic humiliation of the king in which the priest stripped him of his signs of office, made him confess his failures, boxed him on the ears, and only then restored him to his position as king. Some people think that the king then shared in a sacred marriage, representing Marduk, so as to ensure the fertility of the land for another year. An important part of each New Year festival was the reading of the story of creation, which emphasized the importance of the part which Marduk played.

STUDY SUGGESTIONS

REVIEW OF CONTENT

1. Which of the following statements are true and which are untrue?
(a) The kings of Assyria ruled over the whole of the ancient Near East.
(b) The Egyptians often failed to give the help they promised to smaller nations in return for support against Babylonia.
(c) The kings who followed Nebuchadnezzar were more successful than he had been in maintaining the power and prosperity of Babylon.

2. (a) Which were the three 'great nations' who were strong and powerful in the Near East after the Assyrian empire was overthrown?
(b) Which two nations shared out the defeated Assyrian empire between them, and which territory did each take?

3. Which nation had the greatest influence over the people of Judah in the eighth and seventh centuries BC?

4. (a) Who were the Chaldeans?
(b) Which of them overthrew Assyrian rule in Babylon, and in what year?
(c) By what year did Nebuchadnezzar defeat the Egyptians at Carchemish?
(d) What event in what year encouraged him to attack Egypt itself?

5. Explain why the Babylonians were willing to be ruled by the Median king Cyrus rather than their own king Nabonidus.

6. (a) What was the name of the chief god of the Babylonians?
(b) Retell in your own words the Babylonian 'creation myth' outlined on p. 134.
(c) 'The Babylonian New Year festival involved the renewal of the appointment of the human king of Babylonia' (p. 134). What form did this 'renewal' take?

FURTHER STUDY AND DISCUSSION

7. Read again the passage about myths, p. 6, lines 22 to 35 above. The Babylonian creation story is an excellent example of a myth.
(a) What is your opinion of the ideas which it teaches?
(b) What is the value of studying it for us today?
Give reasons for your answers.

8. *Monotheism* is the belief that all things which exist came originally from the activity and purpose of one God alone. *Dualism* is the belief that there were two forces at work in creation: one good, the other evil.
(a) Which of these ideas was accepted by the Babylonians? How do you know?

(b) What do Christians believe about this matter?

(c) What view is accepted by those who are not Christians in your own country?

9. Use a concordance to find at least one Bible passage containing evidence for the reign of each of the kings of Judah listed in Time chart 5 (p. 137).

2. 'CARRIED AWAY CAPTIVE TO BABYLON'

Three verses in the last chapter of the book of Jeremiah clearly summarize the events of this period as they affected the people of Judah (see Time chart 5, p. 137). These verses, Jeremiah 52.28–30, describe three successive deportations: in the years 597, 587, and 582 BC, and one of the editors of Jeremiah's prophecies seems to have felt that they sum up all that the prophet had foreseen, and all that had happened to Judah. Jeremiah seems to have warned the people again and again that God was going to deliver Judah 'into the hand of the king of Babylon' (e.g. Jer. 21.7; 22.25). No doubt the people were reluctant to hear these warnings, but Jeremiah believed that his message was from the LORD.

I. THE FIRST DEPORTATION 597 BC

Look again at the account of King Josiah's death (p. 123). Even after Josiah had been killed, the people of Judah tried to save their newly-found independence by appointing Jehoahaz, Josiah's son, to be their new king (2 Kings 23.31). But Pharaoh Neco was still powerful enough to take the new king prisoner, and to appoint Eliakim in his place (2 Kings 23.33f). It is a sign of the Pharaoh's diplomatic skill that he renamed this man as Jehoiakim, which means 'the LORD has set him in authority'. The writer of the book of Kings did not share this idea about Jehoiakim's appointment (2 Kings 23.36f). Jeremiah tells how Jehoiakim tried to build himself a costly palace using forced labour (Jer. 22.14–19). The people went back to pagan ways of worship in his reign, perhaps because they saw that Josiah's reforms had not brought him long life and prosperity (Jer. 7.18–20; 11.9–13). Jeremiah warned the people that this false worship would bring down God's judgement on Judah, which the Babylonians would carry out for God (Jer. 1.13f; 16.10–13).

When the Babylonians defeated Egypt at Carchemish and Hamath, they claimed authority over the lands of Palestine, including Judah. At first Jehoiakim accepted the Babylonian overlord. But later, in 601 BC, when Egypt seemed stronger again, he rebelled against Babylonia (2 Kings 24.1). For a time Nebuchadnezzar was too busily occupied in other parts of his empire to take action against Judah, but in 598 BC

TIME CHART 5: The Babylonian Empire

Year BC	EGYPT	JUDAH	BABYLON	MEDIA/PERSIA
620			Nabopolassar	
610	Neco II			Cyaxares (Media)
600		Jehoahaz / Jehoiakim	Nebuchadnezzar	
590	Psammetichus II / Apries (Hophra)	Jehoiachin / Zedekiah		
580		Gedeliah / End of independence		Astyages (Media)
570	Amasis			
560			Avil-marduk	
550			Labish-marduk / Nabonidus / Belshazzar	Cyrus (Persia/Media)
540			End of Independence	
530	Psammetichus III / End of independence			Cambyses (Persia)
520				

137

he sent his troops against Judah and Jerusalem. Jeremiah saw this as God's punishment upon Judah for the disobedience of His people (Jer. 35.17). While Jerusalem was being attacked, Jehoiakim died. Perhaps he was assassinated by those among the people of Judah who were willing to submit to Babylon (see the prophecies in Jer. 22.18f, and 36.30).

Jehoiakim's son, Jehoiachin, became the next king of Judah, but he only ruled in Jerusalem for a few months of the siege. Then he submitted to Nebuchadnezzar, and was taken prisoner to Babylon together with members of his court and many of the leading people (2 Kings 24.8 and 15f). This was known as the 'first deportation'.

Jehoiachin remained in prison in Babylon for the rest of Nebuchadnezzar's reign, i.e. for thirty-five years. The next king of Babylonia set him free, and gave him a position of some independence and authority in Babylon among the exiles there (2 Kings 25.27–30). There is evidence that he continued to be regarded as king of Judah even while he was in prison, and his successor acted as a kind of regent in Jerusalem.

2. THE SECOND DEPORTATION 587 BC

After they had deported Jehoiachin the Babylonians appointed his uncle to rule in Jerusalem. His name was Mattaniah, but Nebuchadnezzar renamed him Zedekiah, meaning 'the justice of the LORD'. Perhaps Nebuchadnezzar had heard about the prophecies of judgement proclaimed by Jeremiah.

Zedekiah inherited a divided people. Some believed that Judah should accept Babylonian rule, others that Egypt would help them to break free. Zedekiah seems to have been driven to action first by one group, and then by the other; his policy toward Babylonia kept changing. As early as 594 BC, representatives of some of the small nations gathered in Jerusalem to plan a revolt (Jer. 27.3), and prophets came forward who promised the defeat of Babylonia (Jer. 28.1–4). The exiles from Judah in Babylon seem to have expected a quick return to freedom. But Zedekiah sent envoys to Babylon to show his loyalty to Nebuchadnezzar, and Jeremiah sent a letter to the exiles warning them to settle peacefully there (Jer. 29.3–9).

Zedekiah may even have gone to Babylon himself to prove his obedience (Jer. 51.59). Yet when Apries became Pharaoh in 588 BC, Zedekiah joined in a revolt against Babylonia. Jeremiah immediately denounced Zedekiah, and proclaimed God's judgement on him (Jer. 24.8–10). When Nebuchadnezzar sent troops against Jerusalem, the Egyptians did try to help Judah (Jer. 37.5), but the help they sent was inadequate, and they soon withdrew again (Jer. 37.7–9). Jeremiah warned that trouble would follow the rebellion, and that Jerusalem would be burnt down in punishment (Jer. 34.22). He was right (2 Kings

25.8–10). Zedekiah attempted to escape, but was captured and severely punished (2 Kings 25.4–7), and many of the people were taken into exile. This was the 'second deportation', in 587 BC. It was not so severe as the first, but it had a lasting effect upon the Israelites because this time the Babylonians destroyed the temple and the city of Jerusalem.

3. THE THIRD DEPORTATION 582 BC

After Jerusalem was captured and destroyed, the Babylonians appointed a governor for the people who still remained in Judah, named Gedeliah. He ruled from Mizpah (2 Kings 25.22). A descendant of the house of David called Ishmael plotted to assassinate Gedeliah. He was supported by the Ammonites (Jer. 40—41). When Gedeliah was dead, many of the Jews fled into Egypt to escape the anger of the Babylonians (2 Kings 25.25f). The third deportation to Babylon may have been in punishment for this deed but the precise order of events is not known.

The prophet Obadiah denounced the Edomites at this time, which suggests that they rejoiced in the downfall of their ancient enemy of Judah (Obad. 1.10–14). In one of his prophecies Jeremiah went so far as to suggest that Edom claimed possession of some of the territory of Judah, and he declared that they would be punished for it (Jer. 49.1–6). But evidence from the time of Persian rule suggests that any control over Judah was probably exercised from the provincial headquarters at Samaria. In other words, Judah ceased to exist as an independent political unit, and became part of the larger Babylonian province to the north.

Exile in Babylon was not too harsh an experience, for the people taken into captivity were allowed to form their own communities, and to build their own houses. They took part in the trade of their new homeland, and some became wealthy. We shall trace the experiences of the exiles more fully in the next chapter. Note, however, that when the people of Judah went into exile they kept themselves apart, and did not lose their identity by intermarriage with the people of the land, as had probably happened to exiles from the northern kingdom of Israel under the Assyrian rule. People from Judah also settled in Egypt, and later a strong Jewish community developed there.

STUDY SUGGESTIONS

REVIEW OF CONTENT
1. Read Jeremiah 52.28–30.
   (a) What events was the prophet describing in these verses?
   (b) In what year BC did each of these events take place?
2. Reference is made on p. 136 to Pharaoh Neco's 'diplomatic skill'. What evidence of this do we find in 2 Kings 23.34?

3. In each of the following groups of people, three had something in common which the fourth did not share. Say in each case which one was different from the others.
   (a) Nebuchadnezzar, Sargon, Sennacherib, Tiglath-Pileser.
   (b) Isaiah, Jeremiah, Obadiah, Zedekiah.
   (c) Amasis, Neco, Raamses, Apries.
   (d) Jeremiah, Micah, Hosea, Isaiah.
   (e) Jehoash, Jehoahaz, Jehoiakim, Jehoiachin.
4. Compare the stories about the defeat of Israel and those about the defeat of Judah. Make a diagram to show clearly the following information about the two countries:
   (a) By what people was each conquered?
   (b) In which year was the capital city of each destroyed?
   (c) Who was the king of each at the time of their defeat?
   (d) Which prophets warned them that God would punish them by allowing their defeat?
   (e) Did the people taken into exile ever return to their own country? If not, why not?
5. 'The second deportation from Judah to Babylon was not so severe as the first, but it had a lasting effect on the Israelites' (p. 139). Why did it have a lasting effect?

BIBLE

6. In what way does Jeremiah 22.13–19 confirm the opinion of the writer of the book of Kings as expressed in 2 Kings 23.36, 37?
7. Read Jeremiah 32 and 34. Which verses in those two chapters contain the same message as Jeremiah 20.4; 27.6; and 38.3?

FURTHER STUDY AND DISCUSSION

8. Jerusalem played an important part in the history and theology of the people of Israel.
   (a) Summarize what we have seen so far of the history of this city.
   (b) In what way was each of the following connected with the city?
   David   Solomon   Sennacherib   Josiah   Nebuchadnezzar
9. 'Exile in Babylon was not too harsh' (p. 139).
   Give examples, if you can, of any deportation or exile of conquered tribes or peoples in recent times, in which (a) the exiled people intermarried and became integrated in their new land, and (b) the exiled people kept themselves separate in their own communities.

3. 'THE LORD'S SONG IN A FOREIGN LAND'

I. BEFORE THE FALL OF JERUSALEM

In many ways events in Judah and Jerusalem in the time of Babylonian

140

power were similar to events in Israel in the earlier time of Assyrian power. Jeremiah was the great prophet of this time, just as Isaiah had been great in the earlier period. The message of Jeremiah was in many ways similar to that of Isaiah. But Jeremiah was a much lonelier figure, for he had much opposition from false prophets of his day.

Besides Jeremiah, only Ezekiel seems to have recognized and declared God's anger against Judah, but Ezekiel worked in Babylon among the exiles there. His prophecies against Judah were harsher in tone, and stronger in judgement than Jeremiah's; but his purpose was to assure the exiles that they were the ones who would inherit God's promises, and on whom the future of God's rule among men depended. It is uncertain how much of Ezekiel's message was known to the people living in Judah.

Jeremiah stands almost alone as the great prophet who foretold Judah's doom. Jeremiah declared that God would use Babylonia to punish Judah, because His people were disobedient, and evil-doers. They did not honour God, but served false gods, and acted without compassion or justice (Jer. 1.16; 7.5–10; 7.13, 24, 26). So God was giving His people 'into the hand of the king of Babylon' who would make them serve Him and 'wear His yoke', i.e. obey His rule (see p. 136 and Jer. 25.11; 27.8, 11, 12). In this Babylonia was only carrying out the Lord's judgement, and the Babylonians themselves would be punished if they overstepped the measure of true justice in dealing with Judah (see Jer. 50.11–16).

The people of Judah did not want to listen to Jeremiah's warnings. They looked back to the faith which had given them hope in the days of the Assyrian Empire and to their belief in the 'day of the Lord' when God would show His power, in a righteous king who would reign over them, in a righteous remnant who would be saved, and in the Holy City which God would establish (see p. 128). They trusted in these things to save them from the power of Babylon, and forgot that God had also shown them how they must live in His service if they wanted to remain strong and free.

But Jeremiah did not encourage them to look for causes of hope. He made it quite clear that none of these things could save an unrighteous and disobedient people.

(a) For Judah the *day of the Lord* would be a day of judgement (Jer. 12.3). Jeremiah seems to have taken the view that *every* day is 'God's day'. There had been 'day after day' when God had been active among His people (Jer. 7.25), and He had already given them plenty of opportunity to respond, and serve Him (Jer. 11.4, 7; 25.3). God had given Jeremiah a message suited to his day (Jer. 1.10), and it was clearly a message of judgement on Judah, and on other nations as well (Jer. 46.10, 21). So Jeremiah warned the people of Judah to recognize that

7.1 Marduk, the ancient god of the city of Babylon, was thought to be an appearance of the sun god, and creator and ruler of the world. The drawing is taken from an engraving on lapis lazuli, made in the ninth century BC: it shows Marduk with a horned demon beside him.

7.2 The kings who followed Nebuchadnezzar were less successful than he, and eventually the Babylonians surrendered their empire to the Persian king Cyrus without much fighting (p. 133). Parts of the walls of the ancient city of Babylon are still standing today.

God judges His people according to the way in which they behave. For them this judgement meant that they would suffer at the hands of the Babylonians as a consequence of their disobedience.

(b) The *kings of the line of David* could only bring hope to Judah if they were righteous and obedient (Jer. 17.24f; 22.2–5). Disobedient kings should not expect God's blessing and protection (Jer. 21.12), so there was no hope for Judah while her kings continued to be greedy and lustful (Jer. 13.13), even though a righteous king would rule God's people in later times (Jer. 23.5f).

(c) Jeremiah gave a new significance even to the idea of the *Remnant*. He seems to have used this word more than any other prophet in the Old Testament, but most often he used it to mean the folk left in Judah after each of the deportations. Jeremiah did not believe that God's purposes would be fulfilled through them, for they were still disobedient, and could not escape punishment. 'None of the remnant of Judah who have come to live in the land of Egypt shall escape or survive or return to the land of Judah' (Jer. 24.8–10).

(d) The *Holy City* would eventually have a place in God's plans (Jer. 3.17), but not while the citizens there continued to be disobedient and sinful (Jer. 11.9–11). They could expect only punishment, ending in the destruction of Jerusalem (Jer. 6.1f). It was useless for them to suppose that God would save the city just for the sake of His temple (Jer. 7.4), or that the Ark of the Covenant would necessarily be saved from destruction (Jer. 3.16). The only hope for the future was for the people to change their ways, and live according to God's law (Jer. 4.4, 14; 18.11). Jeremiah understood that God's care for His people is not sentimental; He does not save them from the results of their sin so that they may go on sinning (Jer. 13.14). God's care is righteous, and He blesses those who respond to His call and live in obedience to Him (Jer. 9.24).

2. AFTER THE FALL OF JERUSALEM

The exiles in Babylon faced a time of great difficulty. Even if they wanted to serve God, many of their traditional religious practices were impossible there. The city of Jerusalem had been destroyed. There was no longer any independent territory which could be recognized as the place of God's rule. King Jehoiachin was a prisoner in Babylon, and remained so for many years. And even after his release he could only do what the king of Babylonia allowed him to do. He could not exercise any real rule over the people of Israel.

Since Josiah's time the Temple had been the only place where sacrifices could rightly be made, and now it had been destroyed. So the whole ritual of sacrifice was impossible, and the priests were left without work. The Ark of the Covenant was finally destroyed by the

Babylonians at this time, if it had survived so long, and could no longer stand as a symbol of the rule of the LORD and of the unity of His people. Even the prophets were under suspicion, because so many of them had proclaimed hope for Judah at the time of Babylonian attack, and were now proved wrong.

Clearly the religion of Israel went through a severe crisis, in which there was no longer a place for many of the ideas and objects which had previously been regarded as precious and significant. New ways of worship and of obedience had to be found. Perhaps it would be right to regard these new developments as the beginnings of *Judaism*, and to begin calling the people by the name that began to appear at this time in the biblical records: the Jews.

There were some matters of long tradition which could still be observed among the Jews:

1. *Circumcision*. This custom could be traced back to the time of God's covenant with Abraham (see p. 36). It helped to distinguish the Jews from the people they lived among in exile; for the Babylonians did not practise it. Jeremiah warned the people of Jerusalem against depending on this sort of outward sign, so it is clear that there was a great interest in the custom in his time (Jer. 4.4; 9.25,26).

2. *The Sabbath*. Observance of the Sabbath was included among the Ten Commandments in the time of Moses (see p. 60). Jeremiah too supported the custom, and it is mentioned several times in the book of Ezekiel, where its neglect is said to be one reason for God's judgement (Jer. 17.19–27; Ezek. 20.12, 20, 23f).

3. *The Psalms*. Not all the Psalms now in the Bible had been composed by the time of the exile, but many individual Psalms were already known, and perhaps the first small collection had been made. Psalm 137 describes the feelings of the Jews in exile, when the people of Babylon asked them to use their Psalms as an entertainment. But no doubt Psalms were often used in Jewish worship even in exile.

4. *The Laws*, which had been gathered through the centuries, and were the basis of Jeremiah's complaints about the disobedience of the people (e.g. Jer. 2.8; 8.8; 9.13; 26.4). The Jews in exile must have valued the book of Deuteronomy, at least in its earliest versions. This book gave the people of Israel the belief that sacrifices should only be made in Jerusalem, and had led the exiles in Babylon to give up sacrifice as a means of worship. The teaching about God and His ways which is contained in Deuteronomy would have been an encouragement to the Jews in exile. And instructions like Deuteronomy 6.4–9 must have been very important to the Jews in Babylon, even though they did not yet take the last two verses literally.

5. *The histories*. Probably none of these had yet been written down in the form in which we know them in our Bibles today. But the people

must have treasured the traditions preserved in J (see p. 110), and later in another group of stories known as E. And the written records which were a basis for the books of Samuel and Kings must have been well-known, and closely studied.

There were in fact a great number of traditions which needed to be preserved because they could nourish the faith of the Jews in exile. During the years in Babylon the Jews clearly did much to gather material from earlier ages which the community would value, and would pass on to later generations. They were writing history. They were recording the life and teaching of the great prophets. They gathered the Laws into more orderly collections, and the Psalms into groups for use in worship. Centres were needed among the exiles where the traditions of the nation could be discussed, and records preserved. The first *synagogues* were probably built at this time, and the first Sabbath gatherings of the Jews held in them. This was a new element in the religious life of Israel, and it was to play a very important part in the lives of the Jews in the time of Christ.

STUDY SUGGESTIONS

WORDS

1. 'God's care is righteous, and He blesses those who respond to His call and live in obedience to Him' (p. 143).
   (a) In what ways were they to 'respond'?
   (b) Which four of the following words are nearest in meaning to the word 'respond' in the sentence quoted?
   Accept assent consent observe rejoice repent reward thank
2. Jeremiah emphasizes the 'sinfulness' of the people of Judah. From a concordance, find out how often Jeremiah uses each of the following words in describing the behaviour of the people of Judah.
   Falsehood iniquity shame sin wickedness
   List the three which he uses most often, and look up the references, to discover what kinds of behaviour he used each to describe.
3. What did Jeremiah chiefly use the word 'remnant' to mean?

REVIEW OF CONTENT

4. (a) Which other prophet besides Jeremiah recognized and declared God's anger against Judah?
   (b) What attitude did the people of Judah take toward Jeremiah's warnings?
   (c) What four things did the people of Judah trust in to save them from the power of Babylon?
5. 'Many of the Israelites' traditional religious practices were impossible in Babylon' (p. 143).

(a) Explain this statement.

(b) Name three traditional practices which the Israelites *could* carry on during their exile.

BIBLE

6. Read Jeremiah 17.21–23 and Ezekiel 20.11–13.

    What religious custom were both Jeremiah and Ezekiel accusing the people of neglecting, in these passages?

FURTHER STUDY AND DISCUSSION

7. Read the article on the Synagogue in a Bible dictionary.

    (a) Why were the first synagogues probably built outside of Palestine?

    (b) What part, if any, did the priests have in the life and work of the synagogues?

    (c) Were synagogues likely to be found anywhere else than Babylon in the earliest days? If so, where?

    (d) What singing, if any, was there in the synagogue worship?

    (e) In what ways, if any, was the book of Deuteronomy, or part of it, important in the synagogue worship at later times?

8. The early Christian author Tertullian wrote, 'the blood of Christians is seed', meaning that when Christian communities suffer persecution they only gain in strength.

    In what ways, if any, did the Israelites 'gain in strength' while suffering exile in Babylon?

CHAPTER 8

The Persian Empire

1. PERSIA'S AUTHORITY IN THE WORLD

While the Babylonians were ruling the southern part of the old Assyrian Empire, the Medes were in control of the north. For about seventy years these two empires existed side by side without openly fighting each other. The kings of Media (Cyaxares and Astyages) were too busy trying to gain power over other neighbouring nations to be concerned with affairs in the Babylonian empire. And the Babylonians did not usually interfere in the affairs of the Median empire, except that in 585 BC Nebuchadnezzar prevented the Medes from seizing the kingdom of Lydia, in the area now known as Turkey.

However, in 550 BC great changes came. Astyages led the Median army against the Elamites, who were ruled at the time by a Persian king called Cyrus. The attack was disastrous for the Medes; Cyrus was too powerful and too popular to be defeated. He was able to drive off the Medes, and he then went on to attack and conquer them in their own territory. Soon Cyrus had made himself king in Ecbatana, and also claimed authority in the Median empire (see Map 7).

Nabonidus of Babylonia rightly feared that Cyrus would go on to attack his empire as well. He therefore formed a defence league with Amasis of Egypt and Croesus of Lydia, who were both on friendly terms with the Babylonians. Cyrus first captured Sardis, the capital of Lydia. This was in 547 BC. He may have claimed the right to rule other areas to the north at the same time. Then he turned eastward, and captured large areas of territory not previously ruled by any Near Eastern nations, including the country now called Afghanistan.

Then in 539 BC Cyrus made a direct attack on Babylonia. By that time Nabonidus had become very unpopular among his people in Babylon. He was not a descendant of the Chaldean royal family of Babylon, but an Aramean from Haran. He failed to give supreme honour to the god Marduk, so the priests of Marduk disliked him. Nabonidus preferred to worship the moon-god, Sin, whose temple was in Haran. He claimed that 'Marduk said to me, "Nabonidus, king of Babylon, on thy cart-horses bring bricks, build the House of Joy, and let Sin, the great Lord, take up his residence within it".'

Many years earlier, before Cyrus captured Ecbatana, Nabonidus had left Babylon in the care of his son Belshazzar. As a result the annual New Year festival had not been held for a long time, since the

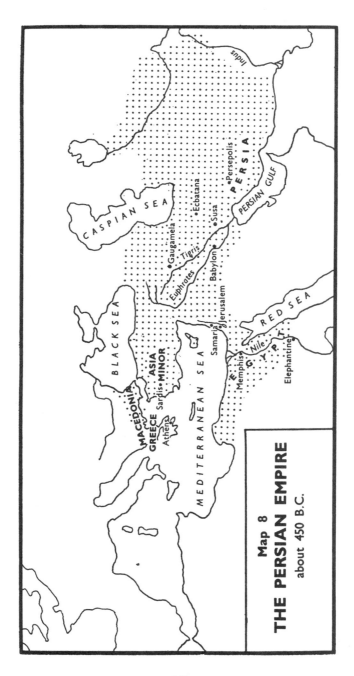

Map 8

THE PERSIAN EMPIRE

about 450 B.C.

customary rites depended on the king's fulfilling the leading role (see p. 134). This did not please the people of Babylon.

Because Nabonidus had become so unpopular, his people were not prepared to fight strongly under him against Cyrus. Nabonidus tried to defend himself by gathering together in Babylon images of all the gods of the various towns of Babylonia, but this only served to anger his people more.

Cyrus defeated the Babylonians at Opis on the River Tigris in 539 BC, and his army commander captured Babylon itself a few days later, without much fighting. Nabonidus fled, but was captured. The Babylonians welcomed Cyrus as a great hero, and as a servant of the god Marduk. He himself had the story of this victory recorded on a stone cylinder (now known as the Cyrus cylinder). According to this inscription, Marduk had 'scoured all the lands for a friend, seeking for the upright prince whom it would have to take his hand. He called Cyrus, king of Ashan. He nominated him to be ruler over all' (cf. Isa. 45.1). To show his loyalty to Marduk, Cyrus re-established the New Year festival, and returned the idols to their normal shrines. We have no details of how Cyrus took charge of the Babylonian empire. But as soon as he had the home country of Babylon in his power, the rulers of the foreign provinces gave him their allegiance. In this way the Persian empire was established, which combined the empires of Media and Babylonia, and also other territory that was much further from the capital at Ecbatana.

This Persian empire lasted for about two hundred years. The kings who followed Cyrus were not all such good rulers as he was. Probably the most important of them was Darius I, who ruled from 522 to 486 BC. Darius divided the empire into twenty areas of government, each called a 'Satrapy'. He appointed Persian rulers (Satraps) over these Satrapies, but made the Persian army independent of them and directly responsible to himself. This meant that the rulers and the army could keep a check on each other's activities, and so prevent plotting and rebellion. Darius also introduced many improvements in the social life of his people: such as good roads and a standardized coinage.

The Persians' most dangerous enemies were Egypt and Greece. Cyrus's son, Cambyses, managed to conquer Egypt in 525 BC. But the people of Egypt were never content to remain under Persian rule. They frequently rebelled, often with help from Greece, and between 401 and 342 BC the Egyptians regained their independence. They lost it again, however, before the Persian empire was eventually destroyed.

The Greeks were even more troublesome, and the Persians never conquered them. Xerxes I was the first to attempt to do so. He set out against Greece in 480 BC, and was at first very successful. He even captured the important city of Athens, where he burned down temples and public buildings on the hill called the Acropolis. But soon afterwards the Greeks destroyed a large part of his fleet of ships, his army was decisively defeated in battle, and he himself was assassinated.

Artaxerxes I continued the war, but eventually made a peace treaty with Greece in 449 BC. The Greeks then started fighting among themselves, and the Persians sat back and watched them tear one another to pieces in the Peloponnesian War (431–404 BC). At the time it did not seem necessary for the Persians to intervene. The Greeks were too busy fighting each other to cause trouble in the Persian empire. But the final result was disastrous for Persia. Once the war between them was over, the Greeks continued to stir up trouble for the rulers of Persia, and the Egyptians made the situation worse. Eventually Alexander the Great of Greece destroyed the Persian empire, and ruled the whole of the known world from the Danube to the Indus and beyond. But that story we shall study in the next chapter.

RELIGION OF THE PERSIANS

The early religion of the Persians had been simple pastoral and agricultural cults. But a new and important religion (Zoroastrianism) developed from the work of a man named Zarathustra. Like Judaism, Islam, and Christianity—and indeed like many of the religions of the east—Zoroastrianism centred upon a holy book. It was called the Avesta. It has been difficult to discover exactly when Zarathustra lived, or exactly when the Avesta was written. But there are inscriptions which show that Darius I was a Zoroastrian, and perhaps all the rulers of the Persian empire practised this religion.

Zoroastrianism was—and is—a 'dualistic' religion (see p. 134), that is to say, its followers believe in the two powers, of good and of evil. They believe in the supreme god of goodness, Ormazd, and his court of archangels and angels. They also believe in a god of evil, called Ahriman, and his court of demons. Unlike the Babylonians, the Persians believed that this conflict between good and evil was still in progress. They believed that there was a continuing celestial warfare, though the victory would go to Ormazd in the end of all things. According to Zoroastrian teaching men should serve the god of goodness, and follow a high code of conduct which expresses the value of a gentle morality. Followers of this religion are confident that death is not the final end, and that there will be new life for the righteous in the time of Ormazd's victory.

This kind of religion clearly influenced the style of rule adopted by the kings of the Persian empire, who were compassionate and considerate toward the people they ruled. They always encouraged the

8.1   Darius reorganized the government of Persia, so that the rulers and the army could keep a check on each other's activities (see p. 149). Statues of the Persian Royal Guard adorn the staircase to the audience hall of Xerxes I, built at Persepolis about 470 BC.

8.2   A slab from the platform in the hall of Xerxes shows Syrians bringing tribute to the Persian conqueror.

people whom they conquered to continue to follow the culture and customs of their own nations. Cyrus's adoption of Marduk, and his reverence for the LORD, can both be explained by his desire to enable the peoples he ruled to follow their own cults, and to live up to the best ideas of their own national heritage.

STUDY SUGGESTIONS

WORDS

1. Who or what were the following?
   Sin   The Cyrus cylinder   Satraps   The Avesta

REVIEW OF CONTENT

2. Each of the ancient empires established in the Near East was larger than the empire which preceded it. New territories were conquered which had not been part of earlier empires. Look at Maps 7 and 8.
   (a) With which countries were the following towns associated before the Persian conquest?
   Ecbatana   Memphis   Sardis
   (b) Which towns outside Palestine on map 8 have *not* been mentioned in our studies of the Persian empire? Find out, if you can, why they were important.

3. Why did the Babylonians and the Medes remain at peace with each other in the first half of the sixth century BC?

4. (a) To what nation did Cyrus belong?
   (b) In what year did Cyrus make a direct attack on Babylon?
   (c) Name three important cities where Cyrus was victorious.

5. (a) Give two reasons why King Nabonidus of Babylon was not popular with his people.
   (b) For what chief reason did the Babylonians welcome Cyrus as their ruler?

6. There is a Latin saying: 'Divide and rule.' What did Darius I do during his government of the Persian empire which suggests that he agreed with this saying?

7. (a) Which two nations were the most dangerous enemies of the Persians?
   (b) What part if any did the Persians play in the Peloponnesian war?

8. (a) What religion did the Persians practise at this time?
   (b) In what chief way was this religion like the religion of the Babylonians?
   (c) In what way was it unlike?
   (d) In what way did their religion influence the way in which Persian kings ruled over the peoples whom they conquered?

9. Use a concordance to discover:
   (a) Which of the kings of Persia listed on the time chart on p. 157 are also mentioned in the Bible.
   (b) In which book or books of the Bible each is mentioned.
   (c) In which books, if any, it is possible to know which king of several with the same name the writer is mentioning?
10. In many parts of the world today national governments are trying to revive the ancient cultures and customs of their people.
   (a) Do you think it is right for Christians to support these activities?
   (b) Are there any limits to the support which Christians should (i) give in their own lives, and (ii) encourage in the life of the community, in response to government schemes of this kind? Give reasons for your answers.

2. THE REBUILDING OF JUDAH

Jeremiah had taught that hope for the future of God's people lay with those who had been taken away into exile in Babylon (Jer. 24.4-7). Even after the third deportation some of the people were still left in Judah, but these were the least skilled or qualified. All their leaders had been taken to Babylon, or else had escaped as refugees. Some form of worship was probably continued in the ruined temple in Jerusalem (Jer. 41.5), but there was little there which could give hope for future days (Ezek. 33.24-29).

In Babylon, too, the morale of the Jewish community was very low, even though the leaders were introducing religious practices which the people could follow when they were away from Judah and Jerusalem. The exiled Jews were still downhearted about the destruction of Jerusalem, and especially of the Temple (Isa. 63.18f; 64.10f). Many of them could not believe that God still cared for His people, and they lost hope (Isa. 40.27). They doubted whether God *could* do anything for His people, even if He chose to. The victories of the Babylonians and the security of their rule seemed to show that Marduk was more powerful than the LORD (Isa. 42.17).

So there were great difficulties to be overcome if a new community of God's people was to be established. But step by step the way was prepared for that new community in Judah and Jerusalem.

I. REVIVED HOPE

Two prophets were active during the exile in Babylon. They did not try to destroy the belief that God had deliberately punished His people by allowing Babylon to conquer them. But they spoke and wrote of a future time when men would acknowledge the LORD's authority, and His people would once again know that they had His blessing.

(a) *Ezekiel* was one of these two prophets. He had been taken to Babylon with the first group of exiles, and had become a prophet there. Ezekiel reminded the people of all the warnings which God had given through His prophets in Jerusalem, and tried to convince them that it was really part of God's plan that they should come to Babylon. Some of the Jews were interested in gathering together the Laws by which God made His will known in earlier times (see pp. 54, 144). Ezekiel supported and encouraged this interest by reminding the people that they were being punished because they had ignored these Laws (Ezek. 5.6–8; 11.12; 20.11–26). Ezekiel believed firmly that God is just: 'the soul that sins shall die' (Ezek. 18.4), and it was this belief which gave him hope for those who repented and turned back to God. He believed that God would restore them, and give His people a home in Jerusalem again (Ezek. 33.19; 36.24–28). The last part of the book of Ezekiel contains his vision of the new community in Jerusalem, with its life centred on the Temple (Ezek. 40—48).

(b) *Deutero-Isaiah* (meaning 'Second Isaiah') is the name which some scholars give to the second of the two prophets who worked at this time. His real name is not known, but his writings are contained in the book of Isaiah, chapters 40—55 (and possibly 56—66 also). Probably he wrote and circulated his book at a time when his words would have brought trouble upon him from the Babylonian authorities if his name had been known.

The writings of Deutero-Isaiah show that he had a specially deep understanding of the ways and purposes of God. He was completely convinced that God is more than the supreme God and Creator of all things (Isa. 45.18): He is the *only* God (Isa. 44.6; 46.9). Marduk and the lesser gods which the Babylonians worshipped really were nothing at all (Isa. 40.18–20). They could not even know the events of history, and certainly could not influence them (Isa. 41.21–24).

Deutero-Isaiah looked back into history and saw God choosing Abraham to be the founder of the people of God. He assured the people of his own day that God had not given up His purposes (Isa. 41.8–10). The people of Judah had suffered the consequence of their sin (Isa. 40.2), and now God was sending Cyrus the Persian to rescue them (Isa. 41.25; 45.1–7). There would be a new Exodus: from Babylon back to Jerusalem (Isa. 43.16–21; 48.20f; 55.12,13). God would enable them to rebuild Jerusalem in great glory, and as a result all peoples would be able to share His salvation (Isa. 45.22; 49.6; 54.11–14).

2. THE RETURN TO JERUSALEM

The challenging words of these two prophets should have brought hope and enthusiasm to all the Israelites, but as far as we can tell they did not. Cyrus did come to Babylon in 539 BC, as we have seen. He did authorize the Jews to rebuild the Temple in Jerusalem; and he decreed that the sacred vessels which the Babylonians had looted from the Temple should be returned, and that money for the rebuilding should be provided from the royal treasury (Ezra 6.3–5). Cyrus also authorized those who were willing among the Jews to return to their own land to carry out the work, and encouraged those who remained in Babylon to contribute to the cost of their going (Ezra 1.2–4). Yet few Jews responded to this new opportunity to serve the LORD.

Sheshbazzar, the prince of Judah (Ezra 1.8), probably the son of Jehoiachin, was leader of the first Jews who did return to Jerusalem. Strangely, later historians knew so little about this man and the group which he led, that they confused his activities with those of Zerubbabel, who led another group back to Palestine at a later time. So we do not know which of these two men laid the foundations of the new temple (Ezra 5.16; Zech. 4.9). It seems probable that only a few Jews returned with Sheshbazzar, and that they found Jerusalem in such ruins that it was difficult for them to re-establish life there. It was as much as they could do to find shelter and food for themselves. Many Jews remained in Babylon, where they were already living comfortable and prosperous lives. An early historian records that they were 'not willing to leave their possessions'.

Zerubbabel, grandson of Jehoiachin, led a second, larger group of Jews back to Palestine, perhaps close to the time that Cambyses conquered Egypt (525 BC). This group also found life difficult, and had little time for anything but the necessities of life. Droughts seem to have added to their hardships. Some people used the droughts as an opportunity to make themselves rich, by profiting from those whose crops were most severely damaged. So there were some in Jerusalem who were able to live in luxury, while others starved (Hag. 1.4–6, 9–11; 2.16f).

3. THE REBUILDING OF THE TEMPLE

In the year 520 BC two prophets, Haggai and Zechariah, came to Jerusalem urging the people to rebuild the Temple (Ezra 5.1f). They believed that the hardships and difficulties which those who returned from the exile had suffered were the direct result of their selfishness and greed. If they would only think about God instead of themselves, and rebuild the Temple, all would be different (Hag. 1.8f; Zech. 1.16). Both men taught that God was about to upset the nations of the world (Hag. 2.6; Zech. 2.9). The unrest in the Persian empire in the years when Darius I became king was a sign of new and great changes in political power in the world. The day would soon come when

Zerubbabel, who was of the family of David, would rule the world (Hag. 2.20–23; Zech. 3.8). (In Zechariah 6.9–15 the writer has corrected the prophecy because he knew that Zerubbabel did not become king of a world empire.) Both prophets foretold that when that day came the Temple would be established in all its ancient glory, and all nations would share in the worship of the LORD (Hag. 2.1–9; Zech. 2.11; 8.22f).

The people of Judah responded to this challenge, and they rebuilt the Temple in four years. But they did not achieve this without difficulty. When Darius established his Satrapies, Palestine became part of the province called 'Beyond the River' (i.e. beyond the Euphrates). The Persian ruler of this area, Tattenai, was greatly disturbed by the rebuilding activity in Jerusalem. He reported the matter to Darius, who checked the court records, and found proof that Cyrus had authorized the rebuilding of the Temple. Darius instructed Tattenai to pay the expenses involved in the work being done by the Jews 'from the royal revenue, the tribute of the province from Beyond the River' (Ezra 5.3—6.12).

So the Temple was completed. It did not have the same beauty and strength of design or richness of decoration as the first Temple, built in Solomon's time. But at least the Jews had a proper centre for sacrificial worship again.

4. THE DISTRICT OF JUDAH

Life in Judah and Jerusalem was still very difficult. Most of the city was still in ruins, and few of the Jews were willing to live there (Neh. 7.4). They settled instead in other towns, including Bethlehem, Geba, Bethel, and Jericho (see Ezra 2.20–35 and Map 4). The total population was probably about 50,000. Political administration was still in the control of the Persian governor of the Province Beyond the River, with a sub-provincial governor at Samaria. Simple local government, and care of the religious affairs of Judah, were in the hands of a series of High Priests: Jeshua, Joiakim, and Eliashib (Ezra 3.2; Neh. 13.28. See also Neh. 12.10).

There was continual trouble between the returned exiles, and the people who had remained in Palestine or had moved in before the exiles returned. The Jews believed that only those who had been in Babylon could be relied upon to follow the traditional patterns of worship for the LORD. Those who had lived in Palestine in the time of the exile had served other gods, as well as the LORD (2 Kings 17.27–34). Unhappily the governors of the sub-provinces of Palestine and across the Jordan (Sanballat, Tobiah, and Geshem) were more sympathetic to those who had never been in exile, and did what they could to make life difficult for those who had returned from Babylon (Neh. 6.10–14,

TIME CHART 6: The Persian Empire

Year BC	EGYPT	JUDAH	PERSIA
530			Cambyses
520	Psammetichus III End of independence		Darius I
510			
500			
490			
480			Xerxes I
470			
460			Artaxerxes I
450		**Province established** Nehemiah	
440			
430			
420			Xerxes II Darius II
410			
400	Freedom won	Ezra	Artaxerxes II
390			
380			
370			
360			Artaxerxes III
350			
340	Freedom lost		Arses Darius III
330			

17f, etc.). Things thus turned out differently from what Deutero-Isaiah, Haggai, and Zechariah had promised. The rebuilding of the Temple did not result in a revival of national life among the Jews, many of whom were in despair.

Two new prophets played their part in the history of Israel at this time. We do not know the names of either of them.

One was the author of the major part of Isaiah 56—66. Some people think that this was Deutero-Isaiah, working after the return to Judah. But it could have been somebody else who had taken up some of Deutero-Isaiah's ideas, but who expressed also a sense of disappointment, and a concern at the carelessness and incompetence of the service offered to the LORD in Jerusalem (Isa. 56.1f; 58.9b–14). At the same time, he believed there was still reason for hope (Isa. 61.1–4). (Scholars who think that Isaiah 40—55 and 56—66 were the work of two different people sometimes call the author of the later chapters 'Third' or 'Trito-Isaiah'.)

The other prophet working at this time was the writer of the book known to us as Malachi. The title simply tells us that it is concerned with 'My Messenger' (that is, God's Messenger). This 'Messenger' sharply rebuked the people for the way in which they were using the Temple. The sacrifices which they made there were no honour to God (Mal. 1.6–8, 13). Priests were failing to give the people proper guidance in worship and the people were breaking the Laws of God and finding excuses for doing so (Mal. 2.8f, 17; 3.13–15).

The prophet seems to have been in continual heated argument with the people he taught. He quoted their own words again and again to show them their lack of faith and reverence (Mal. 1.2, 6, 7, 12f; 2.14, 17; 3.7f, 14). Yet this writer too had a message of hope, if only the people would respond to God with sincerity (Mal. 3.1–4, 10–12).

5. INDEPENDENCE FOR JUDAH

At the end of 445 BC, messengers came to the Persian court at Susa, with news of the difficulties which the Jews were facing in trying to establish a community to serve the LORD in Jerusalem and Judah. Nehemiah, an important court official, was a Jew. He was deeply distressed by all he heard, and longed to be able to do something for his people (Neh. 1.1–4). King Artaxerxes I allowed Nehemiah to go to Jerusalem and help rebuild the old capital (Neh. 2.4–6). He even went so far as to appoint Nehemiah governor of Judah, and so created a new sub-province in the Satrapy Beyond the River. This naturally displeased the governors who already had some power in that area, especially as the new arrangement favoured the Jews who had returned from exile (Neh. 2.10).

The book of Nehemiah tells the story of the way in which two of the governors, Sanballat and Tobiah, tried to prevent the rebuilding of Jerusalem, and of how Nehemiah overcame all the difficulties which they created for him. The detailed eye-witness account in the book of Nehemiah was taken from Nehemiah's own personal diary. He recorded that the work on the wall of Jerusalem was finished in fifty-two days (Neh. 6.15). Probably a whole plan of reconstruction took place inside the city walls, for Josephus, an ancient historian, records that the work took more than two years to complete.

Nehemiah then turned to the social and economic problems that the Jews were facing, and carried out some important reforms so that Jerusalem and Judah could become a happy and prosperous community. Many of the Jews were very poor. Some were getting deeply into debt while others made themselves rich as money-lenders. Nehemiah dealt sharply with those who were making such profits, and set an example himself by limiting his own salary (Neh. 5.1–19).

In 433 BC Nehemiah returned to Susa to report the success of his work, but after a few years he was sent back for a second tour of duty as governor in Jerusalem. Again he found many problems to be dealt with. The Temple buildings were being misused (Neh. 13.4–9), and the Jews were not paying their proper share of farming profits to the Temple authorities for the use of the Levites (Neh. 13.10–14). They were failing to observe the Sabbath (Neh. 13.15–22), and many of them were marrying foreign women and turning away from the service of the LORD (Neh. 13.23–7). Nehemiah took what action he felt to be necessary to deal with these evils.

The solemn agreement recorded in Nehemiah 10 probably belongs to this time. The compilers of the book of Nehemiah thought that it was Ezra who brought in this agreement, but Nehemiah heads the list of those who shared in it, and Ezra is not named. The matters covered by the agreement were the same problems which Nehemiah had tried to settle. It seems probable that he introduced the agreement and it is unlikely that Ezra had anything to do with it.

6. THE LAW OF THE LORD

At some time in this period another great leader came to Jerusalem. His name was Ezra, and he brought from Babylon a Law Book to guide the life of the people of Judah. Scholars are puzzled where to place Ezra's arrival in the order of events of this time. The people who collected records together to form the books of Ezra and Nehemiah seemed to have thought that Ezra came before Nehemiah, but most scholars agree that he came later than Nehemiah.

The evidence provided by the Bible itself is not straightforward. It is probable that the compilers of the books of Ezra and Nehemiah were confused by mention of King Artaxerxes in the records which they used (Ezra 7.1, 6–10). They supposed this was Artaxerxes I, and because they believed this, they placed Ezra before Nehemiah. We shall need to examine some of the details more closely in the second volume of our course. Meantime we shall assume that his visit was later: probably in 397 BC, which is the seventh year of King Artaxerxes II.

Ezra was a religious leader rather than a political leader. He was appointed by Artaxerxes, whose decree is recorded in Ezra 7.12–26. John Bright calls him 'the Minister of State for Jewish Affairs'. The king told Ezra to teach 'the law of your God, which is in your hand' (Ezra 7.14), and to punish Jews who were disobedient, including perhaps those not actually living in Judah (Ezra 7.25f). Thus the Persian king added his own authority to that of Ezra (Ezra 7.26).

Nehemiah 8.1–3 records the first public reading of the Law. It had to be interpreted from Hebrew into Aramaic, as this was the language known in Judah, and widely used in the Persian empire (Neh. 8.8), and Nehemiah 8.13–18 tells how the people held the feast of the Tabernacles to celebrate the reading of the Law.

We cannot be sure what Law Book was read by Ezra. But in later times the Jews came to call the first five books of the Old Testament by the title 'The Law'. It may have been these books which Ezra read. Certainly these books were fully accepted as divine scripture less than fifty years later. At that time the people who had never been in exile, and who had never been accepted as true Jews by those who returned from exile, cut themselves off from the main body of the people of Israel, and formed themselves into a community called the *Samaritans*. They accepted the first five books of the Old Testament as authoritative for themselves, as well as for the Jews, and it is highly unlikely that they would have done so if these books had been introduced after the time of Ezra, i.e. closer to the time of the final split between the Jews and the Samaritans.

Even in Ezra's time the division between these groups was a serious one. The Samaritans built themselves a rival temple on Mount Gerizim in about 400 BC, and carried on their own worship of God there. Not every Jew was happy about the growing split between the Jews and the remainder of mankind including especially the Samaritans. Two books were written to challenge the distrust and neglect of foreigners: Ruth and Jonah. We shall study these more closely in Volume 2.

STUDY SUGGESTIONS

REVIEW OF CONTENT

1. List the following prophets so as to show the order in which they appear in the history of Israel.

   Separate your list into three groups: those who worked mainly

before the exile, those during the exile, and those after the exile. Mark those whose names have been given to books in the Bible.
Elijah Ezekiel Haggai Hosea Jeremiah Malachi Nathan

2. Which two events in particular made the exiled Jews lose hope?
3. 'Two prophets were active during the exile' (p. 153). The name of one of them is not known.
(a) In which book of the Bible do we find his writings?
(b) What is the probable reason why he wrote 'anonymously', i.e. without letting his name be known?
(c) What message of hope did both these prophets give to the Jews in exile?
(d) In what ways did Cyrus help to fulfil their message of hope?
(e) How did the Jews repond?
4. (a) Name two men who led groups of Jews back from Babylon to Jerusalem.
(b) What did they find when they got there?
5. (a) How long did the people of Judah take to rebuild the Temple in Jerusalem?
(b) What sort of difficulties do you think they had to face in completing the task?
(c) Name one unexpected sort of help they received.
6. (a) Under what political authority did the Jews live when they first returned to Judah and Jerusalem?
(b) Under what religious authority did they live at that time?
7. (a) Who was Nehemiah?
(b) In what ways did King Artaxerxes I support Nehemiah in his work of rebuilding Jerusalem?
8. Read Nehemiah 4 and 5; 7.1–5a; 11.1, 2; 12.27–30; 13.
(a) Describe how the jealous governors Sanballat and Tobiah were prevented from hindering the work of rebuilding.
(b) Give examples of some of the reforms which Nehemiah carried out in Judah.
9. The Persian King Artaxerxes I supported Nehemiah in his work of reconstruction in Judah.
Which king probably supported Ezra, and in what ways?
10. What language was used for the first public reading of the Law, as recorded in Nehemiah 8.1–3?

BIBLE

11. Read Haggai 1.13–14; Zechariah 4.8, 9 and Zechariah 6.15.
(a) What do these three prophecies foretell?
(b) In what way is the third prophecy different from the other two?
12. Read 2 Kings 17.27–34; Nehemiah 6.10–14; Isaiah 58.1–5 and Isaiah 59.1–15.

Then explain in your own words why 'the rebuilding of the Temple did not lead to a revival of national life among the Jews' (p. 158).
13. Who was guilty of misusing Temple buildings, according to Nehemiah 13.4–9, and in what way were the buildings being misused?

FURTHER STUDY AND DISCUSSION

14. Which, if any, of the following prophets believed that God still had a plan to fulfil through the life and service of the people of Judah, and especially those who had been in exile? Give chapter and verse from the books of each prophet to support your answer:
Jeremiah Ezekiel Deutero-Isaiah Haggai Zechariah Malachi
15. Politicians and government officials often say that Christian preachers should not concern themselves with politics or affairs of state.
(a) What is your opinion?
(b) Which of the prophets mentioned in this chapter were most concerned with politics?
(c) Which if any of these prophets were able to influence the people of their time sufficiently to change the course of events?
16. (a) Who were the Samaritans, and why did the separation come about between them and the rest of the people of Israel?
(b) Describe any peoples you know of today who have separated themselves from other sections of the nation to which they belong, or who separate themselves very strictly from foreigners.
(c) What effect do you think such separation has on the life and character of the separated peoples?

3. 'AS IT IS WRITTEN'

Ezra's work was in many ways the result of the Exile. In Babylon the Israelites had tried to keep up their religious life. They could still keep up some of their ancient traditions, such as the Sabbath and circumcision. But there were other traditions which they could only keep in mind for the day when life would begin again for them in Jerusalem. Many of the festivals could not be held while the Temple was in ruins, but the priests in exile made records of the way things should be done. Ezra brought the book of the Law to Jerusalem to regulate the life of the new community living round the new Temple. The Law was also a guide for the religious life of the many Jews who still lived in foreign countries, such as Egypt and Babylon.

Religious life in Judah at this time was a combination of customs and practices established in earlier ages. Some of these had to be changed because circumstances had changed. For example, during the Exile there were no kings to act as God's representative. The people hoped one day to have a new ruler chosen by God, but they expected this to happen in the far future, rather than in their own lifetime.

Many of the religious customs and practices we have studied in earlier chapters of this book were, however, revived in Judah. The writers who described these patterns of worship and of religious thought were recording memories preserved by the Israelites for long periods of time. It is not always clear exactly when the various customs were first introduced, or what form they originally took. The most detailed records were made in the latest period, when the things remembered had been changed and adapted in the light of the beliefs and practices followed in those later times. We can, however, be fairly sure about the way in which the Jews took up these practices in Jerusalem after the Exile.

RELIGIOUS LEADERS AND THEIR DUTIES

The leaders of the new community in Jerusalem were the priests (e.g. Ezra 3.2, 10), with a High Priest as chief among them (Neh. 13.28). This High Priesthood was a new appointment after the Exile. There were also Levites, who were a lower rank of Temple workers (e.g. Neh. 8.7; 10.8f).

Various sorts of sacrifice were customary. Burnt offerings were made twice daily (Ezra 3.3, 6). Peace offerings were given on joyful occasions as voluntary expressions of thanksgiving (Neh. 13.43). Two other forms of sacrifice, the sin offering and the guilt offering, are mentioned in the book of Leviticus as being important (Lev. 4 and 5). These seem to have been new customs, though some scholars suggest that they had been introduced at the time of the first kings. Certainly it would have been natural for a people who had already experienced the results of disobedience to God in the time of the Exile to recognize the possibility of 'national' sin, and the danger of breaking God's commandments 'unwittingly' (Lev. 4.2). They would see the need for a way of showing repentance for the wrong which the nation as a whole had committed.

REGULAR FESTIVALS

The three regular festivals observed before the Exile became customary when the Jews returned to Jerusalem: the Passover, Pentecost, and the Feast of the Booths (Ezra 6.19f; Neh. 10.35; Ex. 23.16; Neh. 8.13–18). These three festivals were times of pilgrimage, when Jews living outside Judah would visit Jerusalem.

A new festival seems to have been introduced into the Jewish calendar

Xerxes set out against Greece, and even captured Athens, where he burned down temples and public buildings on the hill called the Acropolis (see p. 149).

8.3 The Acropolis today.

8.4 The 'Porch of the Maidens' on the Acropolis was burned down by the Persians, and rebuilt soon afterwards.

some time after the return from Exile, the Festival of the Day of Atonement (Lev. 23.26–32). It is not mentioned in the books of Ezra and Nehemiah, and may have come into use later than their time. The details are given in Leviticus 16.

At the Festival of the Day of Atonement the High Priest made sin offerings for himself and also for the people, and so made 'atonement for the holy place' itself (Lev. 16.3, 5, 16). Part of the ritual at this festival was unlike other Jewish custom: it included the provision of *two* goats, one for the LORD, and the other for 'Azazel', the name used for a desert spirit or for the leader of evil angels. The goat given to the LORD was a pure sacrifice, worthy for use in His worship. The goat given to Azazel carried with it 'all the iniquities of the people of Israel, and all their transgressions' (Lev. 16.21).

The origin and inner meaning of the goat sent to Azazel is not known for certain, though similar customs exist in some tribal religions today. Some scholars believe it was a very ancient custom preserved from the days when the people of Israel believed in the existence of many gods beside the LORD. But Deutero-Isaiah was so emphatic about other gods being nothing, that it is difficult to believe that such a custom would have been allowed to continue if the Jews had interpreted it in this way. Perhaps some of the Israelite leaders had been influenced by Persian ideas of a battle between the forces of good and evil. If so, the goat was used for the LORD's purposes, to deal with evil. The goat was presented alive to the LORD before being sent away on its errand (Lev. 16.10).

JEWISH CUSTOMS

After their return, the Jews seem to have continued many of the customs which had helped to preserve their independent spirit while in exile. Among these were circumcision, the Sabbath, and the synagogue. Unlike most other nations of the time, the Jews regarded circumcision as a custom for early childhood. This may be one reason for their Laws against marriage with non-Jews. Such marriages would lead to conflicts over the proper time for circumcision. If the foreign wives had their way in the matter, this would have destroyed an important distinction between the Jews and other peoples. The foreigners in Judah did not recognize the Sabbath, and this became another cause of trouble (Neh. 10.31; 13.15–22). Ezra's introduction of the book of the Law encouraged the establishment of synagogues where the sacred records could be preserved and read. These records became the ruling influence in the lives of the Jews as the years went by. Judaism gradually became a religion of written law, and one of the most important functions of Jewish religious leaders was that of interpreting this Law.

STUDY SUGGESTIONS

WORDS

1. The festival of the Day of Atonement was introduced some time after the return of the Jews from exile (p. 165). Read Leviticus 16.
(a) Who or what can receive 'atonement', according to this chapter?
(b) Which one of the following words most helps us to understand the meaning of the phrase 'to make atonement'? Give the reason for your choice.

   To compensate   to reconcile   to compromise
   to reinstate   to propitiate

REVIEW OF CONTENT

2. For what reason is it not always clear when the various religious customs of the Israelites were first introduced?
3. (a) Who were the Levites?
(b) When was the office of High Priest first instituted, and where?
4. Which three festivals, which had been observed before the exile, again became customary after the return to Judah?

FURTHER STUDY AND DISCUSSION

5. Reference is made on p. 163 to the danger of breaking God's commandments 'unwittingly', i.e. accidentally or unintentionally, without realizing it.
   What would you reply to someone who said, 'There is no such thing as "unwitting sin". If I didn't intend to do something, then I am not to be blamed for doing it'?
6. What difference is there, if any, between believing in the existence of many gods besides the LORD, and making use of the idea of 'a battle between the forces of good and evil'? Do you think that a belief in Satan is compatible with belief in the Unity of God?

CHAPTER 9

The Greek Empire

1. UNITED, THE GREEKS CONQUER THE WORLD

The people of Greece had a long recorded history, going back at least to the time of the Exodus, yet in the Bible they are only mentioned in writings from after the Exile. The reason for this is that in earlier times the Greeks had no strong central government, and were unable to influence world affairs. There had been a number of city-states, each with its own independent life. There had been conflicts between these city-states, but none of them had become strong enough to rule the others and create a Greek nation.

Some scholars believe that the Philistines came from Greece and had been driven out of their homeland by stronger groups of Greeks. If so, the first meeting between Greeks and Israelites took place at the time when God's people were settling in Palestine. Later there was trade between Palestine and Greece. Greek pottery was brought into Palestine, and it seems that the Phoenicians sold Jews as slaves to the Greeks (Joel 3.6; see also Ezekiel 27.13, where the ancient name 'Javan' is used for the Greeks). And Greek soldiers were employed as mercenaries in the armies of Egypt and Babylon. But the first important contact between the Jews and the Greeks came toward the end of the fourth century before Christ. At that time, for the first time, the city-states were united into a powerful league under a single ruler.

By 338 BC King Phillip II of Macedonia had conquered the city-states of Greece, and had brought them all under his rule. Two years later he was assassinated, but his son Alexander took his place as leader of the Greeks, and ruled from 336 until 323 BC. Alexander took up again the unresolved conflict with Persia (see p. 150). In 334 BC he entered Asia Minor and drove the local Persian forces out of that area. A year later he defeated the main Persian army at Issus, north of Antioch, and then led the Greek army southwards toward Egypt (see Map 9). The city of Tyre resisted his siege for seven months, and Gaza did so for two months (Zech. 9.1–8); but when Alexander reached Egypt the people welcomed him as the one who had come to set them free from Persian rule. Judah and Samaria came under Alexander's control at this time. Then in 331 BC Alexander led his army against the Persians in Mesopotamia, and finally defeated Darius III at Gaugamela, east of the River Tigris (see Map 9). Alexander marched victoriously into Babylon, Susa, and Persepolis, and Darius was assassinated by some of his own people.

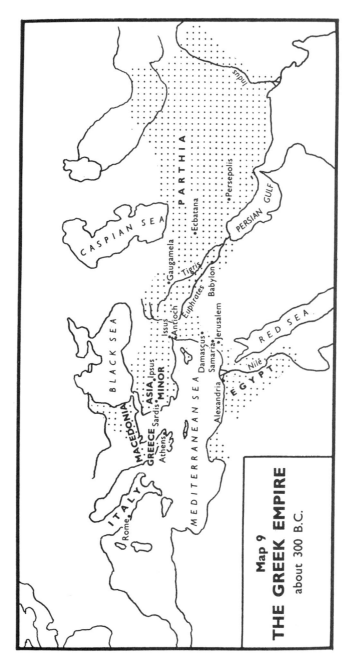

Map 9
THE GREEK EMPIRE
about 300 B.C.

It seemed that Alexander was victorious wherever he went. By 326 BC he had reached the River Indus, which became the eastern border of his empire, and it is said that he wept because he had nowhere else to conquer. In less than ten years he had destroyed the Persian empire, and created the Greek empire, covering a large part of the ancient Near East. In 323 BC he died of a fever in Babylon, aged only 32.

After Alexander's death, the new Greek empire fell to pieces. There was nobody strong enough to take over the rule from Alexander, and the generals in command of divisions of the army in different countries of the empire tried to gain power for themselves over the areas which were in their charge. By 301 BC five areas of government had come into being: Macedonia, Thrace, Asia Minor with Phoenicia, Egypt with Palestine, and Babylon. The ruler in Egypt was Ptolemy. He managed to keep hold of his rule there without much interference from the other generals. The others, however, fought among themselves, and by 281 BC Seleucus, ruler of Babylon, had conquered the other three. In that same year Seleucus was assassinated, and Macedonia broke free from the rule of his successor. Thus there remained three areas of Greek power: *Macedonia* ruled by Antigonus, *Egypt* ruled by Ptolemy, and the rest of the empire ruled from *Antioch* by the Seleucids (i.e. the family of Seleucus).

These three powers continued until early in the second century when the Romans began to compete with the Greeks for control of world affairs. The Seleucids were the first to feel the growing power of the Romans, and Antiochus III received as a refugee a general from Carthage called Hannibal, who had been defeated by the Romans. Antiochus tried to strengthen his own position by capturing the mainland of Greece, but he was driven away by the Romans, and forced to sign a harsh peace treaty in 190 BC.

GREEK RELIGION AND CULTURE

The Greeks believed in many gods. They believed that these gods lived together in a place called Olympia, under the rule of the chief god, Zeus. Many stories of the Greek gods and goddesses have been preserved through the centuries, and are still known today. The Greeks believed that the inhabitants of Olympia often acted on impulse, and did not have any rules of behaviour to guide them.

Many of the most deep-thinking Greeks had rejected the Greek religion, and were more concerned for human achievements. The Greeks of those times were outstanding among men in their study and ability in the arts, sciences, and in philosophy. In the arts they developed special skills in drama, sculpture, and painting. In science they laid important foundations for the study of geometry, engineering, geography, and astronomy. In philosophy they developed ideas about human nature and human society which have continued to have their influence into modern times.

The Greeks were specially fond of discussing ideas of democracy and justice, and they argued fiercely about the principles which should govern people's choice of actions. When they brought the idea of God into these debates at all, it was as an ideal of perfection toward which men should strive. Because they thought of God as perfect, they believed that He had no need for men, and no interest in them, so that He could not be expected to give them aid, or enter into any relationship with them.

Alexander had been a pupil of one of the greatest of Greek scholars, Aristotle. There is no doubt that Alexander believed that he would be serving mankind well by spreading Greek culture across the world. His policy seems to have been to settle groups of retired soldiers in every part of the empire, so that they would introduce Greek ideas, skills, and knowledge to the people among whom they lived. This same policy to spread Greek culture was continued by the other Greek rulers after the partition of the empire into separate states.

Ptolemy and his family in Egypt were especially active in encouraging Greek culture. Alexander had founded a new city known as Alexandria, and under the rule of the Ptolemies this city became a great centre of learning. Many of the greatest Greek scholars studied and taught there, including the mathematicians Euclid and Archimedes.

STUDY SUGGESTIONS

REVIEW OF CONTENT

1. Of what nationality were the following leaders?
   Cyrus   Seleucus   Darius   Nebuchadnezzar   Ptolemy
   Sennacherib
2. Which nations had power over Judah in the following years:
   600 BC   500 BC   400 BC   300 BC
3. Why is it that the Greeks are not mentioned in any books of the Bible written before the time of the Exile in Babylon?
4. (a) At what period did the Greek city-states first become sufficiently united to form a single nation?
   (b) Who was the leader who brought them all under his rule?
5. (a) Who was the Greek general who was victorious wherever he went?
   (b) How long did it take him to conquer the Persians and create the Greek empire?
   (c) When and how did he die, and what happened after his death?
6. What three areas of Greek power continued until the beginning of the second century BC, and by what families were they ruled?

7. 'Alexander believed that he would be serving mankind well by spreading Greek culture across the world' (p. 170).
(a) Give examples of modern nations who have had similar ideas about the value of their culture.
(b) Have they been right in believing that they were serving mankind?
(c) What should our attitude be to the ideas and customs that come from a different culture from our own?

8. Many Greek ideas have influenced European thought down through the centuries since the time of Alexander. Many English words came originally from the Greek language, and are used to express these ideas.
(a) Use a dictionary which explains the origins of words, to discover which of the following words come from Greek:

Art	civics	conquer	defeat	democracy
history	geography	indigenous	industry	justice
languages	mathematics	mercenary	philosophy	physics
scholar	science	surgery	theology	trade

(b) What language are most of the other words derived from? What people or peoples spoke that language?

9. The Greeks believed that God 'had no need for men and no interest in them, so that He could not be expected to give them aid, or enter into any relationship with them' (p. 170).
(a) Were the Jews likely to accept this idea of God? Give reasons for your answer.
(b) Do we as Christians accept this idea about God? If not, what evidence have we that the Greeks were wrong?

2. THE JEWS RESIST GREEK CULTURE

I. JUDAH UNDER THE PTOLEMIES

When the Greek empire broke up into separate kingdoms after the death of Alexander, Palestine was part of the area ruled by Ptolemy and his family. The Ptolemies ruled over Egypt throughout the remaining years of Greek domination in world affairs, but they lost control over Palestine in 198 BC, when the Seleucids took over command of the area.

So far as we know, life in Palestine during the 125 years of the rule of the Ptolemies was peaceful, and without great changes. The High Priest was still the chief authority among the Jews, in both spiritual and political matters, though he was officially responsible to the Ptolemies for what happened in Judah.

The most important development for the Jews in this period was the growth of a strong Jewish community in the new Greek city of Alexandria, in Egypt. These Alexandrian Jews recognized the value of Greek ideas and culture, and were willing to adopt them for their own use. They very quickly forgot how to speak or read the languages of their homeland, and used Greek instead. They found it difficult to maintain their own Jewish heritage of history and faith, because the books of their scripture were written in Hebrew, a language most of them did not understand.

After a time the Jewish leaders came to recognize the need for a Greek translation of the books of the Law. Gradually over the following centuries the whole of what we know as the Old Testament was translated into Greek. At later times other writings were added to the Greek scriptures. These new writings had never been accepted by the Jewish leaders in Palestine, and had never had a place in the Hebrew scriptures. The Greek scriptures were given the name 'the Septuagint', because of a legend that seventy-two scholars had worked to make the translation. The parts of the Septuagint that are not included in the Hebrew Bible are known to us today as the *Apocrypha*. Almost all that we know of Jewish history in the time of the Greeks comes from the Apocrypha. The most important parts are I and II Maccabees, which are two separate accounts of events in Palestine after the Seleucids had taken control there.

2. JUDAH UNDER THE SELEUCIDS

We have seen that after Alexander's death his generals were for a long time in conflict with each other for power over his empire. By 281 Seleucus had defeated them all except Ptolemy, but it was not until 198 BC that Antiochus III, one of the family of Seleucus, was victorious over the Egyptians, and so able to seize control of Palestine.

At first, the Jews were glad about this change. Life was made easier for them. Antiochus charged no taxes in the first three years of his rule, and then only small taxes were imposed. Cult officials and members of the Council of Elders were exempt from taxation, and state aid was provided for repairs to the Temple. But later, Antiochus III was defeated in battle by the Romans, and he began to demand more from the Jews.

The next Greek ruler, Seleucus IV (187–175), continued to help the Jews (2 Mac. 3.3), but was tempted to take for his own use large sums of money which had been placed in the Temple for safe-keeping. According to legend his chancellor, Heliodorus, whom he sent to seize the money, was severely beaten by a spiritual being, and was lucky to escape with his life (2 Mac. 3.4–40). The High Priest, Onias, was accused of causing the injuries which Heliodorus received (2 Mac. 4.1),

9.1   Alexander.

In 331 BC Alexander finally defeated the Persians under Darius III at Gaugamela. A mosaic found at Pompeii portrays the two commanders as they had faced each other in battle two years earlier.

9.2   Darius.

and this led to a long and bitter dispute between the Greek rulers and the Temple officials. It was almost impossible at that time for a man to be loyal both to the Greeks and to his office as High Priest.

The worst time of trouble for the Jews in this period was the reign of Antiochus IV (175–163 BC). He took for himself the title *Epiphanes*, which means 'the bodily appearance of God'. Jason, the High Priest's brother, bribed Antiochus IV to make him High Priest in his brother's place. In return for this honour, Jason promised money from the Temple, and support for Greek culture in Judah (2 Mac. 4.8–10). A sports stadium was set up in Jerusalem, and many of the priests left their Temple duties to join in the Greek sports (1 Mac. 1.14–15; 2 Mac. 4.14–15) which were closely associated with the cult of the Greek god Hercules. Jason even authorized the priests to join in this pagan worship (2 Mac. 4.18–20).

But Jason soon lost his authority as High Priest when another man, called Menelaus, promised Antiochus IV even more money in return for the appointment. Menelaus was dishonest with everyone, and when he was compelled to pay the bribe which he had promised, he robbed the Temple to do so. He also arranged the murder of Onias, who had accused him of the bribery (2 Mac. 4.27–34).

In the meantime Antiochus IV was involved in an attempt to seize control of Egypt. Jason seems to have expected Antiochus to be defeated and killed. He took the opportunity to lead an army against Jerusalem, drove his rival Menelaus into hiding, and massacred many of the people (2 Mac. 5.5–6). Jason was so unpopular that he was unable to stay in Jerusalem in safety. When Antiochus IV returned from Egypt after victory there, he punished the Jews for what he regarded as their rebellion, and robbed the Temple of some of its sacred vessels (1 Mac. 1.20–24; 2 Mac. 5.15, 21).

The climax of trouble came a couple of years later. Antiochus IV had again attacked Egypt and final victory was within his reach when the Romans interfered, ordering him to leave Egypt (Dan. 11.29–30).

Humiliated, Antiochus expressed his anger by attacking Jerusalem (2 Mac. 5.23–26). The city was looted and partly destroyed, and Antiochus built a stronghold to house foreign soldiers in the city (1 Mac. 14.36). He issued an order forbidding the Jews to follow the customs of their religion and forbade Jewish festivals and sacrifices (1 Mac. 1.45). He ordered that all copies of the books of the Law should be burnt (1 Mac. 1.56, 57), and that the custom of circumcision should be forbidden among the Jews (1 Mac. 1.48). The penalty for disobedience was death (1 Mac. 1.50).

Pagan altars were set up all over the land (1 Mac. 1.54), and Jews were forcibly made to eat pork (2 Mac. 6.18–19). Worst of all, an altar to the Greek god Zeus was set up in the Temple at Jerusalem (2 Mac.

6.2). This is what is meant by 'the abomination of desolation' in 1 Mac. 1.54, and in Dan. 9.27; 11.31; 12.11.

In this way Antiochus tried to destroy everything which was distinctively Jewish. He hoped that if Jews were forced to adopt Greek culture they would come to support the Greek rule. Some Jews gave way in face of this persecution (1 Mac. 1.43, 52), but there were many who refused to give up the ways of life which they believed God had given to His people. The centre of the resistance was a group called the Hasidim, that is 'the pious ones' or 'the loyal ones'. Many scholars believe that the book of Daniel was written at this time to encourage the Jews to remain faithful to the Lord. The book describes the great success of Antiochus IV, and his sudden disastrous end (Dan. 8.23–25; 11.40–45).

The Jews soon showed their resistance to the enforcement of Greek culture (1 Mac. 2). The king's officers came to a town called Modin, where they called on an elderly priest named Mattathias to make sacrifice to the Greek gods. He refused, and killed a Jew who offered to act as priest instead. He also killed one of the king's officers, and destroyed the pagan altar.

After this, Mattathias fled into the hills with his sons, and gathered an army of faithful Jews there. They were attacked on the Sabbath day, and many were killed because they refused to fight on the Lord's day. The survivors agreed that they should defend themselves on the Sabbath if the need arose. They caused the Greeks great trouble by frequent guerilla attacks.

When Mattathias died, one of his sons named Judas took command. He had been given the nick-name *Maccabaeus*, which means 'the Hammer', and these independence forces became known as the *Maccabees* as a result. The Greeks tried several times to overthrow the Maccabees, but each time they failed (1 Mac. 3.10—4.34).

Eventually the main part of the Greek army withdrew, and Judas was able to enter Jerusalem freely, and to cleanse the Temple from all the pagan things that had been introduced there (1 Mac. 4.36–61). The Temple was rededicated in 164 BC, and a new feast was introduced to commemorate the event annually. Even so, the stronghold built by Antiochus IV in Jerusalem remained, staffed with foreign troops and with Jews who had adopted Greek culture.

Shortly afterwards, Antiochus IV was killed in battle in the eastern part of the kingdom. A period of conflict followed, when several Greek leaders were fighting among themselves for power. Judas took advantage of this time to show the strength of his own forces in Palestine and across the Jordan. The Greek authorities had to recognize the right of the Jews to follow their own religion and customs, and they withdrew the laws which had been passed forbidding these customs.

175

Many of the Hasidim were content to have religious freedom, and were not much concerned about gaining political power for the Jews. But Judas and his brothers continued to struggle for national independence through all the changing circumstances of Greek rule. Within ten years the Maccabees had managed to capture and disarm the stronghold in Jerusalem. Soon afterwards Jonathan, the youngest of the brothers, was appointed High Priest, with political as well as religious authority (1 Mac. 10.18–20).

Gradually, as a result of continual plots and counter-plots, Greek control of affairs in Palestine grew weaker and weaker, and the Maccabees were able to direct the life of the Jewish nation according to their own wishes, both in Palestine and beyond the Jordan. John Hyrcanus, nephew of Judas Maccabaeus, was able to take for himself the title 'king'. He spread his authority widely, conquering peoples who had not yet submitted to the Jewish rule of the Maccabees. He gave those whom he conquered the choice between becoming Jews, or leaving his kingdom. Many submitted rather than become refugees.

After the death of John Hyrcanus, two of his sons became king in turn, first Aristobulus I, and then Alexander Jannaeus. Alexander Jannaeus spread his rule into Ammon, Moab, and southward to the borders of Egypt.

The more deeply the Maccabees became involved in political matters and in conquest, the more severely the Hasidim opposed them. The great conflict between Pharisees and Sadducees in New Testament times had grown out of the conflict between Hasidim and the Maccabees. Some Jews were so unhappy about the worldly interests of the leaders of their nation that they withdrew altogether from national life, and formed monastic groups in desert places, where they could give attention to the Law, and to worship. Later these groups became known as the Essenes.

STUDY SUGGESTIONS

REVIEW OF CONTENT

1. Prepare a 'family tree', or genealogy, showing the relationships between the various members of the family of the Maccabees mentioned in this chapter. (Begin with Mattathias at the top of your page. Then show his sons on the next line. Below that their sons, and so on. You should include Judas Maccabaeus, Jonathan, John Hyrcanus (whose father was called Simon), Aristobulus I, and Alexander Jannaeus. Draw lines to link fathers with sons, and brothers with brothers. Keep this 'tree'; you will be able to add some more names to it after studying chapter 10.)

2. (a) Who or what were the following?
The Seleucids   Epiphanes*   The Hasidim*   The Essenes
The Septuagint*   Olympia   The Maccabees
(b) Give the meaning in English of those names marked with an asterisk.
(c) What was the chief difference between the Hasidim and the Maccabees?
3. In what writings do we chiefly find the history of the Jews at the time of the Greek empire?
4. What effect did use of the Greek language have on the Jews of Alexandria?
5. 'In 198 BC the Seleucids defeated the Ptolemies and seized control of Palestine. At first the Jews were glad' (p. 172).
(a) For what reasons did the change of rule please the Jews?
(b) What sort of trouble did it cause for them a little later?
6. Read Jeremiah 6.12–15 and 2 Maccabees 4.7–20.
(a) In what ways did the High Priest Jason in the time of Greek power resemble the priests whom Jeremiah was accusing, before the destruction of Jerusalem by the Babylonians?
(b) In what ways was the later action of the Greek rulers in Jerusalem like that of the Babylonians?
7. What is meant by the 'abomination of desolation' in 1 Maccabees 1.54 and Daniel 9.27?
8. Read 1 Maccabees 2. Then rewrite the story of Mattathias in not more than 150 words.
9. What connection, if any, is there between the Hasidim and the Maccabees on the one hand, and the Pharisees and the Sadducees on the other?

BIBLE

10. Read John 10.22. What was the feast mentioned in that verse? When was the feast first introduced among the Jews, and what did it celebrate?

FURTHER STUDY AND DISCUSSION

11. Read the article in a Bible dictionary on the *Apocrypha*, and answer the following questions:
(a) Why are the writings of the Apocrypha not included among the books of the Old Testament in some Bibles?
(b) Why are many Bibles sold which do not include the books of the Apocrypha at all?
(c) What is the view of your own Church about the spiritual value of the Apocrypha?
(d) Why is the Apocrypha important for our study of Jewish history?

12. Use a Bible dictionary and atlas to find out what you can about the city of Antioch in Syria. Then answer the following questions:
    (a) When was Antioch first established, and where?
    (b) Why was it given the name Antioch?
    (c) What was the importance of Antioch in the time of the Maccabees?
    (d) Is Antioch ever mentioned in the Old Testament?
    (e) Were there any Jews settled at Antioch in New Testament times? (See Acts 11.19–21.)
13. (a) Who was the leader of the Maccabees, and why were they given that name?
    (b) In what ways were the Maccabees like or unlike 'freedom-fighters' of the present day? Give examples in support of your answer.

3. RELIGIOUS COLLABORATORS AND FREEDOM-FIGHTERS

We have studied the rise to power of four great empires: Assyria, Babylon, Persia, and now Greece. Always the leaders of such empires have to find ways of gaining obedience from the people they rule. Each of these four empires had its own special answer to this problem.

1. The *Assyrians* relied upon their *military power* to maintain their rule. They enforced their will on the conquered peoples by physical violence.

2. The *Babylonians* tried to break down people's loyalty to their own rulers and replace it by *loyalty to Babylon*. They removed the national leaders of conquered nations, and settled foreigners in their place. People living near one another did not feel they belonged together, and so had to look to Babylon for any political unity.

3. The *Persians* believed in establishing *friendly relations* with the people they ruled. They liked to be regarded as deliverers, rather than as conquerors. They believed that there would be peace in their empire only if they allowed people religious freedom. If men could follow their own culture freely while ruled by the Persians, then they would not want to revolt.

4. The *Greek* way of rule was quite different from any of these. They believed that their own culture was far in advance of any other culture in the ancient middle east. They believed that people would be glad to *share the Greek culture*, with all its great art and knowledge, so they expected people to welcome Greek rule because it would bring the advantages of Greek culture. They deliberately set out to create a new way of life throughout their empire. This presented an entirely new problem for the Jews. What should be their attitude to this new Greek

178

culture? Was it possible to welcome it, and still remain faithful Jews? There were five possible answers to this question:

(a) *Accept* Greek culture wholeheartedly, and break free from Judaism;

(b) *Accept* as much of Greek culture as possible, while still remaining loyal to the LORD;

(c) *Allow* Greek culture a place in national life, without believing that it had anything important to add to Jewish faith;

(d) *Reject* Greek culture, and do everything possible to destroy it, and to replace it by Judaism;

(e) *Reject* Greek culture, and avoid its influence by taking no part in national life, and by forming special communities to follow the Jewish faith.

Each of these five answers was given at one time or another by Jews in the time of the Greek empire. The first answer was given by many Jews (1 Mac. 1.43, 52), but it involved rejection of Judaism, and did not lead to a new religious group among the Jews. At first the new groups that did form within Judaism in this period could be distinguished by their differing attitudes to Greek culture. Later, when Greek power was growing less, the various groups changed their attitudes because they wanted to gain political power.

The Priests in Jerusalem did much to encourage Greek culture, as we have already seen. They believed that Jewish faith and Greek culture could be mixed so as to gain the best of both. But their chief interest seems to have been to gain power for themselves. When the Maccabees gained power in Palestine, the Priests withdrew their support from the Greeks, and supported the Maccabees who had resisted and broken Greek power in Palestine. The Priests eventually formed the party known as the Sadducees, and continued to be chiefly interested in exercising political power.

The Hasidim were willing to allow the spread of Greek culture, so long as it did not interfere with their exercise of the Jewish faith. They actively opposed Antiochus Epiphanes only because he attempted to destroy Judaism. At that time they supported the revolt led by the Maccabees. But later, when the attempt to enforce Greek culture failed, and the Jews were given religious freedom, the Hasidim were satisfied. They did not support the Maccabees' attempts to gain political independence. In fact the Hasidim disapproved of the worldly ways of those holding political power in Jerusalem. Later on, the Hasidim group became the *Pharisees*, who are mentioned in the New Testament.

The Maccabees openly opposed Greek rule and the enforcement of Greek culture in the time of Antiochus Epiphanes. As we have seen, at first they were chiefly concerned to protect the Jewish Faith, at a

9.3　The Greeks believed in many gods, and that they lived together under the rule of a chief god, Zeus. Remains of the temple of Zeus in Athens are still standing today.

9.4　In 198 BC a descendant of Seleucus, Antiochus III—here shown on a coin—defeated the Egyptians and seized control of Palestine. It was under his successor Antiochus IV that an altar to Zeus was set up in the Jewish Temple in Jerusalem (see p. 174).

time when the political rulers were trying to destroy it. When the Jewish Faith was no longer threatened, the Maccabees tried to gain political freedom, and to destroy the remaining power of the Greeks in Palestine. Eventually they joined forces with the Priests, and were content to accept some Greek influence in national life, provided it did not undermine their own power.

The Essenes were a group of devout Jews who became deeply troubled by the way in which men involved in politics could be corrupted. They believed that God's kingdom would never be established on earth by political means. They saw that even when men set out with high ideals, they change and try to gain power for themselves. Only God could bring his rule on earth, and in the meantime all that devout people could do was to keep themselves pure and have nothing to do with worldly men. The Essenes therefore set up religious communities to study God's word, and they separated themselves from all contact with people involved in political activities. The important library of Qumran, which we shall discuss in the second volume of this course, probably belonged to the Essenes.

APOCALYPSE

A new type of literature began to be produced in this period, which took the place of the prophetic writings of earlier times. The new writers were trying to understand history in the light of God's rule, and to declare God's purposes for the future. But they did not believe that human endeavour could ever establish God's rule on earth. Some of their ideas were:

1. Men must wait for God to act, and He will do all that is necessary without the help of men.

2. There will be judgement, with punishment for the evildoers and blessing for the righteous.

3. There will be a new life for those who have died in service of God, and the righteous will be raised to new life in God's kingdom.

These writers usually recorded their teaching in the form of dreams or visions, which they attributed to important men of past ages. They used these famous names to make the Jews take note of what was written. The names of the authors of these books themselves are mostly unknown. The books which they wrote are called 'Apocalypse' or 'Apocalyptic', from a Greek word which means 'unveiling' or 'revelation'.

The visions described in this sort of literature are full of angels and symbolic animals, and world history is seen as a continuing conflict between forces of good and evil, in which the victory already belongs to God. There are not many examples of this kind of writing in the Bible, but early examples are found in Isaiah 24—27, Zechariah 9—14,

181

and Daniel 7—12.There are many examples of apocalypse among the books from those times, which are not included in the Bible, nor in the Apocrypha. In the New Testament the book of Revelation is a good example of this sort of writing.

STUDY SUGGESTIONS

REVIEW OF CONTENT

1. 'The leaders of great empires have to find ways of gaining obedience from the people they rule' (p. 178).
   In what ways did the leaders in each of the following empires maintain their rule?
   Assyria   Persia   Greece

2. 'The new groups within Judaism could be distinguished by the attitude they took to Greek culture' (p. 179).
   Which of the attitudes listed in the second column below was taken by each of the groups in the first column?

1.	2.
(a) The priests	(i) Allowed Greek culture provided it
(b) The Maccabees	did not interfere with Jewish faith
(c) The Hasidim	(ii) Encouraged Greek culture
	(iii) Opposed Greek culture

3. (a) For what reason did the Hasidim oppose Antiochus Epiphanes?
   (b) For what reason did the priests support the Maccabees?

4. Read the articles on Essenes, Pharisees, and Sadducees in a Bible dictionary.
   To which of these three groups does each of the following statements refer?
   (a) They were opposed to the selfish attitudes of the Jewish rulers in Jerusalem.
   (b) They cut themselves off from human society, and lived in desert places.
   (c) They encouraged men to study the Law, and added their own interpretations.
   (d) They enjoyed political power, and were friendly to those in authority.
   (e) They took an attitude to the coming of God's rule on earth similar to that expressed in the Apocalypse.
   (f) They denied that there would be a resurrection after death.

BIBLE

5. Read the following passages and say which of them are examples of 'apocalypse'.

2 Chron. 18.16–19   Ps. 103.1–5   Isa. 10.1–4   Isa. 27.1
Jer. 22.10   Ezek. 44.1–3   Zech. 14.20   Rev. 4.6b–8

FURTHER STUDY AND DISCUSSION

6. The five different attitudes which the Jews took at different times
to the Greek culture are still relevant today. For example, the
Church in each country has to decide what attitude it should take to
the government of the nation.

(a) Which of the five 'answers' listed on p. 179 truly represents the
attitude of your Church to the government of your country?

(b) Do you think this is the right answer?

(c) Can you think of examples of countries where a different answer
would be right?

Give reasons for your answers to (b) and (c).

7. It is difficult today to know exactly what the writers of the 'apocalyptic' books meant by the various signs and symbols which they used.

(a) Look up the notes on Revelation 11.3 in several different commentaries, and compare the interpretations they give of the reference
to 'two witnesses'.

(b) What should our attitude be to Christian sects which base most
of their teaching on apocalyptic writings, and claim to hold the only
true interpretation of such books?

CHAPTER 10

The Roman Empire

1. GREATEST OF THE ANCIENT EMPIRES

While the Greeks were ruling over the eastern part of the Mediterranean, a new nation was forming in the west. In Italy there had been a large number of independent cities, but after a long period of conflict these had been drawn together into a new state. Rome became its chief city, and gave its name to the state. The whole nation was ruled by a Senate, consisting of representatives of the wealthy and powerful families in every part of the country. Later, the leader of the Senate came to be known as the Caesar. This happened after the reign of the greatest of them all: Julius Caesar.

Each of the cities of Italy continued to have some independence. They were able to make local laws, judge cases that arose among them, and tax their own people. But those in authority in the cities recognized the supreme power of Caesar and the Roman Senate. This pattern of government was copied when the Romans began to conquer neighbouring lands and make an empire for themselves. Caesar and the Senate were supreme throughout the empire, but local government was encouraged so long as it did not lead to conflict with those in power in Rome.

The Roman Empire was divided into many provinces. Some provinces were ruled by men appointed by Caesar, called either legates or procurators, while others had governors appointed by the Senate. But local government in each province was organized according to local needs and traditions.

The supremacy of Rome was represented throughout the empire by the presence of the Roman army. Legions of soldiers were stationed in every province, or else there were auxiliary forces of men who were doing military service in order to qualify for Roman citizenship.

We have already seen that the family of Seleucus ruled over the greater part of the Greek empire, but not in Greece itself. The first conflict between the Seleucids and the Romans came when Antiochus III tried to gain control of Greece. He was defeated by the Romans and driven out of Europe. Later, in 190 BC, he was forced to sign a peace treaty which was entirely an advantage to the Romans. Twenty years later, Antiochus IV tried to gain control over Egypt, and would have succeeded if the Romans had not interfered (see p. 174). Judas Maccabaeus, the leader of the Jewish fight for independence, sent envoys to

Rome to seek their support (1 Mac. 8.17–32). After the death of Antiochus IV, the power of the Seleucids gradually diminished and eventually disappeared altogether. This was the result of plots and counter-plots by various members of that family who each looked for power for himself.

In 65 BC the Roman general Pompey set out to gain control of Palestine and Syria, and quickly destroyed the remaining Greek influence in the area. We shall see later how important this change was for the Jewish people. Ten years afterwards Pompey fell out of favour with Julius Caesar, and the Roman Empire was split by civil war. Pompey was defeated at Thessalonica in 48 BC, and he was afterwards murdered.

Four years after that, members of the Senate were involved in the murder of Julius Caesar, and as a result, civil war broke out again. This time there were two leaders on each side. Brutus and Cassius fought against Mark Antony and Octavian. For a time Cassius was successful in controlling Syria, but then he was defeated by Mark Antony. Meantime Octavian had gained mastery in Italy and the west.

Mark Antony then became involved in a love affair with Cleopatra: a beautiful and scheming princess of Egypt. War followed between Octavian and Mark Antony, who both wanted supreme power in the Roman Empire. Mark Antony was defeated at the Battle of Actium in 31 BC, and Cleopatra committed suicide. Octavian became the supreme ruler, and took for himself a new name: Augustus Caesar.

Augustus reigned until his death in AD 14 (see Luke 2.1). Several of his relatives were among the rulers who followed him to power. Tiberius ruled from AD 14 to 37; Caligula from AD 37 to 41; Claudius from AD 41 to 54; Nero from AD 54 to 68, and after a period of confusion, Vespasian, from AD 69 to 79.

ROMAN RELIGION

Traditionally the Romans believed in a multitude of gods and goddesses, ruled over by Jupiter with the help of his messenger, Mercury (see Acts 14.12 NEB). They also worshipped a god of war called Mars, and a goddess of love called Venus.

However, the Romans were much more concerned about military power and systems of justice than they were about the spread of religion. They allowed the peoples whom they ruled to follow their own religious traditions, provided these did not encourage rebellion, or conflict too strongly with Roman social customs. But the Romans did recognize the value of religion as a force to unite people and express their loyalty. From the time of Caesar Augustus, the Romans set up temples throughout their empire, where men were expected to worship the ruling emperor. Anybody who refused to share in this worship was

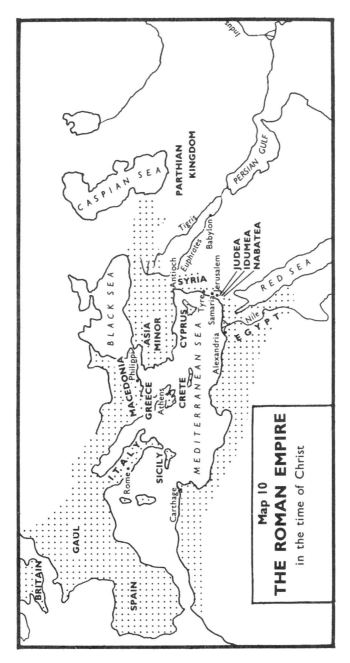

Map 10

THE ROMAN EMPIRE

in the time of Christ

BRITAIN

GAUL

SPAIN

ITALY

Rome

SICILY

Carthage

MACEDONIA

Philippi

GREECE

Athens

CRETE

MEDITERRANEAN SEA

BLACK SEA

ASIA MINOR

CYPRUS

Antioch

SYRIA

Tyre

Samaria

Jerusalem

JUDEA

IDUMEA

NABATEA

Alexandria

Nile

EGYPT

RED SEA

Babylon

Euphrates

Tigris

PARTHIAN KINGDOM

CASPIAN SEA

PERSIAN GULF

Indus

regarded as encouraging rebellion, and was liable to severe punishment. After a time the Jews were freed from this duty of worshipping the emperor, but Christians suffered severe persecution because the Romans would not authorize the worship of Christ.

STUDY SUGGESTIONS

REVIEW OF CONTENT

1. (a) In what ways is it true to describe the Roman empire as 'the greatest of the ancient empires'?
   (b) Which of the following descriptive words could be used in place of the more general word 'greatest'?
   Largest   Most just   Most powerful   Most religious
   Most scholarly   Richest   Most long-lived
2. We have followed the history of Israel through the time of five empires: Assyrian, Babylonian, Persian, Greek, and Roman.
   For each of these empires choose the word from the list below which best describes its character.
   Educated   Just   Religious   Tolerant   Warlike
3. Each one of the five great empires had its own form of religion. In which of them was each of the following gods or goddesses worshipped?
   Ahriman   Ashur   Ishtar   Jupiter   Marduk   Mars   Ormazd
   Venus   Zeus
4. In what way was the early history of the Roman empire similar to that of the Greek empire?
5. Who or what were the following:
   The Senate   Legates   Legions
6. What events brought to an end the power of the Seleucids in the Greek empire?
7. (a) Name two things which Pompey and Julius Caesar had in common.
   (b) In what way was Octavian connected with Augustus Caesar?
8. Describe briefly the relationship between religion and politics in the Roman empire.

FURTHER STUDY AND DISCUSSION

9. The Roman empire used the same months in their calendar as we do. Originally they only included ten months, leaving out July and August. The months July and August are named after two important Caesars. Can you suggest which two, among the Caesars named in this chapter?
10. 'The Romans did recognize the value of religion as a force to unite people and express their loyalty' (p. 185).

(a) To what extent, if any, does religion have this effect in the life of your own country?

(b) Which is likely to be most helpful in this way: a local religion, a national religion, or a world religion?

(c) Is it right to value religion for what it can do in this way? Give reasons for your answer to (b) and (c).

2. ISRAEL UNDER ROMAN RULE

FIRST CONTACTS

The Jews themselves invited the Romans to take an interest in the affairs of Judea. After the death of Alexander Jannaeus (see p. 176), his powerful widow Salome became political leader among the Jews. She made her eldest son, Hyrcanus II, the high priest during her reign. She also became friendly with the Pharisees. Her younger son, Aristobolus II, tried to gain a position of power for himself, and in order to do so he made friends with the Sadducees.

When Salome died there was open conflict between the two brothers, each supported by a Jewish party. Hyrcanus II was defeated in battle near Jericho, and Aristobulus II became ruler in Judea. But Hyrcanus II found a new friend in Antipater, the governor of Idumea (see Map 10). The king of Nabatea also helped him. They attacked Jerusalem, and Aristobulus was only saved from defeat by the help of the Roman general Scaurus. This conflict was going on while Pompey was trying to gain control of Palestine and Syria for the Romans.

Hyrcanus II and Aristobulus II both recognized that the Romans were the new world power. Each planned to gain Roman support for himself and for his rule in Judea. Each tried to bribe Pompey to give his help. Pompey called them both to Damascus in order to decide which of the two he should support. He showed favour to Hyrcanus II who was the rightful heir to the throne.

Aristobulus II withdrew and was defeated in battle in the Jordan valley, but the people of Jerusalem still supported him. So Pompey attacked Jerusalem, and even carried the fight into the Temple, where the supporters of Aristobulus II made their final stand. 12,000 Jews died in the conflict, and Aristobulus II was taken as a prisoner to Rome.

The coastal plain of Palestine, Samaria, and land across the Jordan were then made into a Roman province. Hyrcanus II was allowed to rule in Jerusalem as high priest and Ethnarch—but not as king. 'Ethnarch' seems to have been the title for the ruler of a people who kept their own laws and customs, but who accepted the supremacy of Rome.

From this time onwards the Jewish rulers depended on the support of the Roman authorities for the power which they exercised. Very soon

Hyrcanus II had his political powers removed, and was only allowed to retain his powers as high priest. In his place, Antipater and his family became the civil rulers of Judea.

ANTIPATER

Antipater came to power in Judea at the death of Pompey, when Julius Caesar regained control of the Roman Empire. Antipater helped to make Julius Caesar's rule secure, and Caesar rewarded him by making him a Roman citizen and governor of Judea, and allowing him to rebuild the walls of Jerusalem. Under Antipater's rule the Jews were allowed to hold their own courts, and were exempted from military occupation and from military service. Even so, the Jews hated Antipater. For one thing he was not a Jew, but an Idumean, i.e. a descendant of Esau and the hated Edomites. He was also a representative of Rome, and ruled with severe justice and discipline.

HEROD THE GREAT

Antipater shared his responsibilities with his two sons. He gave his older son, Phasael, authority over Judea and Perea, and his younger son, Herod, authority over Galilee. Herod got into trouble with the high priest and the Jewish court because he executed a robber without proper trial. But he was supported by the Roman authorities, and used the opportunity to gain their approval and friendship.

When Julius Caesar was murdered, the Jews took the opportunity to poison Antipater. But soon Mark Antony took control of affairs in Palestine. He appointed Phasael and Herod as joint Tetrarchs, and confirmed the appointment of Hyrcanus II as high priest. A 'Tetrarch' was a ruler who received his authority from the Romans, and who ruled an area of country on their behalf. A Tetrarch had less authority than an Ethnarch or king.

In 40 BC a people from Persia, called the Parthians, attacked Palestine and took Hyrcanus II as their prisoner to Babylon. Phasael committed suicide, but Herod went to seek help from Rome. In the meantime the Parthians had made Antigonus, a son of Aristobulus II, king in Jerusalem. He ruled there for three years (40–37 BC) and the people readily accepted him as a new king of the Maccabean line.

Octavian and Mark Antony together appointed Herod as king of Judea, and helped him in the battle to regain control of his kingdom. Herod severely punished those who had opposed him, and imposed heavy taxes on the rich. There were many plots and counter-plots during his reign, but he was a ruthless man and overcame them all. During this period Cleopatra (see p. 185) tried to cause trouble, because she wanted power over Palestine, and had great influence with Mark Antony. But, as we have seen, she and Antony both died as a result of their conflict with Octavian. Octavian confirmed Herod's appointment as ruler of Judea, and gave him extra territories as well.

Herod soon began a great series of building schemes: fortresses, palaces, and sports arenas. He rebuilt the Temple in Jerusalem. But he also built temples for the worship of Caesar, and this caused great anger among the Jews. Herod tried to strengthen his position among the Jews by marrying into the family of Hyrcanus and Aristobulus. He took as his wife Mariamne, who was granddaughter to both these leaders. But the marriage was spoilt by Herod's suspicions that his wife was involved in plots against him. Eght years later he had her executed, and then was driven nearly mad by remorse. Later he brought their two sons to trial and had them executed also.

Herod was a man of suspicion and violence, and it was typical of him that he ordered the massacre of young children in Bethlehem after the visit of the wise men at the time of the birth of Jesus (Matt. 2.1–18). He himself died soon afterward, in 4 BC. (It is now widely recognized that Jesus Christ was born before the year which we count as AD 1, but the reasons for believing this are a matter for New Testament study.)

THE KINGDOM DIVIDED

Herod the Great made his own plans for the succession. He had three sons, each of whom was to have part of the kingdom. Herod wanted Archelaus to be the new king, and to rule Judea, Samaria, and Idumea (see Map 10). Herod Antipas was to rule over Galilee and Perea, and Philip was to rule in Iturea, north-east of the Sea of Galilee. This arrangement had to receive Roman approval, and Herod Antipas tried to persuade Caesar to give him the title 'king'. However, Caesar Augustus decided that Archelaus should be called Ethnarch, and that Herod Antipas and Philip should be called Tetrarch; none of them was to be given the title king.

Archelaus was a violent and ambitious man like his father. He was not a good ruler, and within ten years he was deposed, and his part of the kingdom was placed under the rule of Roman Procurators. Among these was Pontius Pilate who tried Jesus and allowed his execution.

Herod Antipas ruled from 4 BC to AD 39 in Galilee and Perea. Little is known of the events of his reign, but this was the Herod who divorced his own wife, and took his brother's wife, Herodias, instead. John the Baptist rebuked him and was eventually executed as a result. Jesus grew up under his rule in Galilee, and according to Luke's gospel was sent to him by Pilate for trial (Luke 23.6–12).

Toward the end of his reign, Herod Antipas went to Rome to ask permission to call himself king. But Caesar Caligula distrusted him, and sent him away into exile.

10.1   The battle of Actium in 31 BC brought civil war in the Roman Empire to an end. Octavian became supreme ruler and took a new name: Augustus Caesar. This heroic statue of him is now in the Vatican museum in Rome.

Philip ruled a territory where most of the people were Gentiles. His reign was peaceful and just, and he rebuilt the cities of Caesarea Philippi and Bethsaida. He married Salome, the girl who asked for the head of John the Baptist on a plate. He died in AD 34.

HEROD AGRIPPA I

Herod Agrippa was the grandson of Herod the Great. He grew up in Rome and became the personal friend of both Caligula and Claudius. When Philip died, his territory was given to Herod Agrippa to rule and when Herod Antipas was sent into exile, his territory too was added to that of Herod Agrippa. Finally, in AD 41, Herod Agrippa was made ruler over Judea and the territories which had been governed by Procurators there. Thus he became king, and ruled over the whole territory which had been held by Herod the Great.

Herod Agrippa gave complete support to the Jews, and was highly regarded by the Pharisees. He opposed the introduction of emperor worship for the Jews, and he also acted against the Christians, when they came into conflict with the Jews (Acts 12.2). Herod Agrippa died suddenly and painfully in AD 44, having allowed the people to praise him with the reverence due only to God (see Acts 12.20–23). His son did not succeed to the kingdom, as he was too young to accept the responsibilities involved. Instead, the whole territory was placed under the rule of a Procurator.

THE END OF JUDEA

This was the beginning of the end for Judea. The men who ruled in turn as Procurator were not Jews, and had no sympathy with Jewish customs, ambitions, or beliefs. Some were violent and wealth-loving men, chiefly concerned with their own advancement. Others were weak and ineffectual in the difficult situations they faced.

The group known as the Zealots became very influential at this time. They believed in using violence to oppose and overthrow Roman authority, and had first acted together in about AD 6, at the time when Quirinius had ordered a census of the Jews (Luke 2.2). At least one of the disciples of Jesus was a Zealot (Mark 3.18, where 'Cananaean' is another name for a member of this group), and Judas Iscariot also may have been a Zealot.

But it was later, under the Procurators, that the Zealots came into open conflict with the Roman authorities. Two of these Procurators are named in the book of Acts: Felix and Festus. Felix was so violent and corrupt that some of the Zealots were forced into extreme and fanatical opposition to him. They became 'dagger-men' (Sicarii), and were ready to kill Romans at any opportunity (Acts 21.38).

In AD 66 another Procurator, Florus, robbed the Temple and went on to a full-scale plunder of the city of Jerusalem. The Jews opposed him and he attempted to overcome them by bringing in Roman troops. The crowds mocked these troops who then attacked them. The Jews withdrew into the Temple and fortified it against attack. Herod Agrippa's son (the King Agrippa II before whom Paul defended himself) tried to pacify the Jews but failed, and a full-scale battle developed. The Romans suffered several severe setbacks, but the Jewish people were unable to keep up their opposition. The Emperor Nero sent one of his best generals, Vespasian, to deal with the situation.

In the midst of the conflict Nero died (AD 69). The army proclaimed Vespasian Emperor, and he left his son Titus to put an end to the rebellion in Judea. Titus attacked Jerusalem, and drove the Jews back into the Temple. He set fire to the gates of the Temple, and the fire spread to other parts of the city. Roman soldiers broke into the Temple, and massacred many of the Jews, and eventually almost the whole of the city was destroyed. A Roman garrison was stationed in the ruins of Herod's palace, and this was the end of the Jewish state. Later the Pharisees established a religious community at a place called Jamnia, to preserve Jewish traditions and their Scriptures.

STUDY SUGGESTIONS

REVIEW OF CONTENT

1. (a) Several different types of ruler are mentioned in this chapter. List the following titles in their order of rank, starting with the highest: Caesar Ethnarch King Procurator Tetrarch
   (b) Name at least one holder of each of these offices, from among the people mentioned in this chapter.
2. List in order the rulers over Jerusalem from the death of Alexander Jannaeus until the siege of Jerusalem and the end of the Jewish state. Say what rank each man held.
3. Read the article on Edom in a Bible dictionary.
   (a) Describe as fully as you can the relationship between Edom and Israel.
   (b) Why did the Jews hate having Idumean rulers?
4. (a) What did Hyrcanus II and Aristobulus II have in common?
   (b) In what ways did they try to gain Roman support, and for what purpose?
5. (a) Herod the Great 'caused great anger among the Jews'. What did Herod do, which caused their anger?
   (b) What two chief things did Herod the Great do to strengthen his position among the Jews?
6. Under which Roman emperor was the Jewish state in Judea brought to an end?

7. The name Herod appears in the Gospels and Acts more than forty times. In some places it stands for Herod the Great, in others for Herod Antipas, and in yet others for Herod Agrippa.

(i) Which of the three Herods was involved in the events recorded in each of the following passages?

(a) Matt. 2.1–22   (b) Matt. 14.1–12   (c) Mark 6.14–29
(d) Luke 3.18–19   (e) Luke 9.7–9   (f) Luke 13.31–33
(g) Luke 23.6–12   (h) Acts 12.1–5   (i) Acts 12.20–23

(ii) Draw a family tree to show the succession to the Herod family from Antipater to Agrippa II. (A Bible dictionary will help you.)

FURTHER STUDY AND DISCUSSION

8. Describe as fully as you can the attitude of each of the following Procurators in their dealings with the Jews, and with Jesus and His disciples:

Pontius Pilate   Felix   Festus

(A Bible dictionary will help you.)

9. (a) Who were the Zealots?

(b) What present-day groups can be compared to the Zealots? If you can, give actual examples, and describe the ideas and practices which they have in common.

3. 'MY TIME IS AT HAND'

The Jews believed that the work of revelation was now complete. They had learnt a great deal about God, the world, and mankind. God had led them through many experiences which He had used as a means to make Himself known to them. He had won response from many men of varying depth of spiritual insight. The Patriarchs, the Kings, the Prophets, the Priests, the Lawgivers, the Historians, the Poets, and many others had helped to make the truth of God known to the Jews. God's people had grasped and shared many insights into His nature and purposes. We shall study these in more detail in the third volume of this course, but briefly we can summarize them as follows.

1. The Jews had learned to believe in One God, the Creator and Sustainer of the universe, who is altogether righteous, and expects men to serve Him in righteousness (e g. Mic. 6.8, Ezek. 18.5–9).

2. They had grasped the idea that God was one who revealed Himself to men, and who calls them into a new society of those who serve Him.

3. They believed firmly that one day God would establish His kingdom on earth, and that Jews would have an honoured place in that kingdom, though other men might share in it as well.

4. They believed that violent and wicked men would be punished, and that the righteous would receive their reward.

Most Jews accepted these ideas as having been revealed by God, although there were some who did not take religion very seriously. Among these were the Herodians, who supported the rule of the family of the Herods. Their chief concern seems to have been to gain political power by supporting the family who had favour among the Roman authorities.

The more faithful Jews were greatly divided among themselves in their attitude to the rule of Rome, and the ways in which they expected God's kingdom to be established. Similar groups existed to those described on pp. 179–181. In fact parties which had begun in the period of Greek power continued under Roman rule: Sadducees, Pharisees, and Essenes. The place of the Maccabees, as violent opponents of foreign rule, was taken by the Zealots, and especially the Sicarii (dagger-men).

It seemed that the process of God's revelation had ended in utter confusion, as each man interpreted for himself the traditions passed on from the past. It was certainly true that men who were deeply concerned to serve God were also deeply divided among themselves as to how this should be done. There was no real harmony or peace between the various parties of the Jews.

The truth was that God's work of revelation was not complete. Throughout the history of the Jews, God had been preparing the way for the fullest revelation this world has ever received. Now was the time for Christ to come to reveal God's purposes to men. God had already taught the great lessons which were necessary as a preparation for the coming of Christ. Now the Jews needed to look to God for the fulfilment of all that had gone before. We cannot in this book survey the whole story of the life and work of Christ, even though it is the most important study for those concerned with religious developments among the Jews in the time of the Roman empire. All the events recorded in the New Testament, and the recording of them, took place within the years of Roman rule. Events, record, and interpretation all belong to New Testament studies, and must be dealt with there.

All we can do here is to review the way in which the various parties among the Jews reacted to the coming of Christ. and so complete the story of Judaism in ancient times. Christianity became a distinct and different religion, because although it was the fulfilment of Judaism, the Jews in general rejected Christ. Each party felt that it had good reason to ignore or to oppose Him.

THE HERODIANS

This party is mentioned in Mark 3.6; 8.15; 12.13 and the parallel passage in Matthew 22.16. At all times the Herodians were in opposi-

'The Roman emperor Vespasian left his son Titus to put down the rebellion in Judea (p. 193).

10.2   Titus, whose bust is shown above, attacked Jerusalem and destroyed almost the whole city. This was the end of the Jewish state.

10.3   The triumphal arch set up in Rome to commemorate Titus's victory shows Romans carrying away the seven-branched candlesticks and other sacred treasures from the Temple in Jerusalem.

tion to Jesus. No doubt they thought of Him as an associate of John the Baptist. John had been a trouble-maker for them, and they would count Jesus the same. John had been a fearless preacher of righteousness, and had publicly criticized Herod; they expected the same from Jesus.

Mark 8.15 is our Lord's comment on the Herodians (see the footnote to this verse in the RSV). Jesus saw their influence as evil, and to be avoided. They had let go of righteousness for the sake of personal gain, and now went on to do what they could to destroy the influence of Jesus (Mark 12.13-17). No doubt they shared merrily in Herod's mockery of Jesus at His trial (Luke 23.6-12).

THE SADDUCEES

These were the priests who served in the Temple in Jerusalem. They believed that the sacrifices which they made were the central part of Jewish life and faith. They were prepared to accept Roman rule, and even to benefit from the added power which it gave them, provided the Romans did not interfere with the worship in the Temple. The Sadducees' attitude was influenced by their belief that human life ends at death, so that if a man is to find blessing at all he must find it in this life through such things as wealth and authority.

The Sadducees did not at first oppose Jesus. But when He cleansed the Temple, and claimed that they had made it a 'den of robbers', they became very angry with him (Matt. 21.12f), and challenged His authority to do such a thing (Matt. 21.15 and 23). They tried to show the people that He did not know what He was talking about, by questioning Him about the resurrection of the dead (Matt. 22.23-33). Eventually they led the Sanhedrin in ordering His arrest (Matt. 26.47), in condemning Him for blasphemy (Matt. 26.63-66), and in persuading the Romans that He was a revolutionary (Luke 23.1-5).

Jesus' comment on the Sadducees is similar to what He had said about the Herodians; their influence was evil, and to be avoided (Matt. 16.6 and 11). They too had allowed personal gain to affect their judgement. They had justified themselves by regarding the ceremonial of the Temple as of supreme importance, but even there their influence was evil, and soon the Temple would be destroyed.

THE PHARISEES

This group stood in great contrast to the Herodians and the Sadducees. They regarded personal righteousness as the most important part of their religion, and of their lives. The Law of God was their most prized possession, and they ordered their lives by it. They worked out in extreme detail the implications of general rules for particular situations. For example, they defined very carefully what activities counted as work, so as to be sure of keeping the law of the Sabbath day. They were proud of their righteousness, and contemptuous of those who broke the Law (Luke 18.9–14). They accused Jesus of breaking the Law, and of encouraging others to do so (Mark 2.23—3.6), and questioned Him closely about the Law and its interpretation (Matt. 22.34–40).

The Pharisees believed firmly in the resurrection of the righteous, and set all other ambition aside in order to gain this prize. Jesus opposed them openly and frequently. He denied that they possessed any special merits which would find favour with God, and described them as blind guides and hypocrites (Matt. 23.1–36). Sinners, He said, were reaching heaven before them (Matt. 21.31); their influence was as evil in its own way as that of the Herodians and Sadducees, and was to be avoided (Matt. 16.6, 11). They had forgotten the mercy of God, and had denied that salvation was part of His purpose for man. Jesus had come to save sinners.

THE ESSENES

There is no mention of the Essenes in the Gospels. They had cut themselves off from human society so completely that the early Christians did not remember any meeting between them and Jesus. They had established their own communities in desert places, and were awaiting God's action in bringing in His kingdom.

It would be foolish to suggest that we know our Lord's attitude to this sect. Some writers have suggested that John the Baptist was an Essene, because he worked in the Judean desert and there was an Essene monastery there. Other writers have suggested that because Jesus did not criticize the Essenes He must have supported their activities and attitudes. Certainly He saw the kingdom of heaven as something given by God, rather than fought for by men. But His love for men and women, His care for the suffering and the sinful, His delight in sharing home life and the fellowship of a meal table, are all in marked contrast to the withdrawal and asceticism of the Essenes. What we do know is that the Essene monastery in the Judean desert was eventually destroyed by the Romans, without the dramatic intervention by God which the Essenes themselves expected.

THE ZEALOTS

The Jews who belonged to this sect believed that men must fight for the coming of God's kingdom. They believed that Roman rule was the worst evil in a corrupt world, and that if any blessing was to be received by men it would be in a kingdom established by the Jews. They believed that the Messiah would come as a military leader, with wisdom and power to overthrow the rule of Rome, and to bring God's kingdom on earth. The events of Palm Sunday were the answer of Jesus to the Zealots. He came to Jerusalem riding an ass, not a war horse; He came humbly, not with military might (Matt. 21.1–9). With deep sorrow he recognized the restlessness of the Jews, and the inevitable result of their attitude to Rome:

O Jerusalem, Jerusalem, killing the prophets and stoning those who are sent to you!
How often would I have gathered your children together as a hen gathers her brood under her wings, and you would not!
Behold, your house is forsaken and desolate.
For I tell you, you will not see me again, until you say,
'Blessed be he who comes in the name of the Lord'. (Matt. 23.37–9)

STUDY SUGGESTIONS

REVIEW OF CONTENT

1. Distinguish between the two names in each of the following pairs by explaining what is important about each.
   (a) Chemosh and Carchemish   (b) Dan and Daniel
   (c) Esau and Ezra   (d) Hyksos and Hercules
   (e) Jethro and Jephthah   (f) Legate and Legions
   (g) Malachi and Maccabees   (h) Neco and Nero
   (i) Raamses and Remnant   (j) Sumerians and Samaritans
2. (a) List the four chief ideas about God and His purposes for men and women, which the Jews had come to accept as having been revealed to them through their history.
   (b) Are they ideas which Christians can accept. Give examples in support of your answer.
   (c) Name one group among the Jews who did *not* take religion very seriously.
3. (a) For what reasons were the Herodians in opposition to Jesus?
   (b) In what way did the action of the Herodians described in Mark 12.13 fulfil the prophecies in Jeremiah 23.11, 16, 17?
4. The Sadducees and the Pharisees disagreed fundamentally in their ideas about life after death.
   What did each group believe on this subject, and what influence did their belief have on their teaching and behaviour?
5. In what way was the behaviour which the Sadducees allowed in the Temple in the time of Jesus similar to that for which the prophet Jeremiah rebuked the people of his time? (See Jeremiah 14.18.)
6. Read the article about the Kingdom of God in a Bible dictionary and look up the Bible references which it gives.
   (a) What ideas did the Jews have on the subject?

(b) In what ways did their ideas conflict with the teaching of Jesus about it?

FURTHER STUDY AND DISCUSSION

7. Jews today continue to practise the religion of their ancestors, based on the writings of the Old Testament. Find out what they believe today. (If there is a synagogue in your town you could visit it and find out their present-day practice.)

8. Many countries today are ruled by foreign overlords, or by governments which represent only a small minority of the people.
(a) What attitude should Christians take to this sort of government?
(b) What if anything can we learn from the attitude of Jesus to the Romans (e.g. as recorded in Mark 12.13–17; Mark 13.9–13; Matthew 26.51, 52, and 27.11–14)?

Key to Study Suggestions

Please Note: This key provides information about where the answers can be found. It does not usually provide the answers themselves. Students should not answer questions by copying out the paragraphs and lines indicated here, but discover the answers and explain them in their own words. No answers are given for questions which direct students to the use of a Bible dictionary, or concordance: since the answers are to be found there. Nor does this key give answers to topical questions which depend on knowledge of the students' own country, customs, etc.

INTRODUCTION: PAGES 4 AND 5

2. See p. 2, para. 3, lines 3–4.
3. (a) See p. 2, para 3, lines 3–4.
   (b) See p. 2, para. 5, lines 3–4.
   (c) See p. 2, para. 3, lines 4–5.
   (d) See p. 2, para. 4, lines 1–4.
   (e) See p. 2, para. 3, lines 3–4.
4. See p. 3, para. 2.
5. (a) See p. 3, para. 4, lines 1–2.
   (b) See p. 3, para. 3, lines 2–4.
6. See p. 3, para. 4, lines 3–6.
7. (a) See p. 3, para. 6.
   (b) See p. 4, para. 2, lines 4–6.
8. receptive, obedient, perceptive, humble, open-minded.

PAGES 11 AND 12

1. Legends: See pp. 6 and 7, section (b).
   History: See p. 7, section (c)   Myths: See p. 6, section (a).
2. See p. 7, last 2 lines, and p. 9, first 6 lines.
3. See p. 6, para. 2, lines 3–6.
4. (a) True   (b) See p. 6, para. 5, lines 3–8.
5. See p. 6, last 8 lines, and p. 7, first 8 lines.
6. (a) See p. 7, para. 3, lines 7–10.
   (b) See p. 7, para. 4, lines 2–4.
   (c) See p. 7, para. 4, lines 7–11.
   (d) See p. 7, para. 5.
7. See p. 9, paras. 3 and 5.
8. See p. 9, para. 5, lines 1–5.

PAGES 18 AND 19

1. (a) Eighth century BC   (b) AD 300–399   (c) 1599–1550 BC   (d) Fifth century AD.
2. Assyria: See p. 17, para. 1.
   Palestine itself: See p. 16, para. 3.
   Greece: See p. 17, para. 4.
   Egypt: See p. 13, para. 6.
   Babylon: See p. 17, para. 2.
3. Alexander: See p. 17, para. 4, line 1.
   The Maccabees: See p. 17, para. 4, line 8.
   Cyrus: See p. 17, para. 3, line 1.
4. The correct order is: h, a, c, e, i, f, d, g, b, j.

CHAPTER 1: PAGES 22 AND 23

1. See p. 20, para. 1, lines 9–10.
2. (a) See p. 20, para. 1, lines 5–9.
   (b) See p. 20, last 9 lines and p. 21, first 4 lines below chart.
   (c) See p. 21, para. 2, lines 1–4.
   (d) See p. 20, para. 2, last 3 lines.
3. (a) See p. 20, para. 2, line 4.
   (b) See p. 20, para. 2, lines 5–7.
   (c) See p. 20, para. 2, lines 3–4.
4. (a) See p. 21, lines 1–4.
   (b) See p. 21, last 3 lines and p. 22, first 3 lines.
5. (a) See p. 20, para. 3.
   (b) See p. 22, para. 3.
6. (a) 8000 BC: See p. 20, para. 2, lines 5–7.
   5000 BC: See p. 20, para. 2, lines 7–8.
   4000 BC: See p. 20, para. 2, lines 8–9.
   3300 BC: See p. 20, para. 2, lines 9–11.
   2900 BC: See p. 20, para. 3, lines 3–4.
   2600 BC: See p. 21, para. 2, lines 1–3.
   (b) (i) See p. 20, para. 2, lines 5–6.
   (ii) See p. 20, para. 2, lines 9–11.
   (iii) See p. 20, para. 3, lines 3–4.
   (iv) See p. 20, para. 3, lines 4–5.

PAGES 30 AND 31

1. The Aramaeans: See p. 23, para. 2, lines 3–8.
   The Negeb: See p. 26, para. 3, lines 1–3.
2. (a) See p. 23, para. 3, lines 3–4.
   (b) See p. 22, para. 3, lines 5–6.
3. See p. 24, first 2 lines.
4. See p. 22, para. 4, lines 1–3.
5. (a) See p. 24, para. 3, lines 1–2.
   (b) See p. 24, para. 3, lines 4–8.
6. See p. 26, para. 3 and para. 4, lines 1–3.
7. See p. 26, para. 1, lines 3–5.
8. (a) See p. 26, para. 5, lines 1–3 and p. 27 first 4 lines.
   (b) See p. 25, para. 6, lines 6–7 and p. 27 lines 4–5.
9. (a) See p. 27, para. 3, lines 1–3.
   (b) See p. 27, para. 3, lines 4–9.
10. See p. 28, para. 2.
11. See p. 28, para. 3, lines 4–8.
12. (a) See p. 28, para. 4, lines 3–7.
    (b) See p. 28, para. 5, lines 1–3.
13. (i) See Gen. 25.19–26.
    (ii) See Gen. 25.21–26.
    (iii) See Gen. 29.10–28.
    (iv) See Gen. 11.27–31 and Gen. 22.20–23
    (v) See Gen. 39.1–6, 19–23.
    (vi) See Gen. 17.15–16 and Gen. 25.1–4.
    (vii) See Gen. 11.27.
    (viii) See Gen. 35.22–26.
    (ix) See Gen. 35.22–26.
    (x) See Gen. 40.1–23.

PAGES 37–39
1. See p. 33, para. 4, lines 5–9.
2. (i) See p. 32, last 9 lines. p. 33, paras. 1 and 2, p. 35, para. 1.
   (ii) See p. 32, para. 5, lines 2–4; and p. 35, para. 1.
   (iii) (a) and (c) Yahweh; (b) and (d) El.
3. (a) See p. 32, para. 4, lines 1–3.
   (b) See p. 32, para. 3, lines 4–9.
   (c) See p. 32, para. 4, lines 7–10.
   (d) See p. 37, para. 2, lines 2–4.
   (e) See p. 36, last 4 lines, and p. 37, first 3 lines.
   (f) See p. 36, para. 1, lines 2–6.
4. (a) See p. 33, para, 4, lines 3–5.
   (b) See p. 33, para. 4, lines 13–15.
5. See p. 35, para. 1.
6. See p. 35, para. 3, lines 2–3.
7. (a) See p. 36, para. 2, lines 4–6.
   (b) See p. 36, para. 4, lines 1–2.
   (c) See p. 36, last 4 lines, and p. 37, first 3 lines.
8. See p. 37, para. 2, lines 8–10.
9. See p. 35, para. 2, lines 7–10.
10. (i) See p. 35, para. 3.
    (ii) (a), (b), and (c) Abraham; (d) Isaac; (e) Jacob.
12. (a) His belief would lead him to think that the god of a place had no power outside that place; though the god of a people would be active wherever those people were.
    (b) God has been associated in history with a particular place (Palestine), and a particular people (the Jews); but He rules over all places, and all peoples as God of Creation.

CHAPTER 2: PAGES 46 AND 47
1. (a) Dynasty (b) Nomads (c) Delta (d) Archaeology (e) Generation.
2. (a) See p. 20, last 2 lines.
   (b) See p. 44, para. 2, last 4 lines.
   (c) See p. 41, section I.
   (d) See p. 42, para. 2, lines 3–4.
3. See p. 40, para. 2.
4. (a) See p. 40, para. 3, lines 1–2.
   (b) See p. 41, para. 2.
5. (a) See p. 41, section I, lines 7–9.
   (b) and (c) See p. 41, section I, lines 2–4.
   (d) See p. 41, section I, line 5.
   (e) See p. 41, section 2, line 1.
6. See p. 42, section 3
7. See p. 42, section 4, lines 1–4.
8. (a) See p. 44, para. 1, lines 5–10.
   (b) See p. 44, para. 3.
9. (a) See p. 45, para. 1.
   (b) See p. 45, section 7, para. 1.
10. (i) (a) See p. 45, last 3 lines, and p. 46, first 2 lines.
    (b) See p. 46, para. 2, lines 1–3.
    (ii) See p. 46, para. 2, lines 4–10.

PAGES 55–57
1. See p. 50, last para., lines 7–8.
2. (c) Presence.

3. (a) See p. 47, para. 1.
   (b) See p. 48, para. 1.
4. See p. 48, para. 2, lines 2–7.
5. (a) E.g. See Exod. 3.14; 4.3; 4.15.
   (b) E.g. See Exod. 9.22; 12.29.
6. (a) See p. 49, para. 2, lines 5–8.
   (b) See p. 49, para. 3, lines 1–4.
7. (a) See p. 50, para. 2, lines 3–8.
   (b) See p. 50, para. 3, lines 1–7.
   (c) See p. 50, para. 4.
8. See p. 50, section 4, lines 1–5.
9. (i) (a) and (d) Moses expected them to share his experience.
   (b) and (c) Moses expected to be the intermediary.
   (ii) See p. 53, lines 6–10.
   (iv) See p. 53, lines 11–17.
10. See p. 53, last 4 lines.
11. See p. 54, para. 1.
13. (a) See p. 54, para. 4, lines 6–9.
    (b) See p. 55, para. 1.
    (c) See p. 54, para. 4, lines 10–15.

PAGES 63–64
1. (b) Agreement.
2. See p. 57, lines 4–13.
3. (a) See p. 58, first 2 lines.
   (b) See p. 58, lines 3–10.
4. See p. 58, paras. 4 and 5.
5. See p. 58, last para., and p. 60, lines 1–5.
6. See p. 60, para. 3, lines 7–10.
7. (a) (i) God. (ii) Parents. (iii) Fellow men.
   (b) See p. 62, para. 3, lines 1–8.
8. See p. 62, para. 3, lines 3–8.
9. See p. 61, para, 3, lines 7–11.
10. (a) See p. 62, para. 4, lines 1–2.
    (b) See p. 62, last 5 lines, and p. 63, first 6 lines.
12. See p. 58, para. 2, lines 4–8.
13. See p. 61, para. 2.

CHAPTER 3: PAGE 68
1. (a) See p. 65, para. 2, lines 2–4.
   (b) See p. 65, para. 2, lines 4–8.
2. (a) See p. 65, para. 3.
   (b) See p. 65, para. 4.
3. (a) See p. 65, para. 5, lines 2–3.
   (b) See p. 66, para. 5, lines 3–4.
4. (a) See p. 66, paras. 2 and 3.
   (b) See p. 66, paras. 4 and 5.
   (c) See p. 66, para. 9.
5. See p. 66, para. 7, lines 3–7.
6. See Map 2, p. 51.
7. (a) See p. 65, last 3 lines, and p. 66, first 5 lines.

PAGES 73 AND 74

1. (a) Three were allotted land of their own, Levi was no:.
   (b) Three were foreign tribes in Palestine, the Danites were Israelites.
   (c) Three were Aramaic-speaking tribes living across the Jordan, but the Ephraimites were Israelites.
   (d) Three were Israelite tribes that settled in northern Palestine, but Judah settled in the south.
   (e) Three were Judges who led the Israelites in battle, but Samson worked alone.
2. (a) See p. 69, para. 4 (1), lines 2–3.
   (b) See p. 69, para. 4 (2), lines 2–3.
   (c) See p. 70, para. 3.
4. (a) See p. 70, para. 2, lines 1–2.
   (b) See p. 70, para. 2, lines 2–3.
   (c) See p. 70, para. 2, last 2 lines.
5. See p. 72, para. 3, lines 4–5.
6. (a) See p. 72, para. 5, lines 1–4.
   (b) (i) Compare the two accounts of: the authority of Sisera; the Israelite tribes involved in the battle; and the death of Sisera.
   (ii) See p. 72, para. 5, line 5.
9. The Israelites were following the generally accepted attitudes of their day to land ownership, and to ways of settling disputes. Many other tribes were doing the same.
11. See p. 70, last 2 lines, and p. 72, first para.

PAGES 77 AND 78

1. See p. 70, last 2 lines, and p. 72, first para.
2. See p. 75, para. 2 (i), last 3 lines.
3. See p. 61, para. 3, lines 5–11.
4. See p. 75, para. 2 (2), line 2.
5. (a) See p. 75, para. 2 (2), lines 4–9.
   (b) See p. 75, para. 2 (2), lines 6–7.
6. (a) See p. 75, last 7 lines.
   (b) See p. 76, paras. 2 and 3.
7. See p. 76, section 3, para. 1.
8. (b), (d), (g), (i).
10. Ex. 22.21–27 describes what must not be done against the helpless, and the needy. Matt. 25.31–46 describes what should be done to help.
11. Passover: replaced by Good Friday. Both celebrate God's deliverance of His people: the former from slavery in Egypt, the latter from sin. Pentecost: replaced by Whit Sunday. Both celebrate God's work of making men righteous: the former through the giving of the Law as a guide, the latter through the giving of the Holy Spirit who brings new life to men.
    The Feast of Booths was similar in origin to the Harvest Festival, but came to celebrate the renewal of God's Covenant and so is similar in purpose to the Methodist Covenant Service.

CHAPTER 4: PAGES 80 AND 81

1. (a) See p. 79, para. 2, lines 3–7.
   (b) See p. 79, para. 2, lines 6–7.
2. See p. 79, para. 7, lines 1–2.
3. See p. 79, paras. 4–6.
4. (a) See 1 Sam. 4.1   (b) See 1 Sam. 4.3–7   (c) See 1 Sam. 4.7–11.
5. See p. 80, para. 3.
6. See p. 80, para. 4, lines 1–2.

KEY TO STUDY SUGGESTIONS

PAGES 89-91
1. See p. 84, para. 5, lines 7-11.
2. (a) See p. 81, para. 1, lines 5-6.
   (b) See p. 81, para. 1, lines 1-3.
3. (a) See p. 82, para. 1, lines 4-8.
   (b) See p. 81, last 2 lines, and p. 82, first 2 lines.
   (c) See p. 82, para. 2, lines 1-2.
4. (a) See p. 82, para. 4, lines 7-9.
   (b) See p. 82, para. 4, lines 9-16.
5. See p. 84, para. 2.
6. (a) See p. 84, para. 3.
   (b) See p. 84, para. 5, lines 1-4.
7. (a) See p. 85, para. 2, lines 10-14.
   (b) See p. 85, para. 3, lines 3-7.
8. See p. 85, paras. 4 and 5 for those that *were* ruled.
9. (a) and (b) See p. 87, para. 2.
10. (a) See p. 87, para. 7.
    (b) See p. 88, lines 1-3.
    (c) See p. 88, para. 6.
11. (a) See p. 82, first 2 lines.
    (b) and (c) See 1 Sam. 16.13; 2 Sam. 2.4, 5.3; and 1 Kings 1.38-39. Also see p. 84, para. 4, and p. 85, para. 2, lines 8-9.
12. See p. 82, last 3 lines; p. 85, para. 5, lines 5-7; p. 88, last line; and p. 89, paras. 1 and 2.

PAGES 94 AND 95
1. (a) Kings: See p. 91, para. 2.
       Prophets: See p. 93, para. 1, lines 3-7.
       Priests: See p. 93, para. 4.
   (b) Kings: David, Saul, Solomon, and Eshbaal.
       Prophets: Nathan and Ahijah.
       Priests: Abiathar, Eli, Zadok.
2. (a) See p. 92. paras. 2-4.
   (b) See p. 92, last 4 lines, and p. 93, paras. 1-3.
3. (a) See p. 93, para. 6.
   (b) See p. 93, para. 5, lines 2-6.
4. (a) See p. 91, para. 4, lines 1-3.
   (b) See p. 92, para. 4, lines 1-4.
   (c) See p. 93, para. 3.
   (d) See p. 93, para. 4, lines 3-4.
5. Ps. 18.43-50; 89.34-37; 132.11-18.
6. See p. 92, para. 4, lines 9-12.

CHAPTER 5: PAGES 98 AND 99
1. (a) See p. 96, para. 1, lines 5-8.
   (b) See p. 96, para. 2, lines 6-8; and p. 98, para. 2, lines 1-4.
2. See p. 96, last 2 lines.
3. See p. 98, first 2 lines.
4. (a) See p. 98, para. 3, lines 4-5.
   (b) See p. 98, para. 3, lines 5-7.
   (c) See p. 98, para. 4.
5. (a) See p. 96, para. 4.

KEY TO STUDY SUGGESTIONS

PAGES 104–106

1. See p. 99, para. 1, lines 3–5.
2. (a) See p. 100, para. 5, line 4; and chart for this date.
   (b) See Bible passage given in chart against this king of Judah.
3. (a) See chart for king of Judah from 913 BC to 873 BC.
   (b) See Bible passage given in chart against this king's name.
4. See chart for king of Israel from 842 BC to 815 BC.
   (a) and (b) See Bible passage given in chart against this king's name.
   (c) See p. 104, para. 4, line 1.
5. None! There were two different kings called Ahaziah, and two called Jehoram. One of each pair in each kingdom.
6. (a) and (b) See p. 100, paras. 2 and 3.
7. (a) See p. 99, para. 2.
   (b) See p. 102, para. 4.
   (c) See p. 103, para. 6, lines 5–6.
   (d) See p. 103, paras. 5 and 6.
   (e) See p. 104, para. 2.
8. (a) See p. 99, para. 2.
   (b) See p. 102, para. 3, lines 1–3.
   (c) See p. 102, para. 4, lines 1–2.
9. (a) See p. 100, para. 4.
   (b) See p. 100 paras. 2 and 3.
10. (a) See p. 103 para. 5.
    (b) See p. 104 para. 4, lines 3–5.
11. (a) and (b) See Time chart 3, p. 101.
    (c) That the kings of Israel ruled by military power rather than popular support.
12. (a) and (b) Compare p. 100, last para., and p. 102, first para., with p. 58, last para.
13. They both rebuked their hearers for attempting to serve the gods that were supposed to provide material prosperity, as well as the true God.
15. Confident, Courageous, Faithful, Obedient.

PAGES 111 AND 112

1. (a) (i) See p. 107, para. 2.
       (ii) See p. 107, para. 3.
   (b) See p. 107, para. 5.
2. (a) See p. 109, para. 1, last 2 lines.
   (b) See p. 109, para. 3 (a) and (b).
3. (a) Not until the time of the Babylonian and Persian Empires.
   (b) See p. 110, para. 3.
   (c) See p. 110, para. 2, lines 5–9.
4. (a) Joshua. (b) 2 Samuel. (c) 2 Kings. (d) 1 Samuel. (e) Judges. (f) Genesis. (g) 1 Kings. (h) Exodus.

CHAPTER 6: PAGES 114 AND 116

1. (a) See p. 114, para. 3.
   (b) See p. 114, para. 1.
   (c) See p. 114, para. 2.
   (d) See p. 113, para. 4, lines 4–7.
2. See p. 113, para. 4.
3. (a) See p. 98, paras. 3 and 4, and p. 113, para. 2.
   (b) See p. 113, para. 2, lines 4–6.
4. See p. 114, para. 2, lines 1–3.

5. (a) They both believed that military leaders must be obedient to their God, to gain victories.
   (b) The Assyrians believed in many gods, the Israelites in one God.

PAGES 123-125

1. Co-regent: Somebody who rules at the same time, and with the consent of the rightful ruler of a country.
   His father was ill. See p. 119, para. 2, lines 8-9.
2. Hezekiah, Josiah.
3. (a) See Time chart 4, entry opposite 'End of Israel'.
   (b) See p. 121, para. 3, lines 1-2.
4. (a) See Time chart 4, p. 118. Entries for Judah (a) between 783 and 745 BC, and (b) after 633 BC.
   (b) See p. 119, paras. 2 and 3, and p. 123, para. 3.
5. (a) See p. 117, para. 2, lines 4-7.
   (b) See p. 117, para. 2, lines 1-4.
6. See p. 117, para. 3.
7. (a) See p. 119, para. 6.
   (b) See p. 119, para. 5.
   (c) See p. 121. para. 2, lines 3-10.
   (d) See p. 121, para. 3, lines 1-2.
8. (a) See p. 121, para. 4, lines 2-3.
   (b) See p. 121, para. 4, last 2 lines.
   (c) See p. 121, last 2 lines, and p. 122, first 2 lines.
   (d) See p. 122, para. 2, line 1.
9. See p. 121, para. 4, lines 3-5; and p. 123, para. 1.
10. See p. 123, para. 2.
11. Hosea: See p. 117, last 2 lines, and p. 118, first para.
    Hoshea: See p. 121, first para.
    Hoshea probably became king toward the end of Hosea's ministry.
12. Jeroboam II 785 BC-745 BC.
13. (a) Hos. 4.1-3; 6.7-10; Amos 2.4-8.
    (b) Hos. 9.1-7; Amos 2.14-16; 3.11-15.
15. Compassionate, Practical, Social.

PAGES 129 AND 130

1. Remainder, Residue, Survivors.
2. (a) See p. 128, para. 2, lines 1-3, and paras. 4 and 5.
   (b) City, a man, God, remnant, king, nation.
      Obedient to the rule of God. And for God: acting consistently with His revealed purposes.
3. (a) The Israelites had rejected God's rule, and had spoilt the life of their nation by disobedience and sin. Their strength and safety lay in serving God.
   (b) The Assyrians had chosen to conquer the world, and had accepted the suffering this ambition involved. God was able to use their plans and activities to punish the Israelites.
4. See p. 127, para. 2, line 6.
5. (a) and (b). See p. 128 (a) to (d).
6. See p. 128, last 5 lines, and p. 129 first 6 lines.

CHAPTER 7: PAGES 135 AND 136

1. (a) See p. 131, para. 1, line 1.
   (b) See p. 131, para. 3, lines 2-3.
   (c) See p. 133, para. 6, lines 1-3.

2. (a) See p. 131, para. 1, lines 10–11.
   (b) See p. 131, last 4 lines, and p. 133, first 2 lines.
3. See p. 133, para. 3, lines 1–2.
4. (a) See p. 133, para. 4, lines 2–3.
   (b) See p. 133, para. 4, lines 5–6.
   (c) See p. 133, para. 2, lines 4–5.
5. See p. 133, para. 7.
6. (a) See p. 134, para. 1, line 10.
   (c) See p. 134, last para., lines 5–3.
8. (a) See p. 134, para. 1, lines 5–10.

PAGES 139 AND 140
1. (a) and (b). See p. 136, lines 3–6.
2. See p. 136, para. 2, lines 6–8.
3. (a) Three were Assyrian rulers, one Babylonian.
   (b) Three were prophets, one a king of Judah.
   (c) All were Pharaohs, but three in time of Babylonian empire, and one at the Exodus.
   (d) All were prophets, but three in time of Assyrian empire, and one in Babylonian empire.
   (e) Three were kings of Judah, and one king of Israel.
4. ISRAEL
   (a) See p. 121, para. 2, lines 1–5.
   (b) See p. 121, para. 2, line 2.
   (c) See p. 121, para. 1.
   (d) See p. 117, last 4 lines.
   and p. 119, first 6 lines.
   (e) See p. 121, para. 2, lines 3–5.
   JUDAH
   See p. 133, para. 3, lines 1–2.
   See p. 139, para. 1, lines 3–5.
   See p. 138, paras. 2 and 3.
   See p. 136, para. 1, lines 7–9.
   See p. 139, para. 3.
5. See p. 139, line 5.
6. See p. 136, para. 2, lines 9–12.
7. Jer. 32.3–5, 28–29, 36.
   Jer. 34.2–3, 21–22.
8. David: 2 Sam. 5.7.
   Solomon: 1 Kings 8.1–21.
   Sennacherib: 2 Kings 18.13—19.37.
   Josiah: 2 Kings 22. 23.1–27.
   Nebuchadnezzar: 2 Kings 24.10–15; 25.8–12.

PAGES 145 AND 146
1. (a) See p. 146, para. 4, lines 7–13.
   (b) Accept, Assent, Observe, Repent.
3. See p. 143, para. 3.
4. (a) See p. 141, para. 2, lines 1–3.
   (b) See p. 141, para. 3, line 1.
   (c) See p. 141, para. 3, lines 3–6.
5. (a) See p. 143, last 4 lines, and p. 144, first 5 lines.
   (b) E.g.: Circumcision, observance of the Sabbath, and use of Psalms in worship.

7. See p. 145, para. 2, lines 8–11.
8. See p. 145, para. 2, lines 1–8.

CHAPTER 8: PAGES 152 AND 153

1. Sin: See p. 147, para. 4, lines 5–9.
   The Cyrus Cylinder: See p. 149, para. 3, lines 1–6.
   Satraps: See p. 149, para. 4, line 5.
   The Avesta: See p. 150, para. 3, lines 5–6.
2. (a) Ecbatana: Media;   Memphis: Egypt;   Sardis: Lydia.
   (b) Elephantine, Gaugamela, Memphis, Persepolis, Susa.
   The Subject Index at the end of this volume will help here.
3. See p. 147, para. 1.
4. (a) See p. 147, para. 2, lines 2–3.
   (b) See p. 147, para. 4, line 1.
   (c) See p. 147, para. 2, lines 6–7 and para. 3, line 4.
   Also see p. 149, para. 3, lines 1–3.
5. (a) See p. 147, last 12 lines; and p. 149, first 2 lines.
   (b) See p. 149, para. 3, lines 3–5.
6. See p. 149, para. 4, lines 4–9.
7. (a) See p. 149, para. 5, line 1.
   (b) See p. 150, para. 2, lines 2–6.
8. (a) See p. 150, para. 3.
   (b) See p. 150, para. 4, lines 1–5.
   (c) See p. 150, para. 4, lines 5–8.
   (d) See p. 150, last 3 lines; and p. 152, first 5 lines.

PAGES 160–162

1. *Before:* Nathan, Elijah, Hosea (Book), Jeremiah (Book). *During:* Ezekiel (Book).
   After: Haggai (Book), Malachi (Book).
2. See p. 153, para. 2, lines 3–9.
3. (a) See p. 154, para. 3, lines 3–4.
   (b) See p. 154, para. 3, lines 4–7.
   (c) See p. 153, last 3 lines; and p. 154, first 2 lines.
   (d) See p. 155, para, 1, lines 2–10.
   (e) See p. 155, para. 2, lines 7–13.
4. (a) See p. 155, para. 2, line 1 and para. 3, line 1.
   (b) See p. 155, para. 2, lines 8–10 and para. 3, lines 3–5.
5. (a) See p. 156, para. 2, lines 1–2.
   (b) See p. 156, para. 2, lines 3–6.
   (c) See p. 156, para. 2, lines 8–10.
6. (a) See p. 156, para. 4, lines 5–7.
   (b) See p. 156, para. 4, lines 8–9.
7. (a) See p. 158, para. 6, line 4.
   (b) See p. 158, para. 6, lines 6–9.
8. (a) See Neh. 4.9.
   (b) See p. 159, paras. 2 and 3.
9. See p. 160, para. 1, last line, and para. 2.
10. See p. 160, para. 3, lines 1–3.
11. (a) The rebuilding of the Temple.
    (b) See p. 156, lines 4–6.
12. See p. 158, para. 3, lines 5–6; and para. 4, lines 5–8.
14. Jeremiah: e.g. Jer. 24.4–7.
    Ezekiel: e.g. Ezek. 36.24–27.
    Deutero-Isaiah: e.g. Isa. 43.16–21.

Haggai: e.g. Hag 2.1–9.
Zechariah: e.g. Zech. 6.9–15.
Malachi: e.g. Mal. 3.1–4.
16. (a) See p. 160, para. 4, lines 5–8, and para. 5, lines 2–3.

PAGE 166
1. (a) See p. 165, para. 2, lines 1–3.
   (b) to reconcile.
2. See p. 163, para. 2, lines 5–11.
3. (a) See p. 163, para. 3, lines 3–4.
   (b) See p. 163, para. 3, lines 2–3.
4. See p. 163, para 5.
5. Sin is anything contrary to the Will and purpose of God. A man may deliberately defy God and sin. He may sin because he is ignorant of God's will for him.
   This is 'unwitting sin'. The results of his action will still be evil, even though he
   does not intend evil. God knows that the man intends to do good, and He seeks
   to make His will known so that the man will be able to avoid evil and do good.
6. 'Many gods' may be in conflict for authority. Belief in the LORD includes the
   knowledge that His authority is eternal, and cannot be destroyed. Evil must be
   conquered in order to fulfil all God's purposes for the world. Satan claims an
   authority which does not belong to him, and he will be defeated in the End.

CHAPTER 9: PAGES 170 AND 171
1. Cyrus: See p. 147, para. 2, lines 3–4.
   Seleucus: See p. 169, para. 2, lines 12–15.
   Darius: See p. 149, para. 4, lines 1–4.
   Nebuchadnezzar: See p. 133, para. 4, last 2 lines.
   Sennacherib: See Time chart 4, p. 118.
2. 600 BC: See p. 136, last para.; and p. 137, first para.
   500 BC: See Time chart 6, p. 157.
   400 BC: See p. 160, para. 1, lines 4–7.
   300 BC: See p. 171, para. 1.
3. See p. 167, para. 1.
4. (a) and (b) See p. 167, para. 3, lines 1–2.
5. (a) See p. 169 para. 1, line 1.
   (b) See p. 169 para. 1, lines 4–6.
   (c) See p. 169 para. 1, line 6.
6. See p. 169, para. 2, lines 12–15.

PAGES 176–178
1. Mattathias had three sons: Simon, Judas Maccabeus, and Jonathan. Simon had
   a son: John Hyrcanus. John Hyrcanus had two sons: Aristobulus and Alexander
   Janneus.
   (a) and (b) The Seleucids: See p. 169, para. 2, last 2 lines.
   Epiphanes: See p. 174, para. 2, lines 1–3.
   The Hasidim See p. 175, para. 2, lines 4–7.
   The Essenes: See p. 176, para. 4, last 5 lines.
   The Septuagint: See p. 172, para. 2.
   Olympia: See p. 169, para. 4, lines 1–2.
   The Maccabees: See p. 175, para. 5.
   (c) See p. 175, para. 1, lines 1–4.
3. See p. 172, para. 2, last 5 lines.

4. See p. 172, para. 1, lines 5–8.
5. (a) See p. 172, para. 4, lines 1–5.
    (b) See p. 174, para. 6.
6. (a) E.g. Jer. 6.13, cf. 2 Mac. 4.7–9.
    (b) E.g. See p. 174, para. 7, line 1; p. 153, para. 1, lines 5–6; and p. 156, para. 5, lines 5–6.
7. See p. 174, last 2 lines; and p. 175, first line.
9. See p. 176, para. 4, lines 3–4.
10. See p. 175, para. 6, lines 1–5.
13. (a) See p. 175, para. 5.

PAGES 182 AND 183
1. Assyria: See p. 178, para. 2.
    Persia: See p. 178, para. 4.
    Greece: See p. 178, para. 5.
2. (a) See p. 179, para. 3, line 1.
    (b) See p. 179, para. 4, lines 1–2.
    (c) See p. 179, para. 5, lines 1–2.
3. (a) See p. 179, last 2 lines.
    (b) See p. 179, para. 3, lines 3–7.
5. Isa. 27.1; Zech. 14.20; Rev. 6.1–8

CHAPTER 10: PAGES 187 AND 188
1. (a) See p. 184, paras. 1 and 2.
    (b) Largest, Most just, Most powerful, Most long-lived.
2. Assyrian: Warlike; Babylonian: Religious; Persian: Tolerant; Greek: Educated; Roman: Just.
3. Ahriman: Persian; Ashur: Assyrian; Ishtar: Assyrian; Jupiter: Roman; Marduk: Babylonian; Mars: Roman; Ormazd: Persian; Venus: Roman; Zeus: Greek.
4. Compare p. 167, para. 3, lines 1–2 with p. 184, para. 1, lines 2–5.
5. The Senate: See p. 184, para. 1, lines 5–7.
    Legates: See p. 184, para. 3, lines 1–3.
    Legions: See p. 184, para. 4.
6. See p. 184, last para.; and p. 185, first para.
7. (a) Both were Romans. Both were murdered.
    (b) See p. 185, para. 4, last 2 lines.
8. See p. 185, last para.
9. See p. 184, line 9; and p. 185, para. 4, last line.

PAGES 193 AND 194
1. (a) Caesar   King   Procurator   Ethnarch   Tetrarch.
    (b) Caesar: See p. 184, line 9.
        King: See p. 189, para. 6, line 1.
        Procurator: See p. 192, para. 6, line 3.
        Ethnarch: See p. 188, para. 5, lines 2–3.
        Tetrarch: See p. 189, para. 4, line 3.
2. See pages 188–193.
4. (a) and (b) See p. 188, para. 3.
5. (a) See p. 192, para. 2, lines 2–4.
    (b) See p. 192, para. 2, lines 2, 4–5.
6. See p. 193, para. 2, lines 1–3.

7. Herod the Great: (a).
   Herod Antipas: (b)—(g).
   Herod Agrippa: (h), (i).
9. (a) See p. 192, paras, 5 and 6.

PAGES 199–200
1. The Subject Index of this textbook will help you discover information about each of these.
2. (a) See p. 194, paras. numbered 1, 2 and 3; and p. 195, para. numbered 4.
   (c) See p. 197, para. 2.
3. (a) See p. 197, para. 1.
   (b) See p. 197, para. 2, lines 2–4.
4. See p. 197, para. 3, lines 3–8; and p. 198, paras. 1 and 2.
5. See p. 197, para. 4.

Subject Index

Please Note: Only the major references to each subject are given in this index. Figures given in italics are the page numbers for maps, illustrations, or time charts in which the subject is mentioned. Countries and their peoples are given as a single entry, e.g. *Ammon, Ammonites.*

Aaron, 49
Abiathar, 87, 93
Abijah, *101*
Abimelech, 26
Abner, 84–5
Abomination, 175
Abraham, *14*, *21*, 22, 26
Absalom, 87
Acropolis, 150, *164*
Actium, 185
AD (Anno Domini), 13
Adadnirari III, 98, *118*
Adam, 6
Adonai, 60
Adonijah, 87
Afghanistan, 147
Agrippa II, 193
Ahab, *101*, 103
Ahaz, *118*, 119, 121
Ahaziah, of Judah, *101*, 104; of Israel, *101*, 103
Ahijah, 89, 102
Ahriman, 150
Ai, 45
Akkadians, 21
Alexander the Great, 150, 167, 170, *173*
Alexander Jannaeus, 176, 188
Alexandria, *168*, 170, 172
Alphabet, 65, *67*
Altars, 36, 62, 76, 119
Amalek, Amalekites, 42, 66, 73, 82, *83*
Amarna, 44
Amasis, Pharaoh, 133, *137*, 147
Amaziah, 117, *118*
Ammon, Ammonites, 26, *51*, 66, 73, 82, 85, 96, 117, 122, 139, 176
Amnon, 87
Amon, *118*, 123
Amorites, 65–6
Amos, *15*, 117
Anat, 65, 109
Angels, 150
Anointing, 81
Antigonus, (a) 169, (b) 189
Antioch, *168*
Antiochus III, 169, 172, *180*, 184
Antiochus IV, 174
Antipater, 188–9
Aphek, 79, *83*, 84

Apocalypse, 181
Apocrypha, 172
Apries, Pharaoh, 133, *137*, 138
Aqaba, gulf of, *51*
Arabah, *51*, 88
Arabia, Arabs, 88, *115*, 117
Aram, Aramaeans, 23, *83*, 147
Aramaic, 160
Archaeology, archaeologists, 7, 79, 88, 113
Archangels, 150
Archelaus, 190
Aristobulus I, 176
Aristobulus II, 188
Aristotle, 170
Ark of the Covenant, 61, 75, 80, 85, 143
Arnon, *83*
Arses, 157
Art, 169
Artaxerxes I, 150, *157*, 158
Artaxerxes II, *157*, 160
Artaxerxes III, *157*
Arvad, 122
Asa, *101*, 102
Ashdod, 66, 79, *83*, 122
Asher, *71*
Asherah, 65, 109
Ashkelon, 66, *83*, 122
Ashtoreth, 109
Ashur (a god), 114, 119, *120*, 125
Ashurbanipal, 114, *118*, 122
Ashur-nasir-pal II, 97, *120*
Asia Minor, *115*, 167, 169
Asshur (a town), 113, *115*
Assyria, Assyrians, *15*, 98, 104, 113, *115*, *120*, 178
Astarte, 65, 76
Astyages, *137*, 147
Athaliah, *101*, 103
Athens, 150, *164*, 168
Atonement, 165
Augustus Caesar, 185, *191*
Avaris, *25*, 41, 42
Avesta, 150
Avil-Marduk, *137*
Azariah, 117, *118*
Azazel, 165

Baal, Baalim, 65–6, *86*, 103, 109

214

Bible Reference Index

Please Note: There are a large number of Bible References in this Guide, but most references to any book of the Bible are in a single chapter, e.g. the references to Genesis are mostly in Chapter 1. This index gives (a) the chapter of the Guide that contains the majority of references, and (b) the page numbers for references which are scattered in other parts of the Guide.

BIBLE REFERENCE INDEX